BARKING & DAGENHAM

THROUGH TIME

Michael Foley

AMBERLEY PUBLISHING

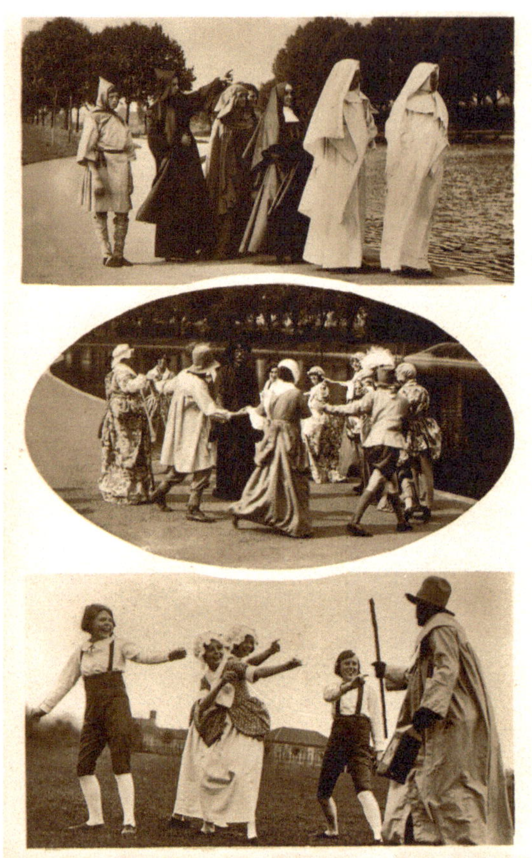

Scenes in Barking pageant.

To
Tich & Alan

First published 2010

Amberley Publishing
Cirencester Road, Chalford,
Stroud, Gloucestershire, GL6 8PE

www.amberleybooks.com

ISBN 978-1-4456-0240-0

British Library Cataloguing in Publication Data.
A catalogue record for this book is available from the British Library.

Typeset in 9.5pt on 12pt Celeste.
Typesetting by Amberley Publishing.
Printed in the UK.

Introduction

Barking and Dagenham have been closely connected throughout history. In the distant past Barking owed its existence to the abbey that stood there for centuries. It was burnt down by the Vikings at one point, but then rebuilt on an even grander scale. It was thought to be a suitable home for a king; William the Conqueror lived there while waiting for the Tower of London to be built. There are also rumours that the king's army was based at nearby Uphall, an ancient fortress site dating back to the Iron Age.

The connection with Dagenham at this time was that the abbey owned much of the land in the area.

The paths of the two towns diverged in later times, as Barking became a centre for industry with a large fishing fleet based around the town quay. As this industry declined, others came to take its place, again mainly based around the river, which was used to transport goods.

Dagenham, meanwhile, was still a small rural village surrounded by farmland. It was to stay this way until after the First World War when the Becontree estate was built to re-house the people from the overcrowded slums of London's East End. It was to become the largest council estate in the world at the time. As the majority of the estate was in Dagenham, both towns developed separate identities.

However, this did not last and the two towns once again came together as the London Borough of Barking and Dagenham. Despite being a London Borough, the area has always retained its aura of being part of Essex.

The last hundred years then have seen many changes, as can be seen from the old images in this book. Many of the rural scenes have vanished under the housing that gives Dagenham its identity. It has been said that all the streets in Dagenham look the same. When one looks closely this is not the case, with several types of housing included in the estate.

A number of the old pubs that survived the coming of the new estate have recently vanished, but in some cases they have left the memory of their names to the areas where they stood. Along with the pubs, many of the shops have disappeared. The recent economic downturn has led a number of shops to bring down the shutters for the last time. This has happened even in Barking's main shopping centre with almost whole streets, once boasting streams of busy shops, shutting down. North Street and London Road are two examples.

It becomes obvious as you look through the images in this book that despite the idea that Dagenham only began life with the Becontree estate, there was much more there before this. No one can dispute Barking's impressive history, and this book shows how much of that history can still be found without too much trouble.

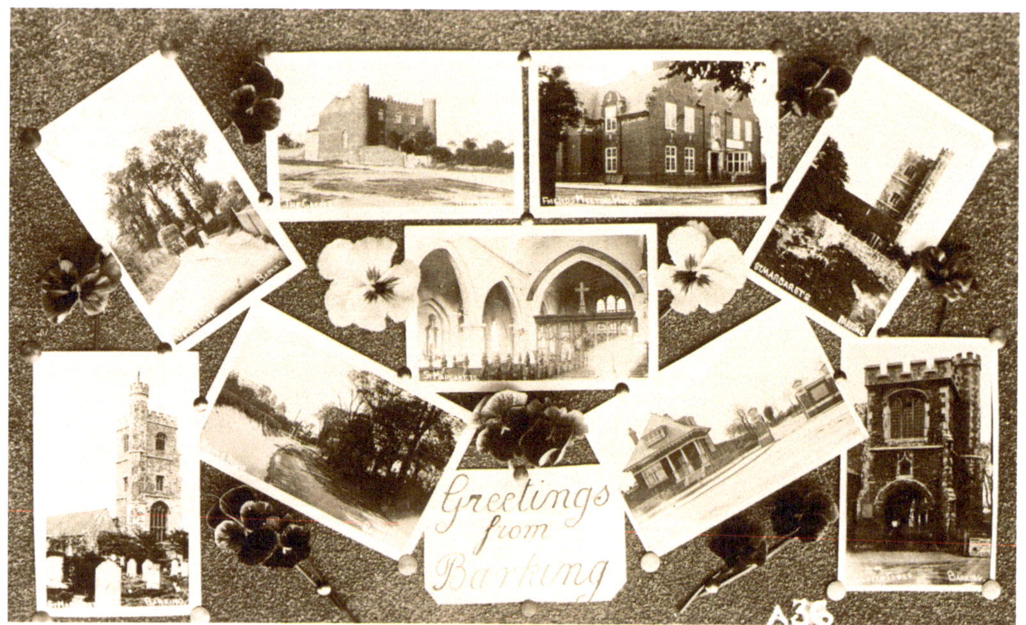

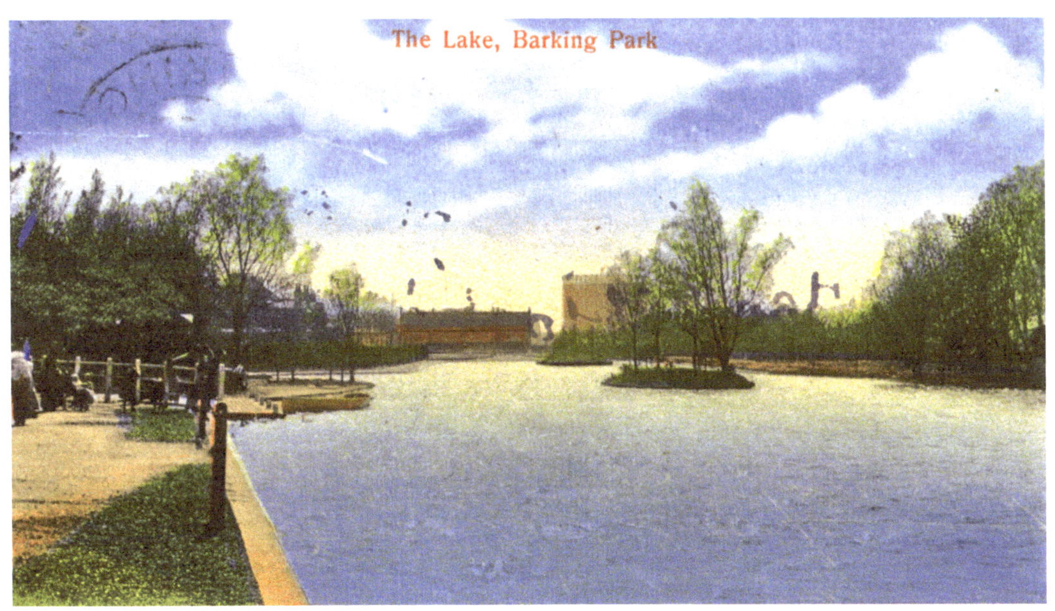

Barking Park

The most striking thing about Barking Park is the boating lake. It is more than half a mile long and around 100 feet wide. It was always a popular and well-used resource in the park until the boats were withdrawn. The lake is one part of the park that has hardly changed.

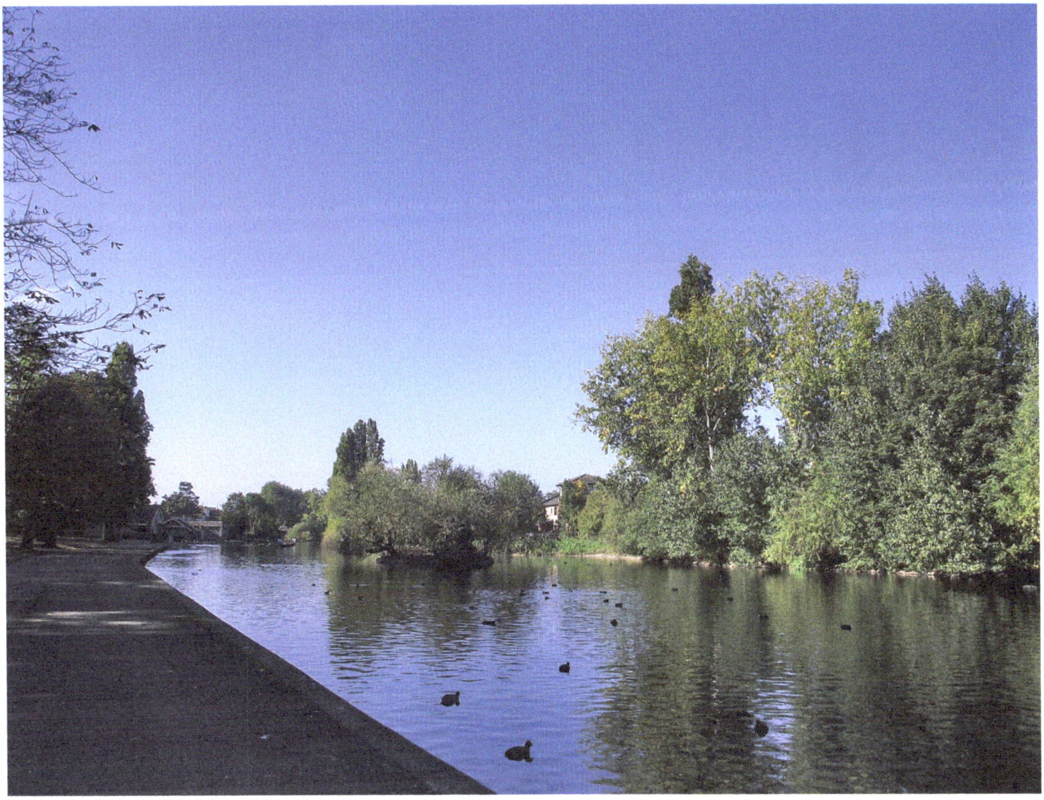

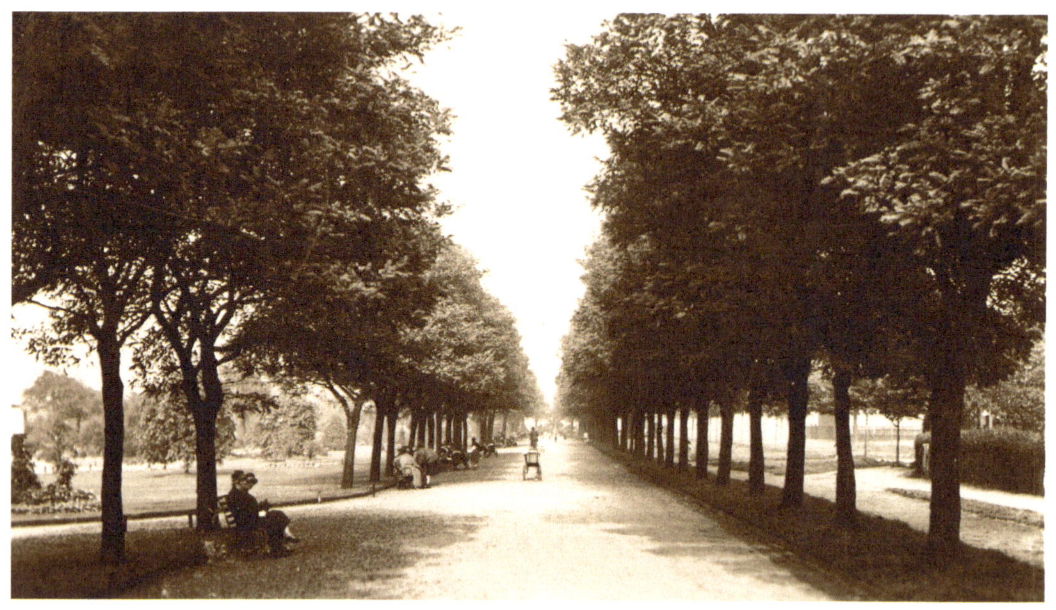

Music in the Park

The park was popular during the First World War, not only for those relaxing in the old image. Concerts were often held in the park by military bands. The local newspapers reported that thousands of people attended the concerts. The bandstand has now gone and been replaced by a car park.

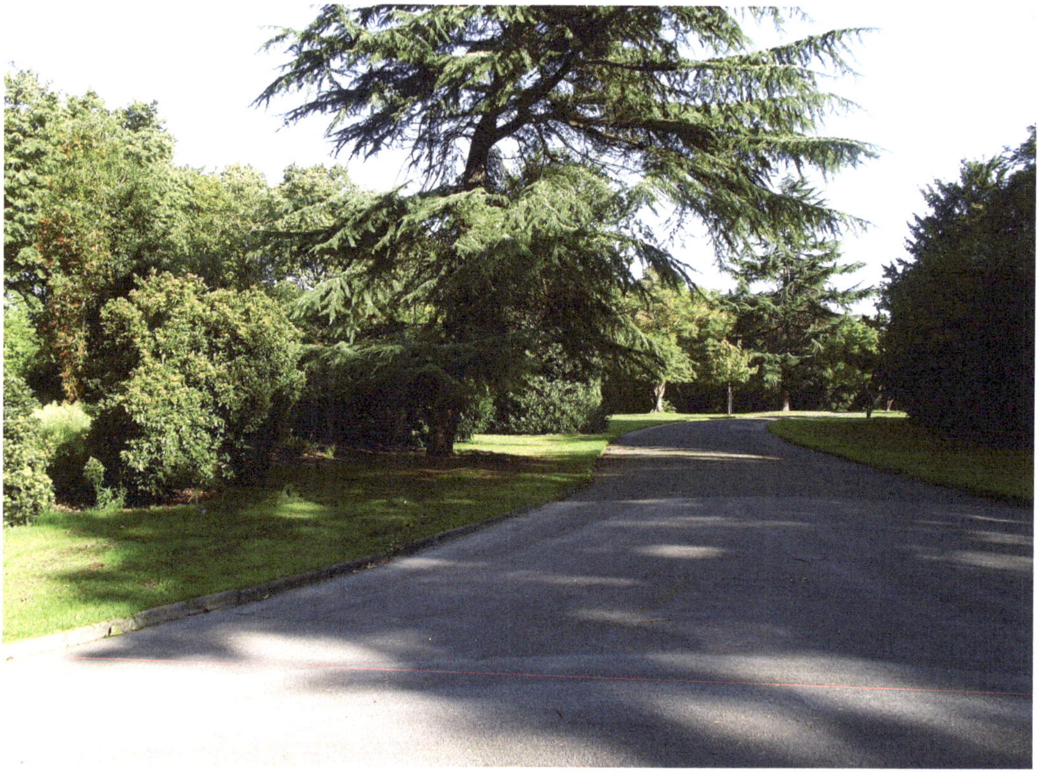

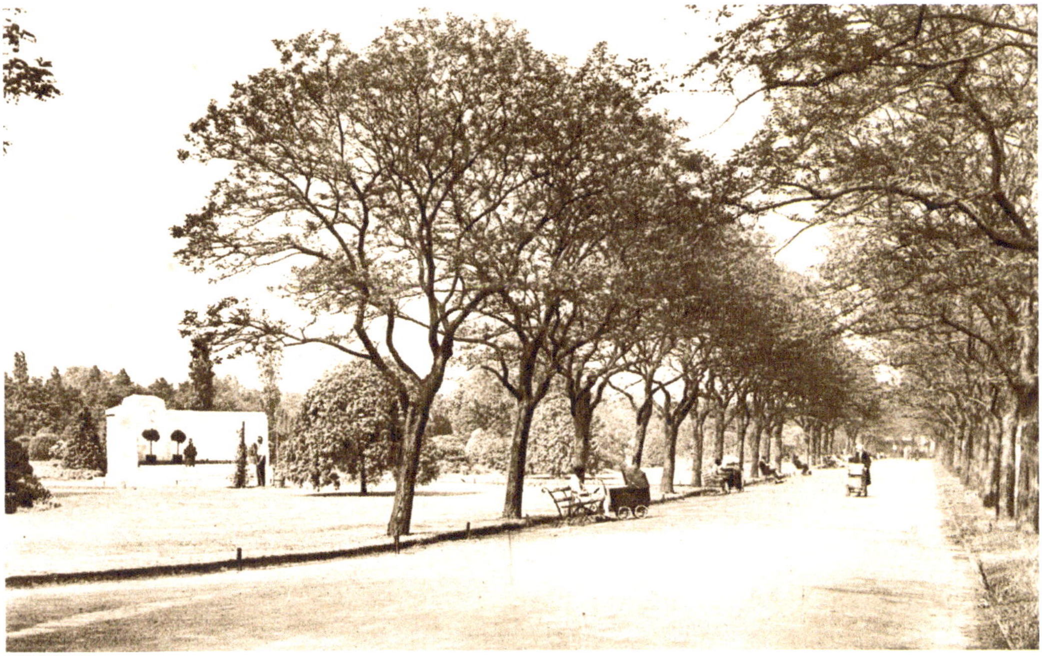

Barking Park War Memorial

Concerts were not the only events held in the park. Just before the First World War, thousands of spectators turned up to watch a flying display by Mr B. C. Hucks in his military-type Bleriot plane. The display was to raise funds for a cottage hospital in the town. Another military connection is the war memorial which now stands in the park.

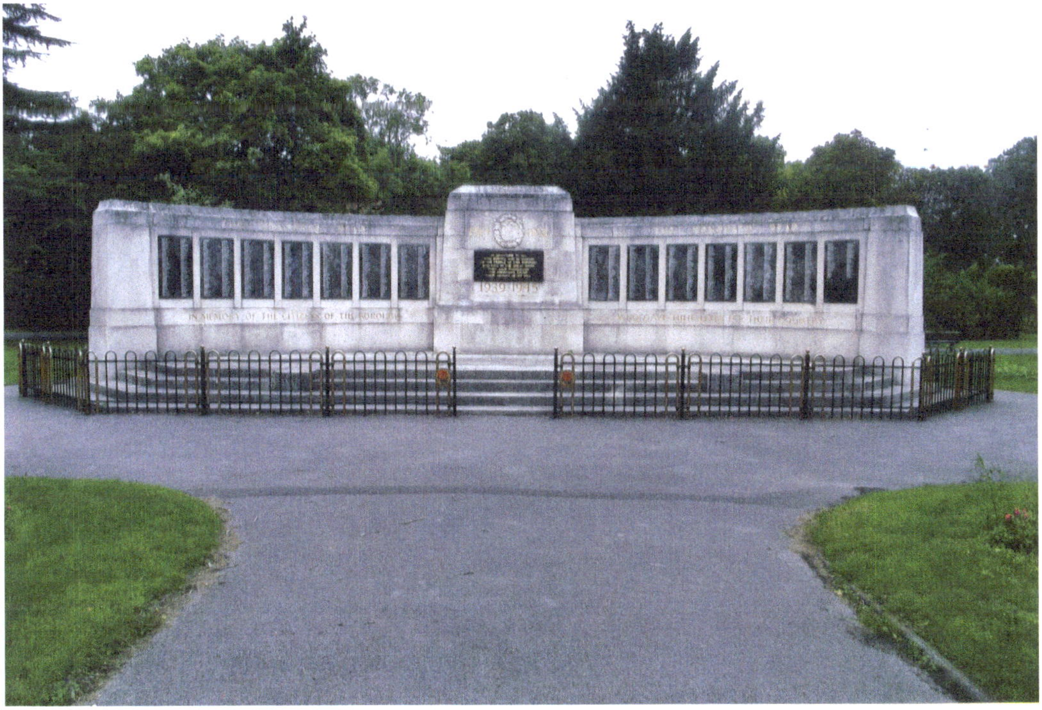

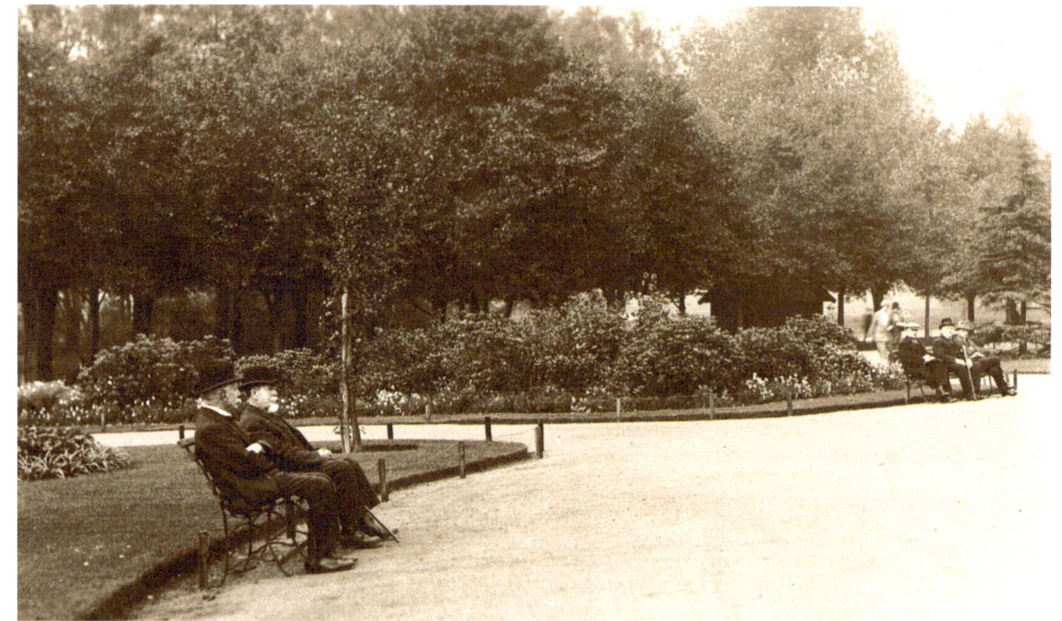

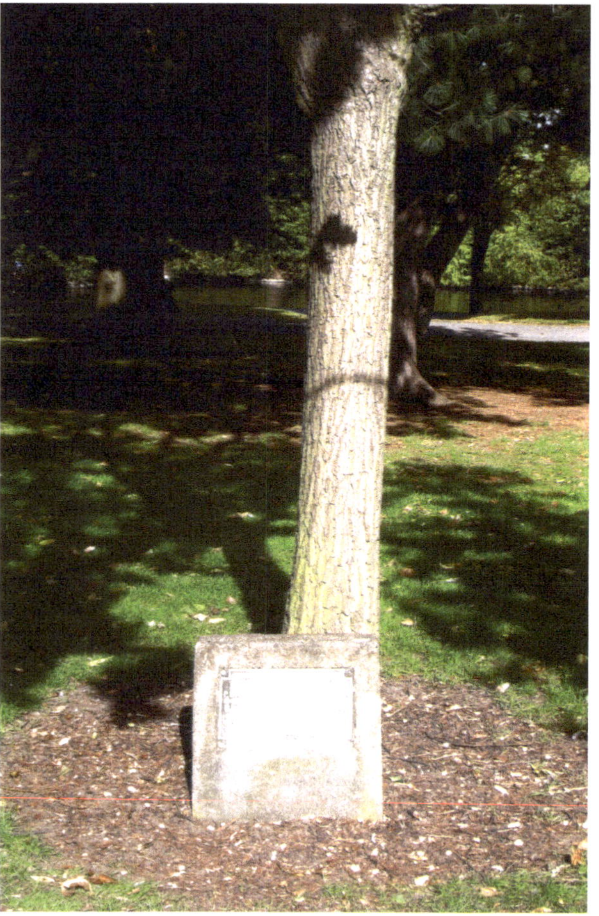

Patriotism

The elderly gentlemen relaxing in the park in the early part of the century would have no doubt been very patriotic, as was the norm in those days. It is no surprise then that a memorial for the Coronation of George V should have been placed by a tree planted to commemorate the event.

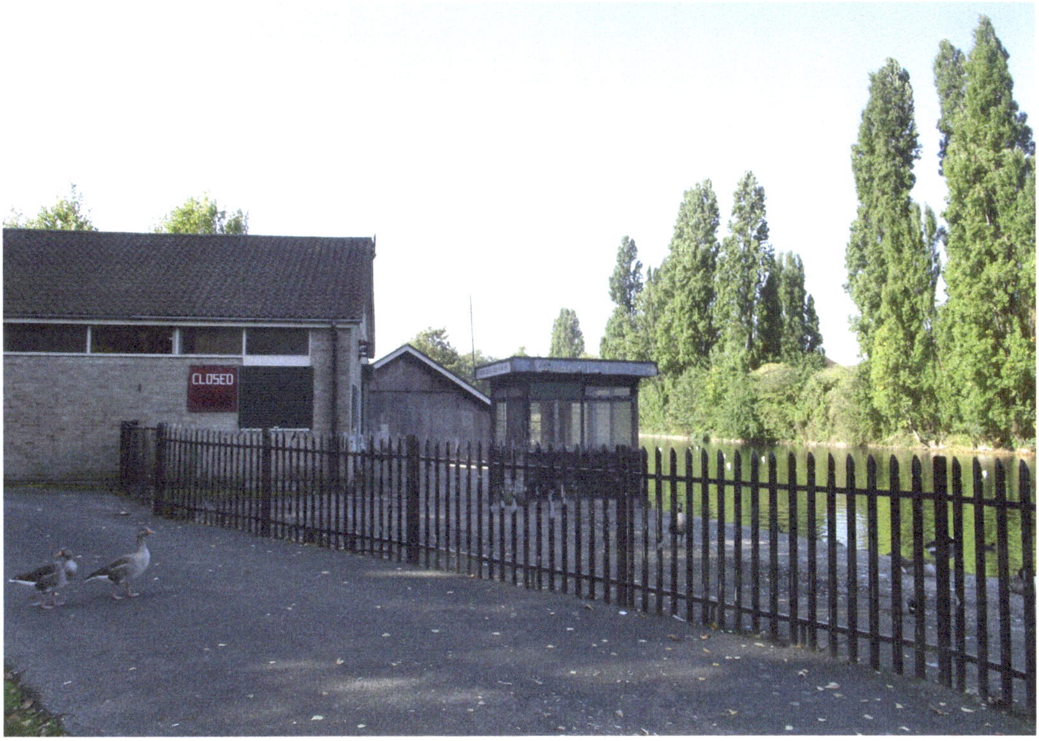

The Boathouse

The boating lake in the park was very popular. Originally, only rowing boats were available, but in 1953 motorboats made an appearance for the first time along with the paddle steamer *Phoenix II*. This lasted until 1967. Unfortunately, the boathouse shown has now been closed.

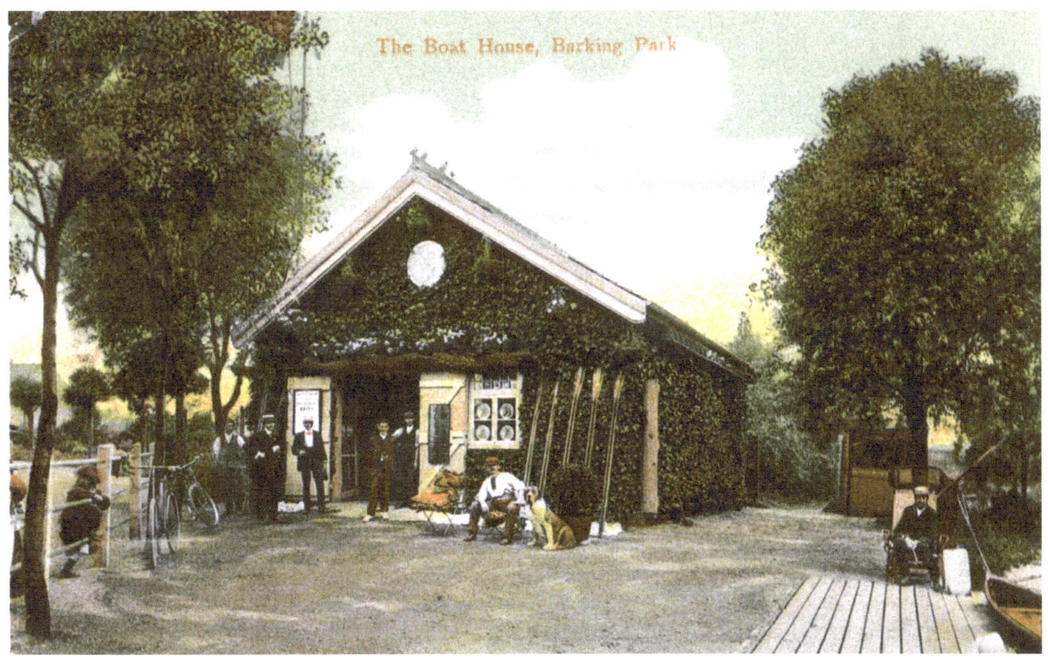

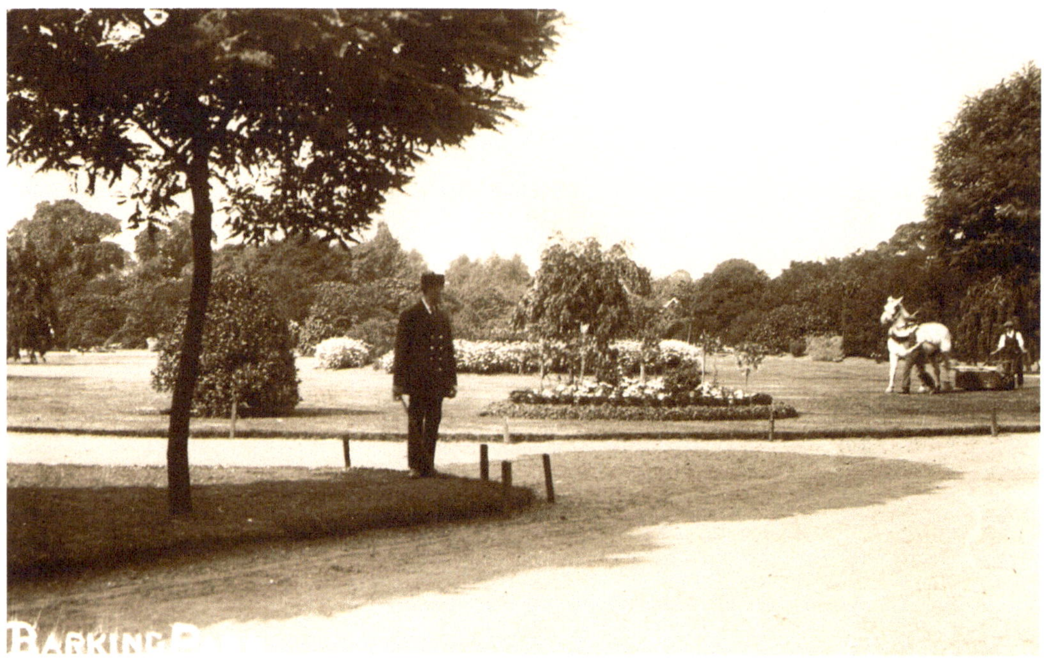

Cutting the Grass

Cutting the grass in the park must have been a monumental task when the mower was drawn by a horse as shown in the old image. The gentlemen in the centre of the photograph looks to be dressed in a uniform, perhaps the park keeper. Cutting the grass must be much quicker today.

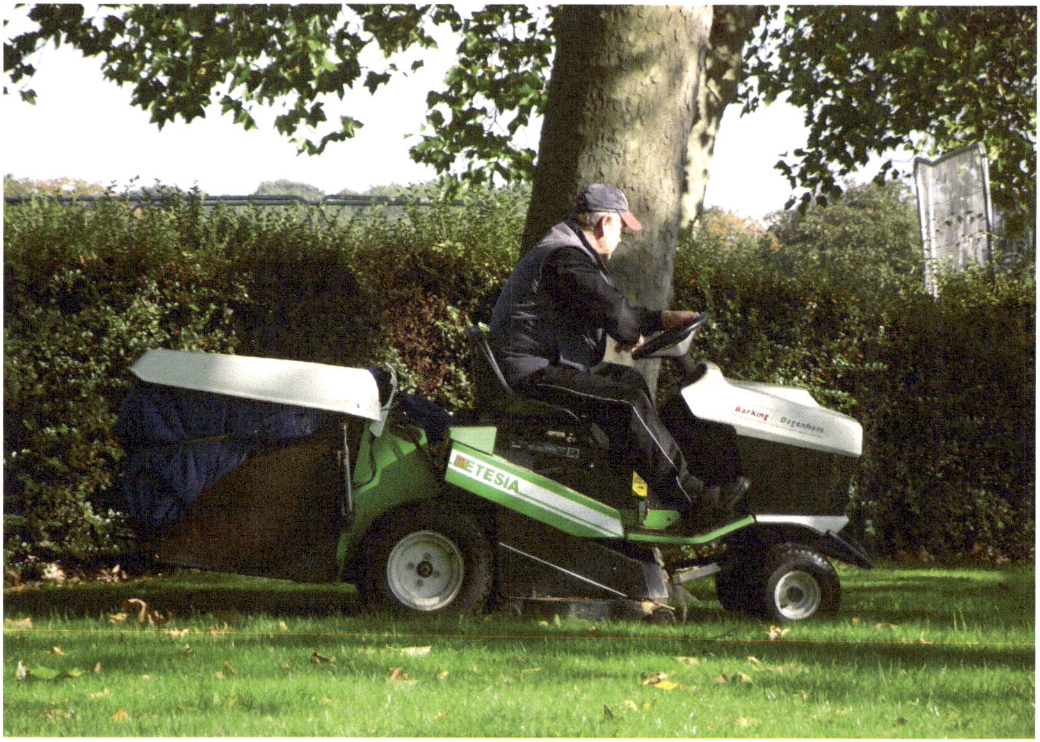

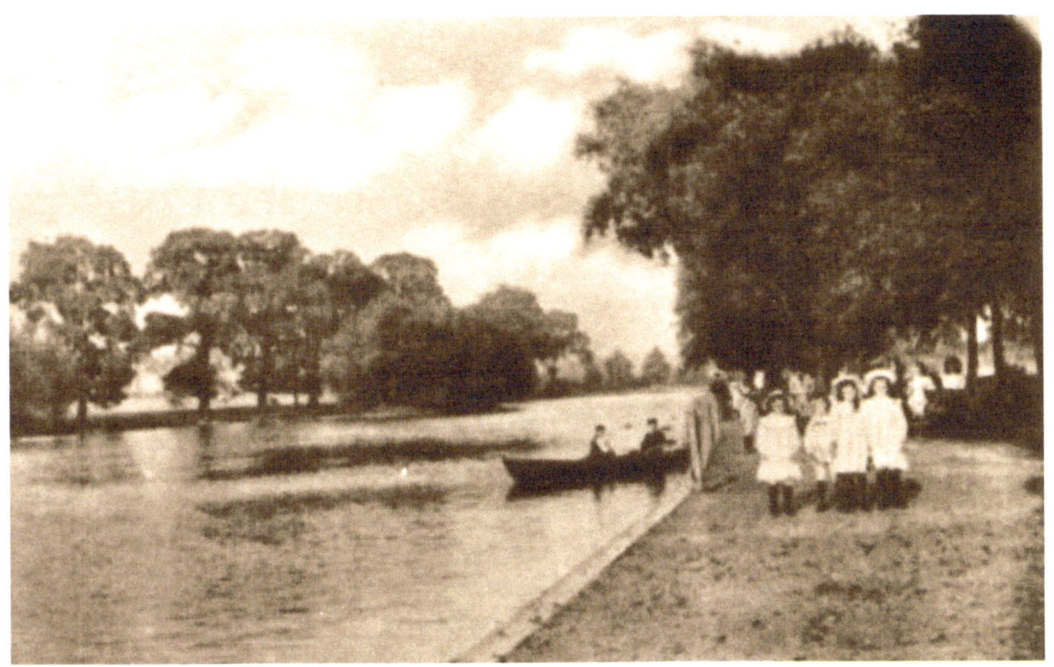

Walk by the Lake

It would be no surprise to see groups of children walking in the park today. Fashions would no doubt be very different from those in the old photograph. It would also be unusual to see a boat on the lake today.

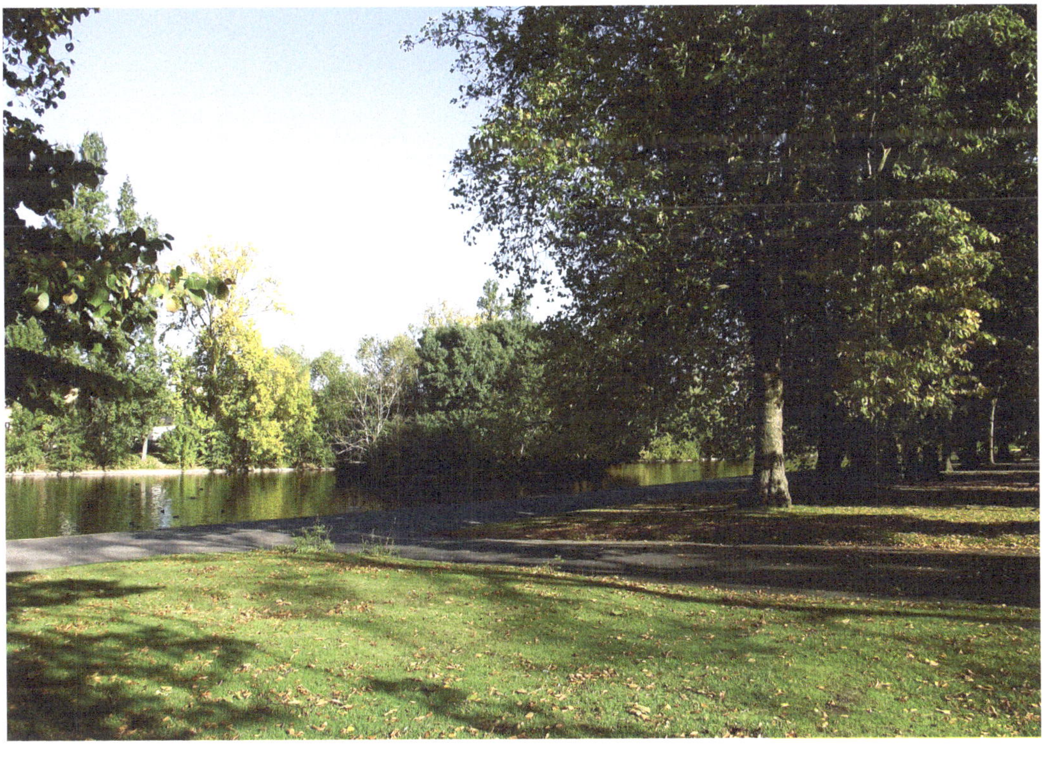

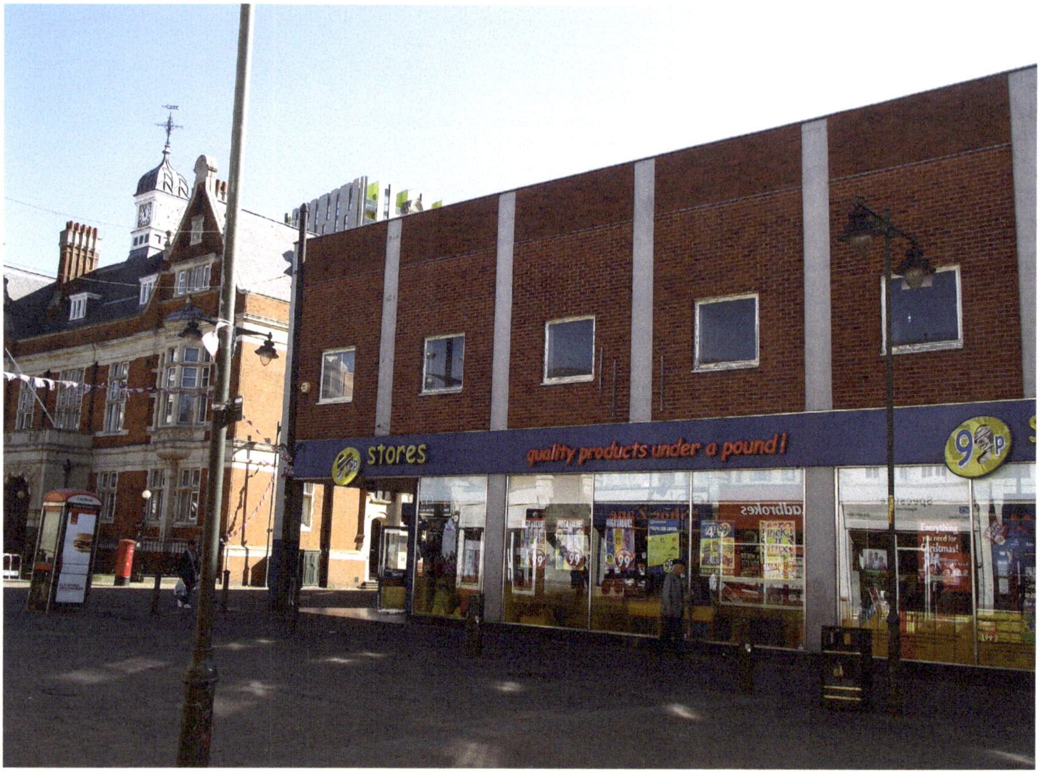

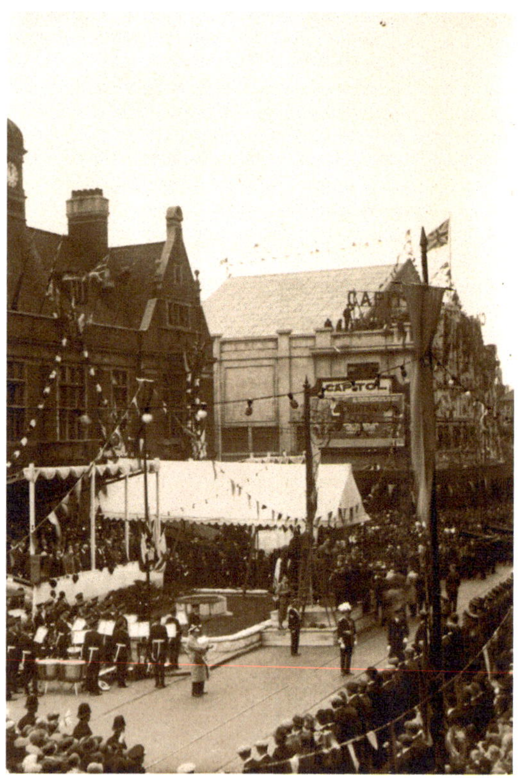

Barking Celebration

I am not sure what this celebration in Barking town centre is about, but it must have been after 1933 when the Capitol Cinema opened and before 1959 when the cinema closed and became part of Marks & Spencer, which has now also gone. The only building remaining from the old image is the magistrates' court.

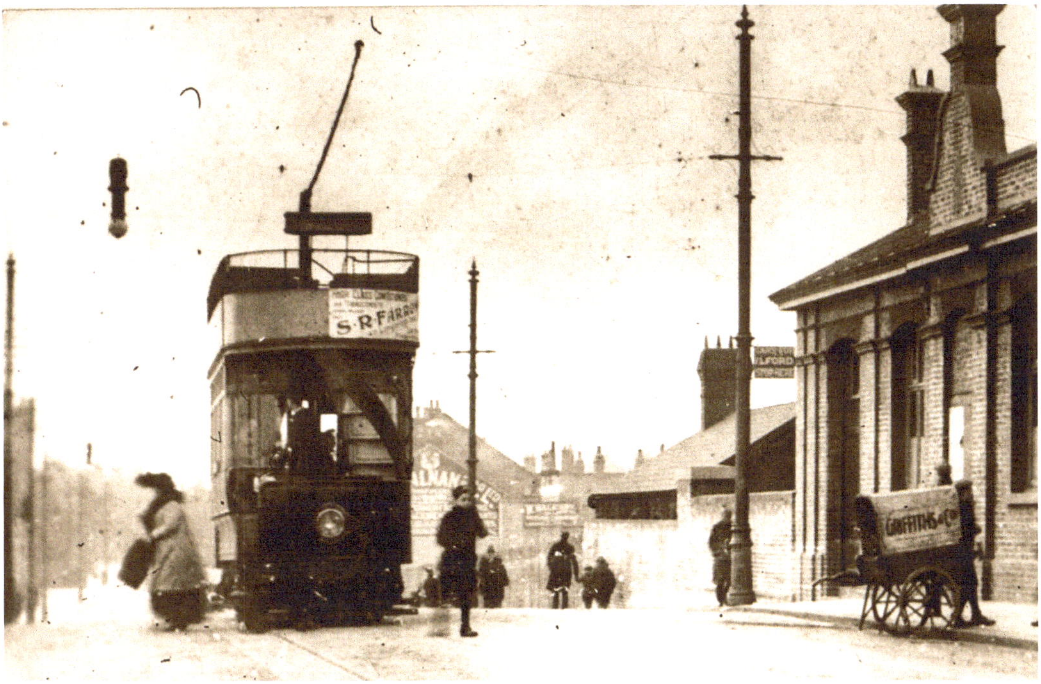

Barking Station

The station was opened by the London, Tilbury and Southend Railway Company in 1854. There were soon sixteen trains a day running between Southend and London that stopped at the station. The type of transport passing the station was very different then as the old tram shows. The old station was demolished in 1959.

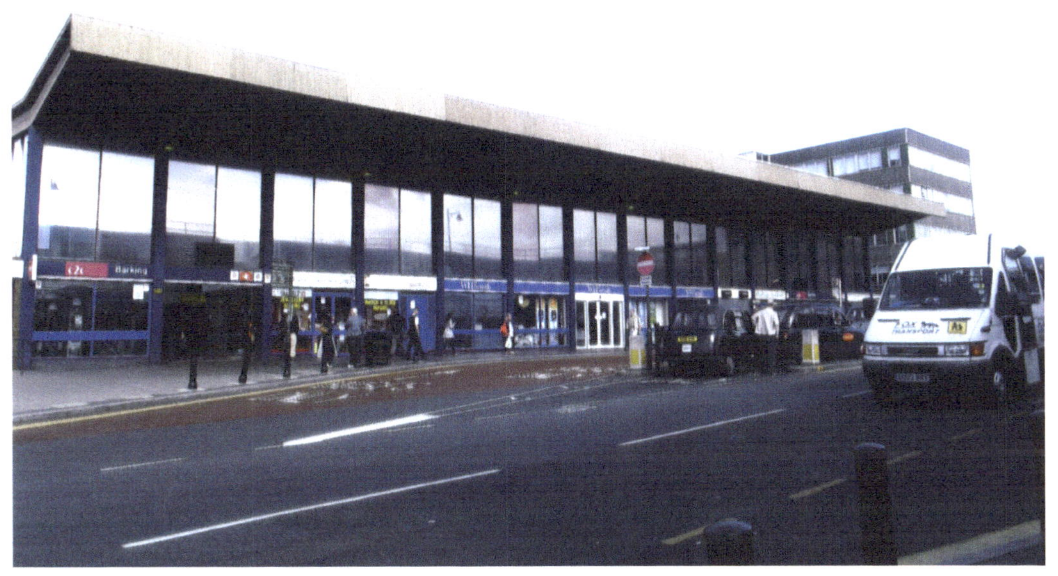

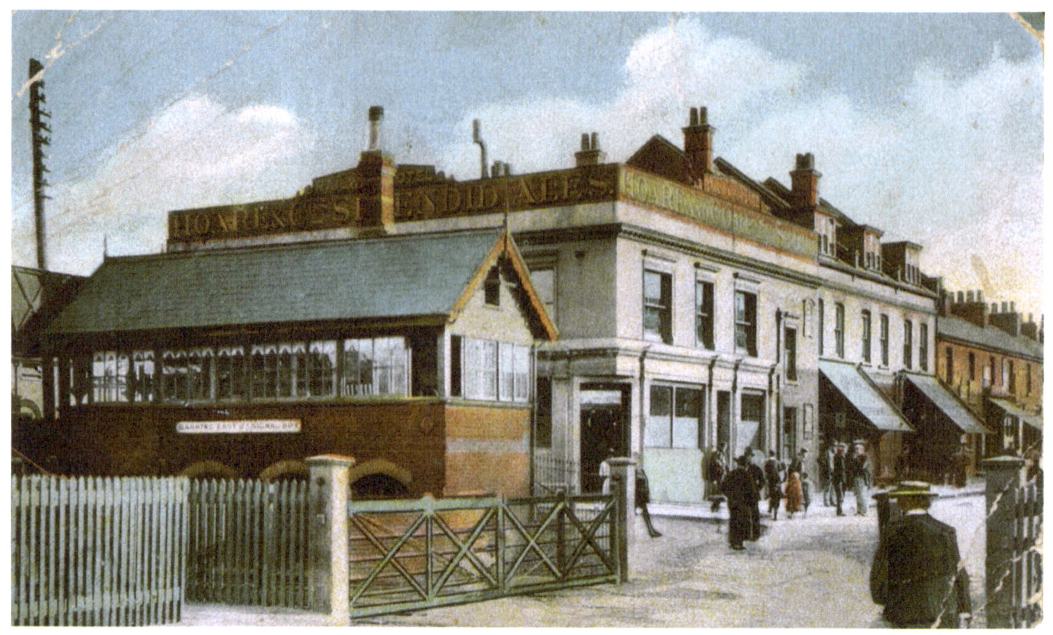

The Old Level Crossing, Barking

The line from Barking station used to run across what was then the area where East Street met Longbridge Road. Because of this, a level crossing had to be installed. How this would have coped with increasing traffic in latterday Barking is unimaginable.

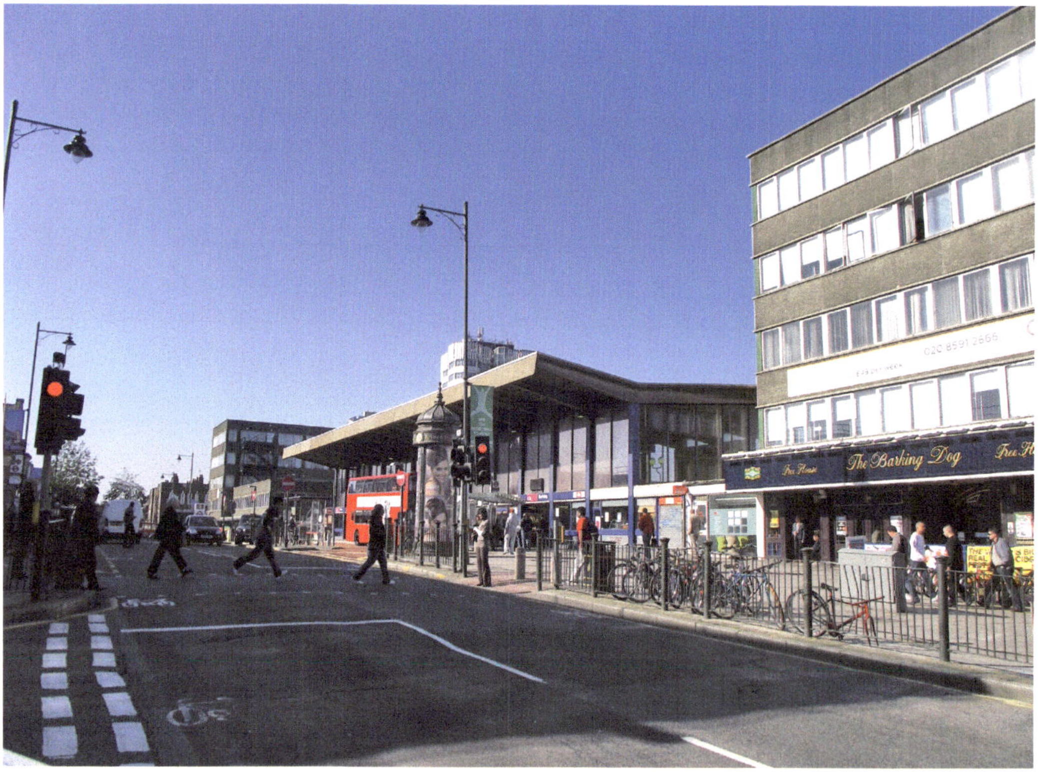

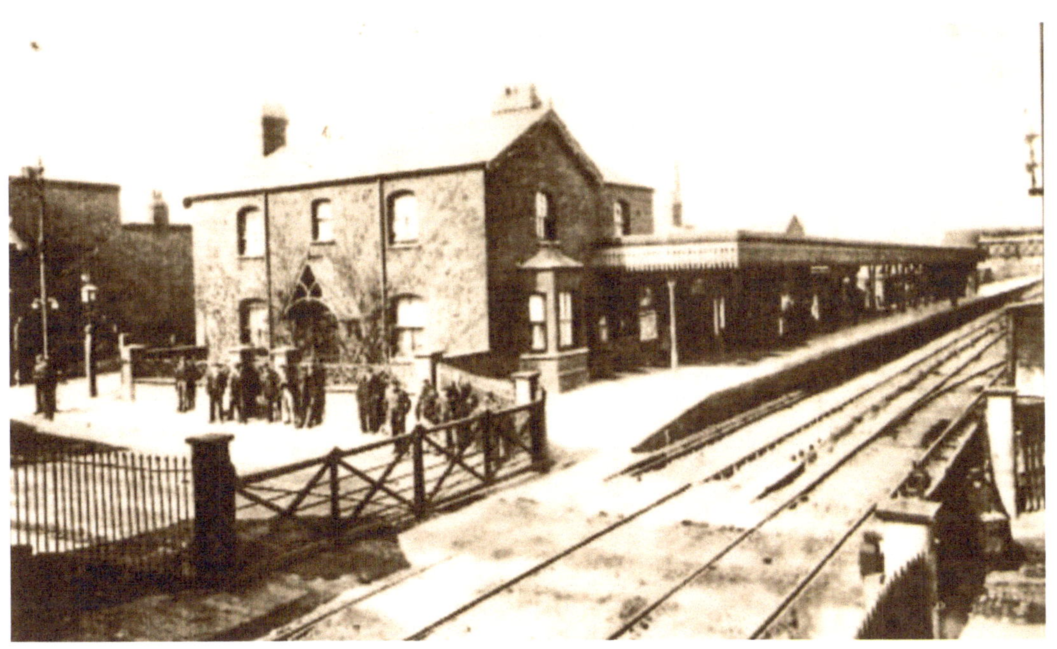

Traffic Through the Ages

Another view of the level crossing and Barking station itself. Traffic across the road which now runs over the rail line has decreased enormously since the part of East Street beyond Ripple Road became a pedestrianised area.

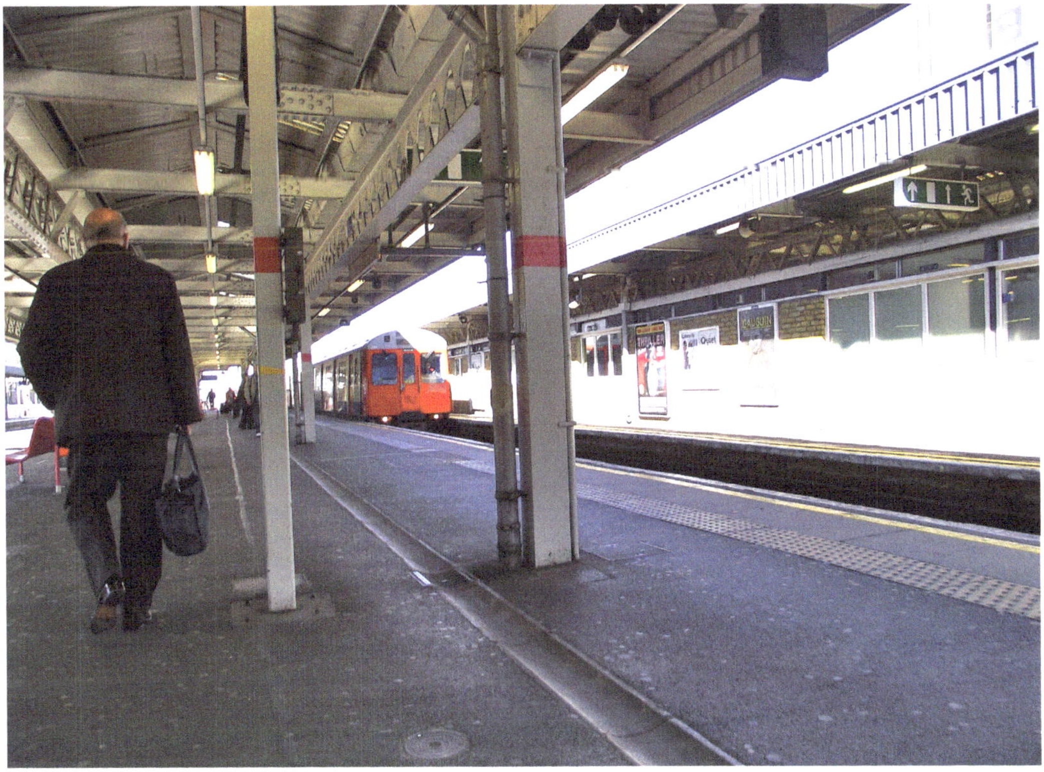

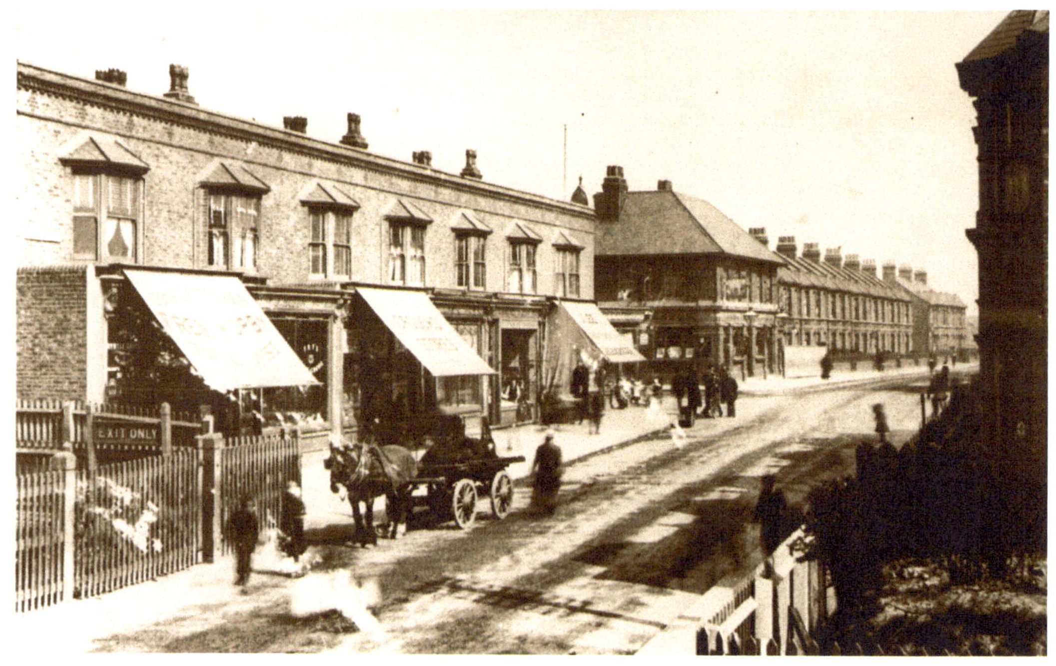

The Spotted Dog

The Spotted Dog has been one building near the station that has changed little over the past century. Everything around it, however, has altered drastically. The surrounding buildings of the old image have all but vanished.

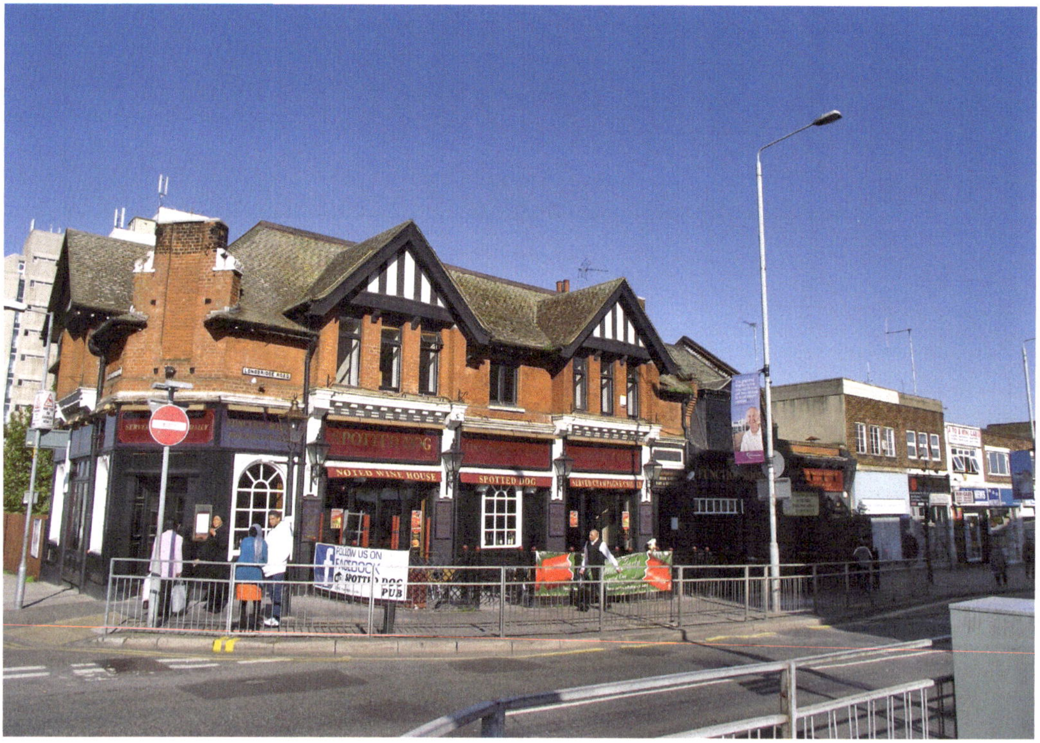

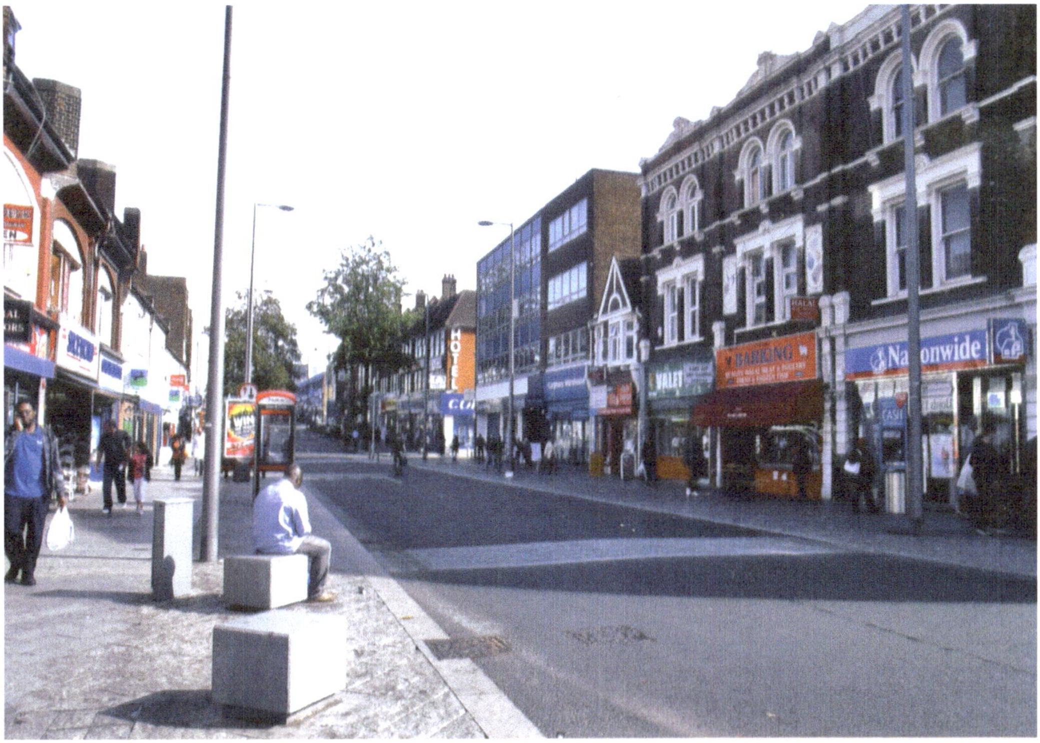

East Street

This part of East Street is now known as Station Parade, which lies between East Street and Longbridge Road. East Street was once the site of the fire station and swimming baths.

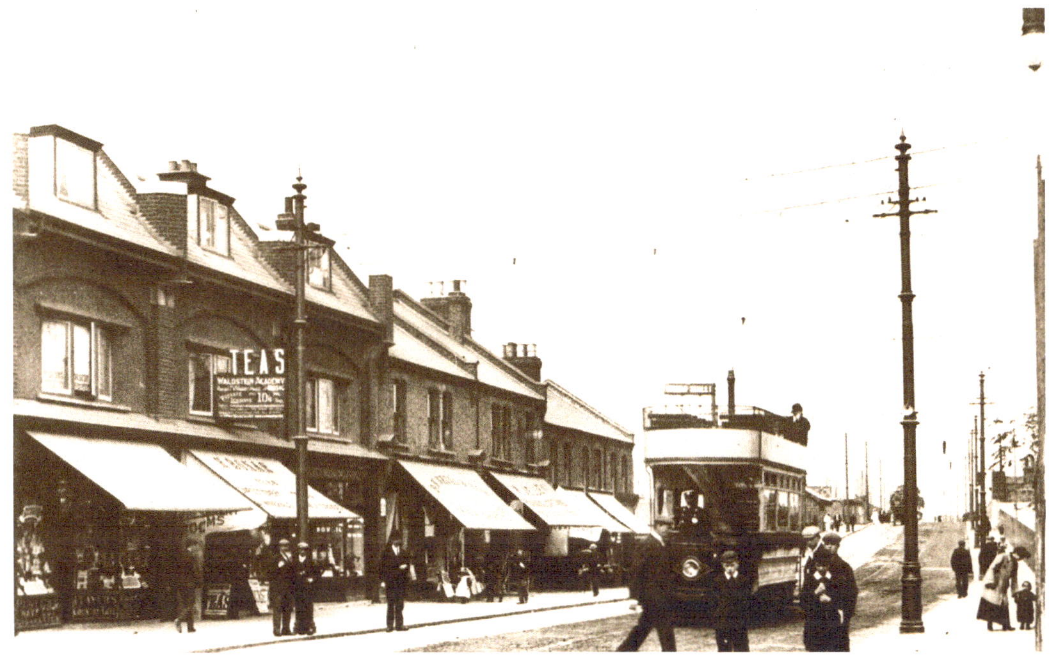

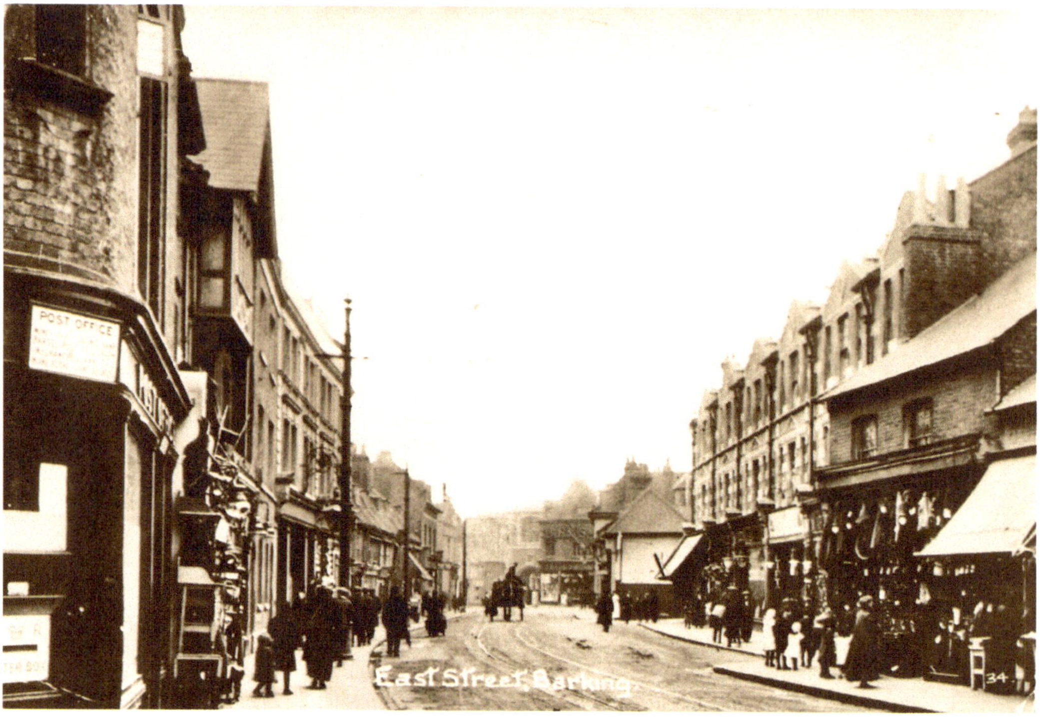

The Site of Barking Market

The main part of East Street is now a pedastrianised area. It is lined with shops and is also the site of much of Barking market. The old Barking market closed some time ago.

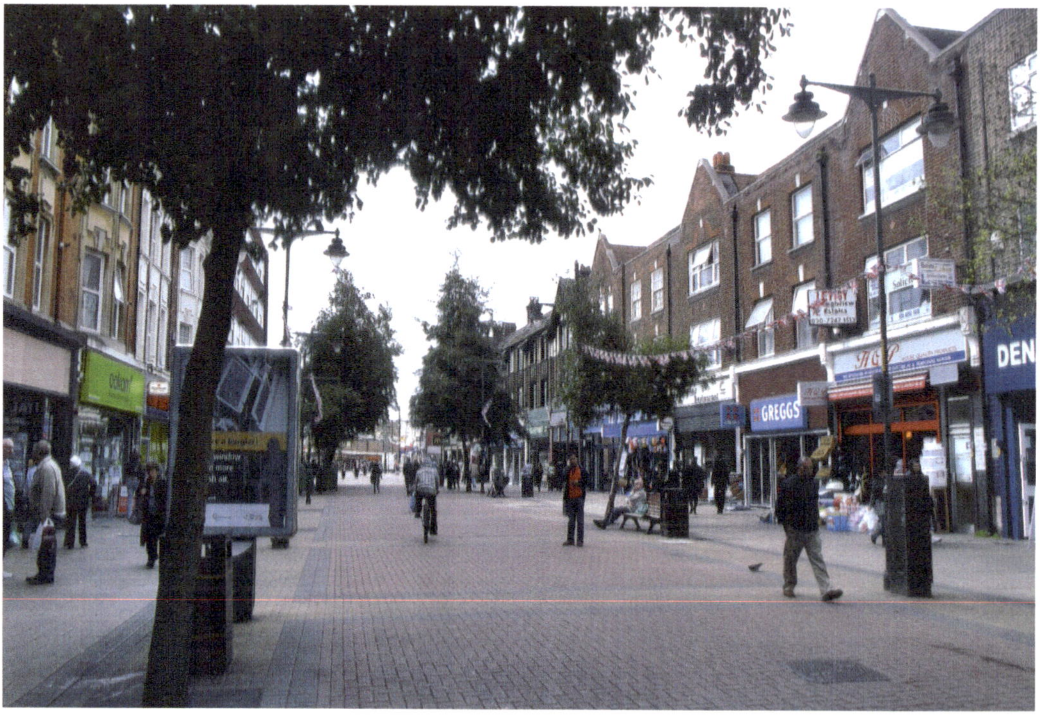

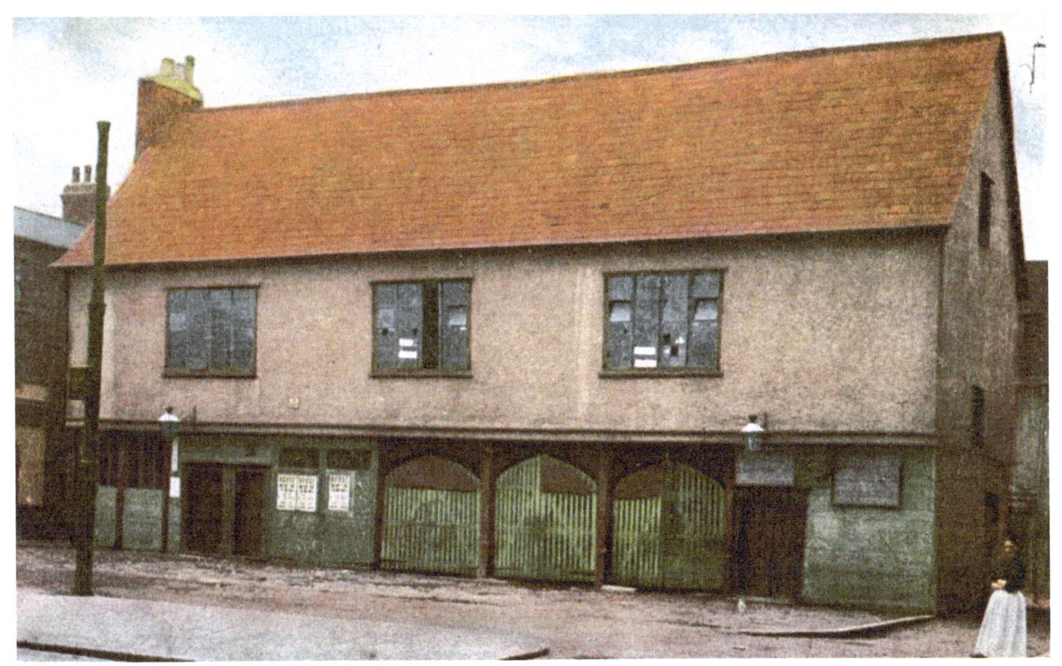

Town Hall

The old town hall had a market hall underneath. It was replaced in the late nineteenth century by a newer version which later became the magistrates' court. The present town hall was built in the late 1950s.

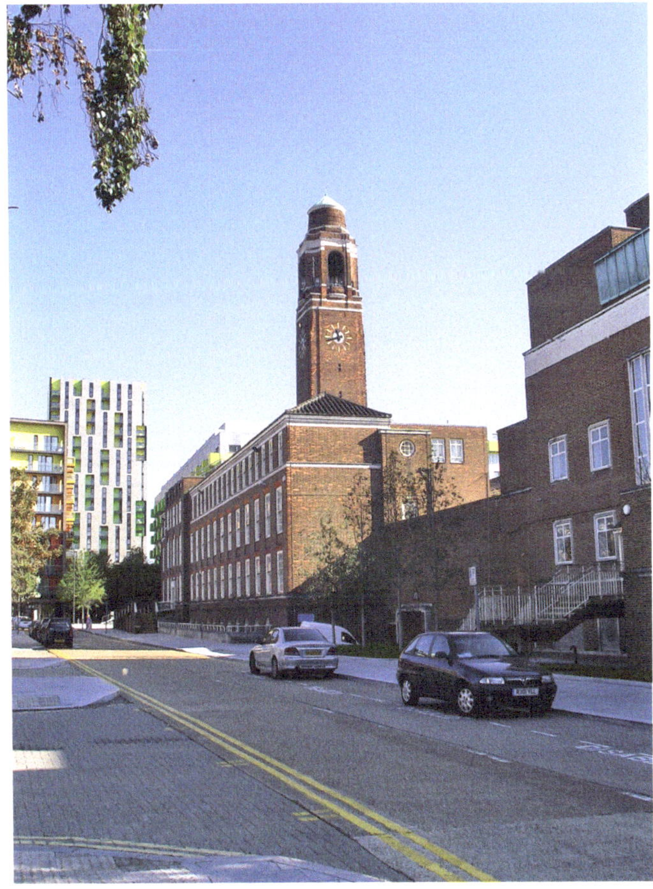

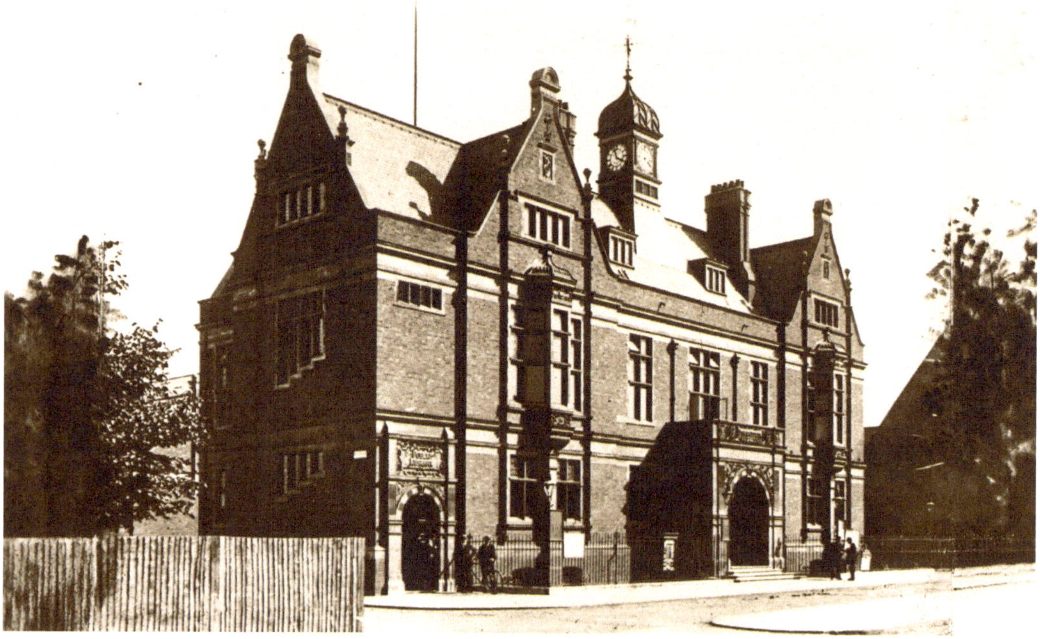

Public Offices

The building standing in East Street was built in 1894. It was originally the town hall. It has been used as the magistrates' court for many years. The new town hall was designed in 1936 but not finished until 1958.

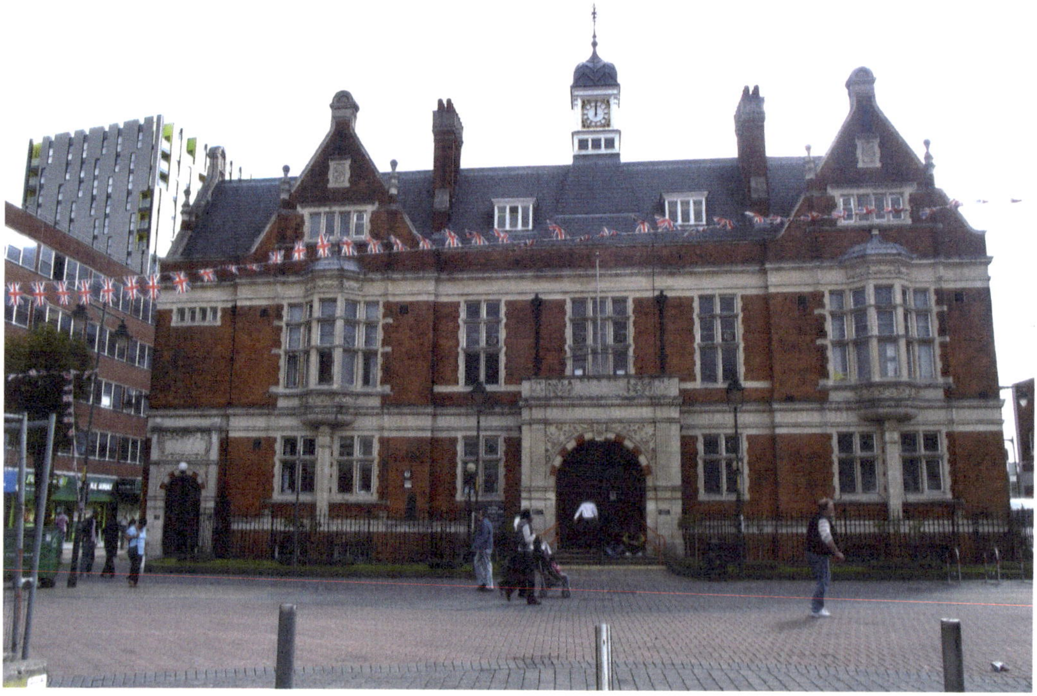

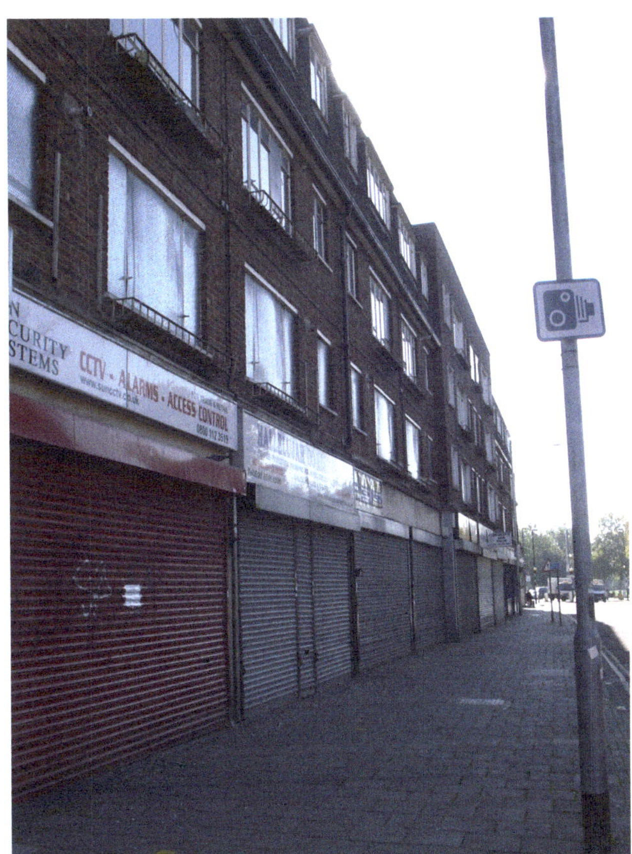

North Street

North Street has changed dramatically. The old police station was demolished in 1955 and many of the shops that stretch from the junction with East Street are now closed. The street leads up to the old Quaker meeting house and burial ground.

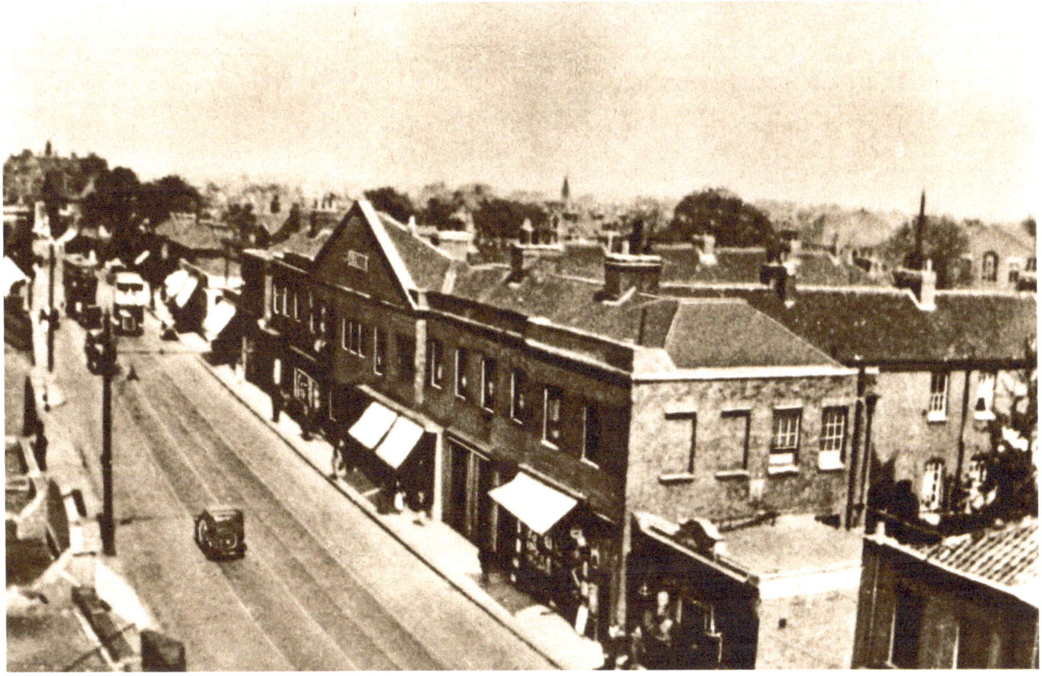

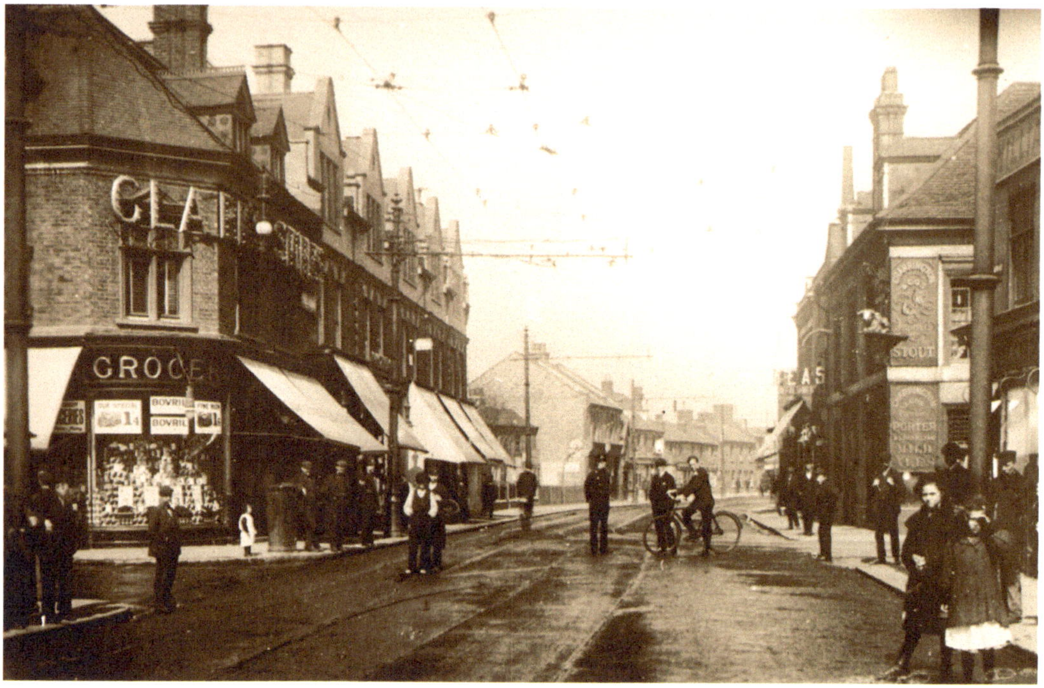

Broadway Assembly Hall and Theatre

The old Barking assembly hall, which opened in 1961 and whose entrance was in the Broadway, replaced many of the old buildings. It has now become the Broadway Theatre with a much more modern face. It now has shows on all year and a regular pantomime at Christmas.

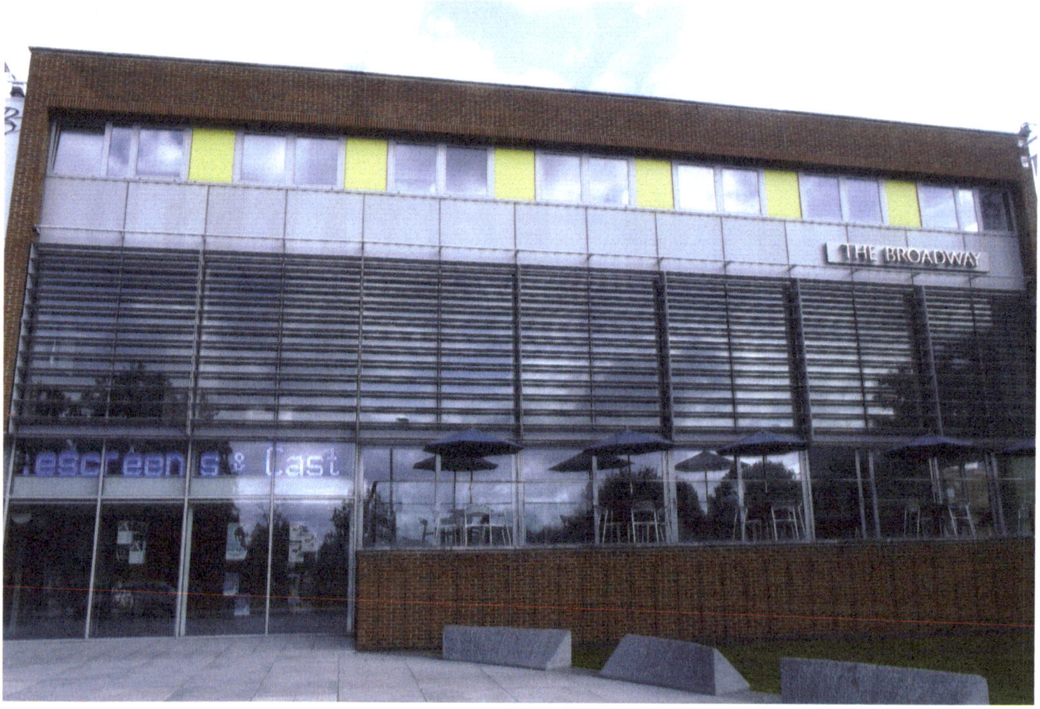

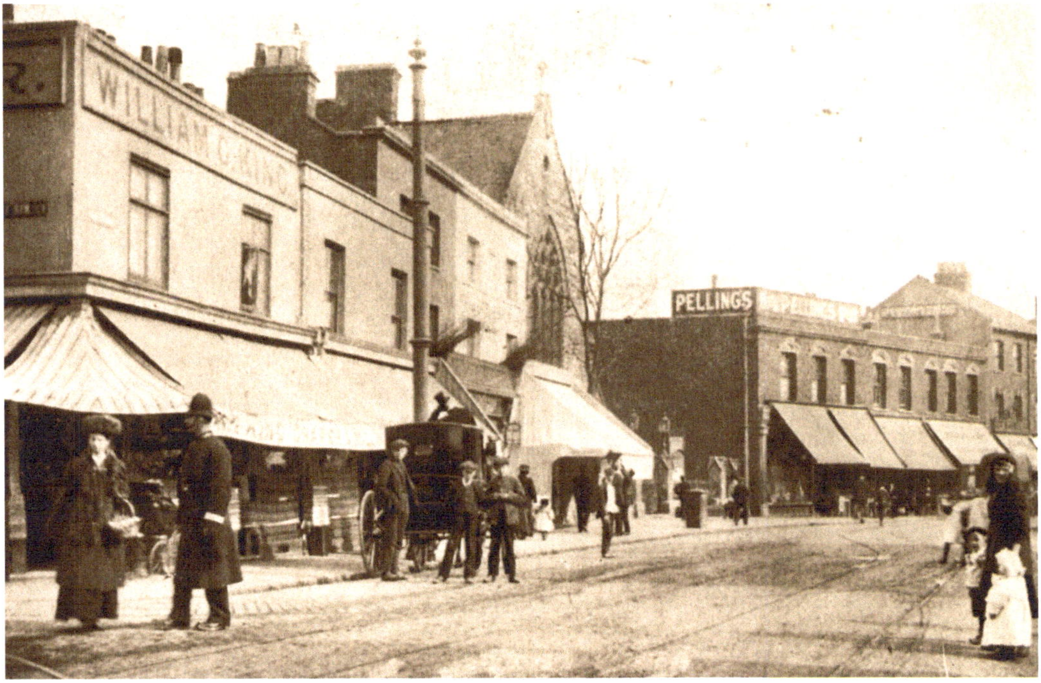

A Changing Urban Landscape

The Broadway was one of the original roads of the town and dates back to the middle ages. It was upgraded in the late nineteenth century when kerbs were added. Many buildings east of the Broadway were demolished in 1937 to make space for the new town hall, which was not built until much later.

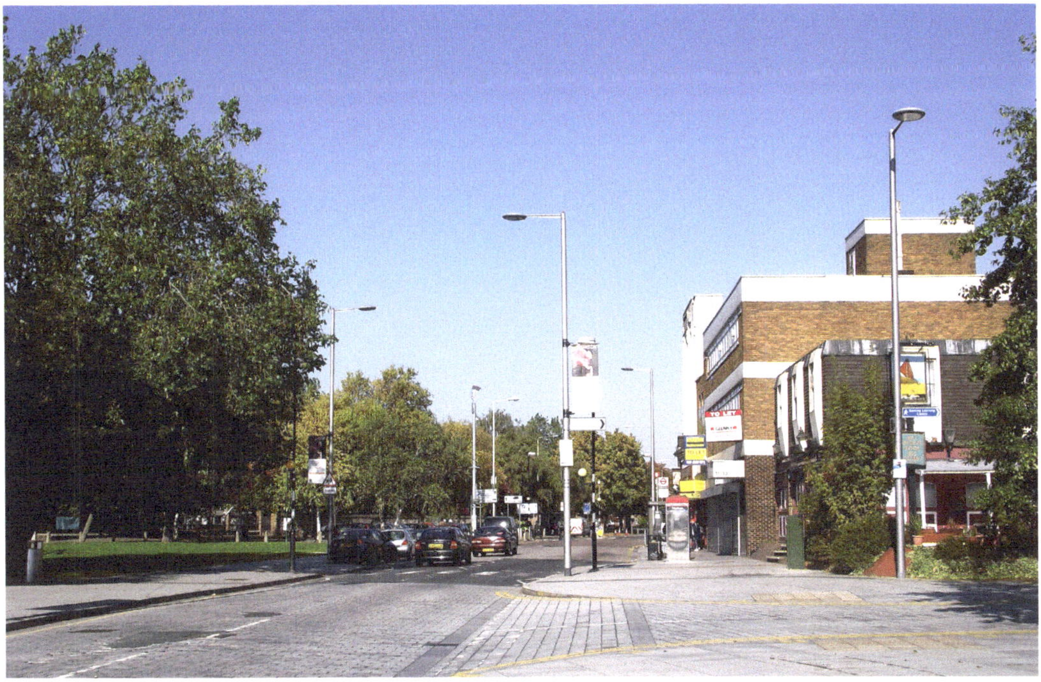

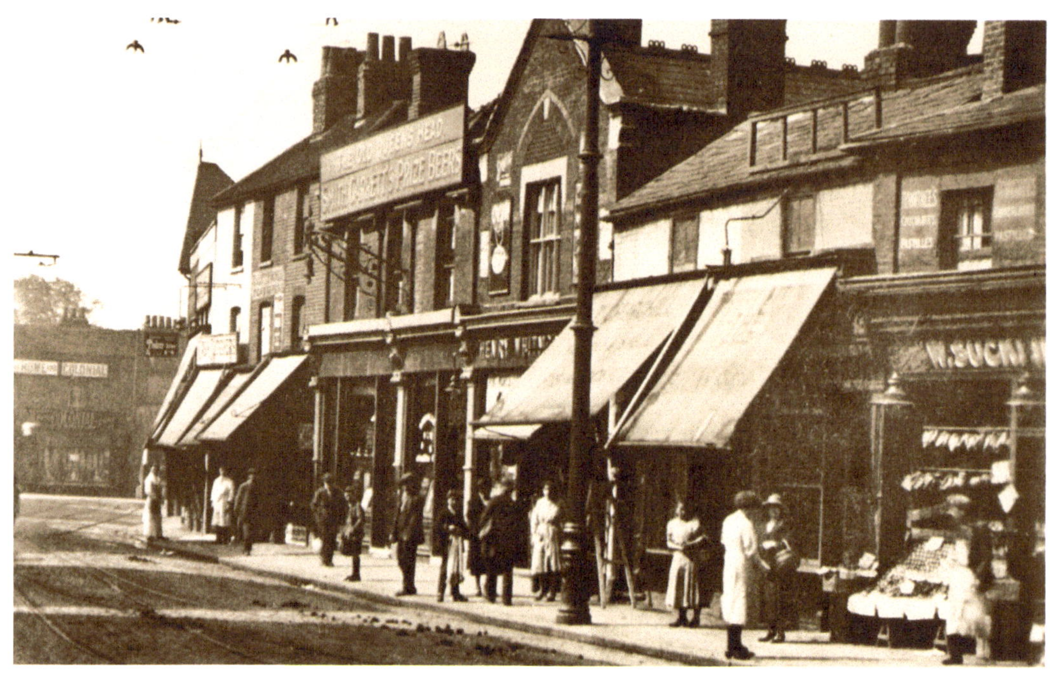

Broadway Shops

Old photographs of the Broadway show a street lined on both sides with buildings and busy shops. Now the area in front of the church is all open parkland giving a clear view across to the old town quay.

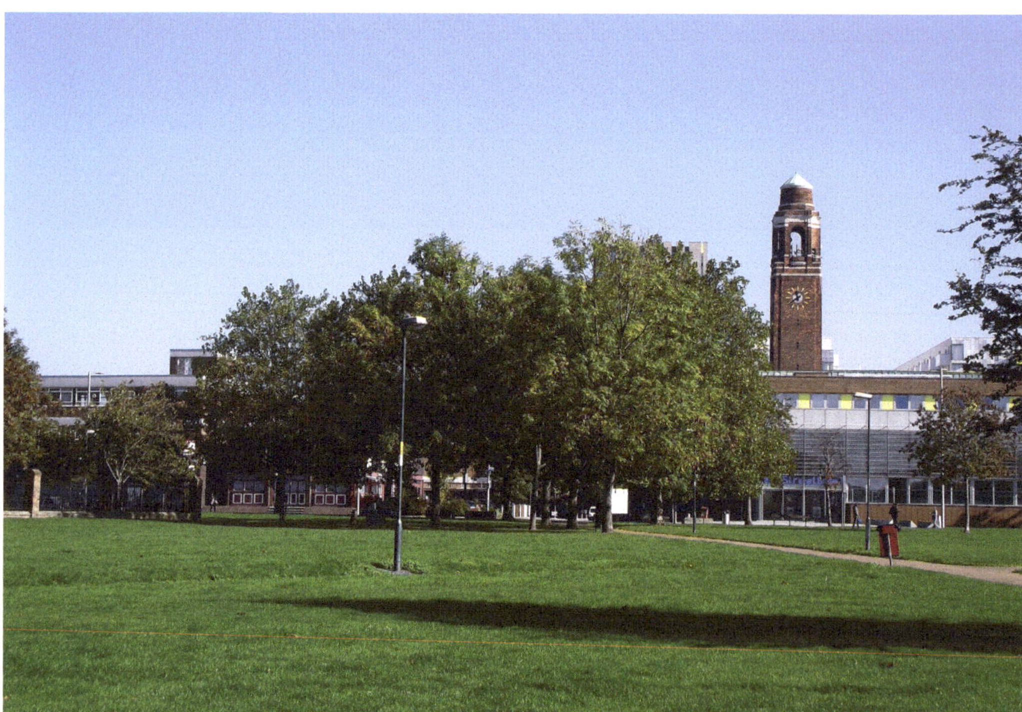

Driver J. H. C. DRAIN, V.C.

Job Drain

Job Drain of the Royal Field artillery was awarded the Victoria Cross early in the First World War. At the age of eighteen he helped to save a gun from the advancing enemy while under fire. He has been honoured by a statue erected outside the Broadway Theatre.

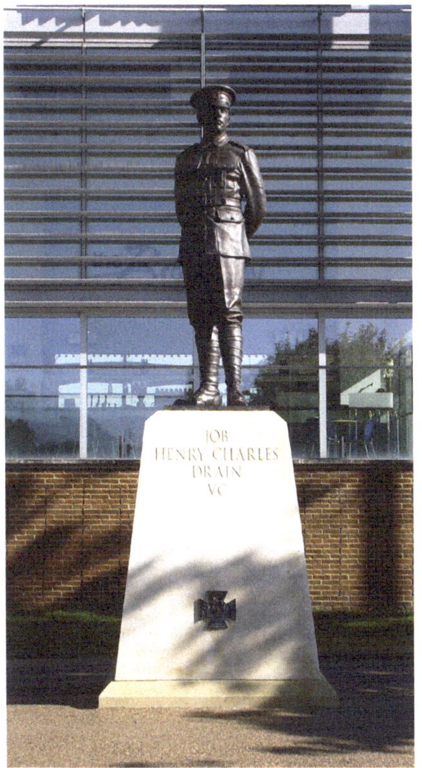

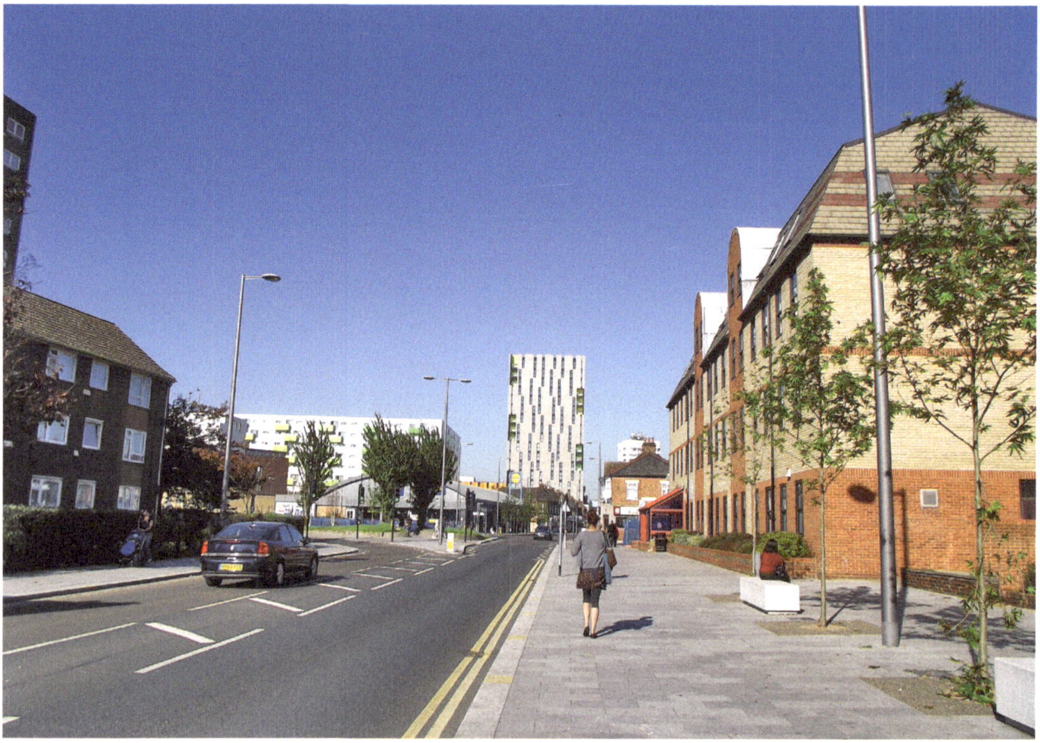

Ripple Road

Ripple Road was very rural in the early part of the twentieth century, leading to the Rippleside cemetery. Houses began to be built as the town of Barking expanded in the 1920s. The road then carried on to Dagenham, later becoming the A13. It has changed dramatically in recent years.

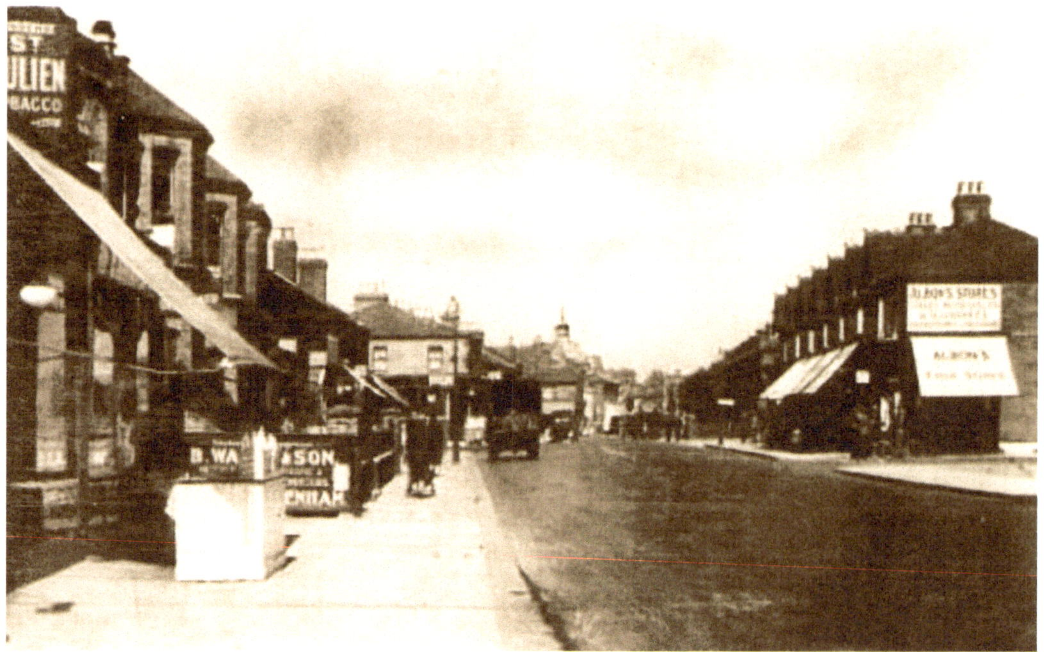

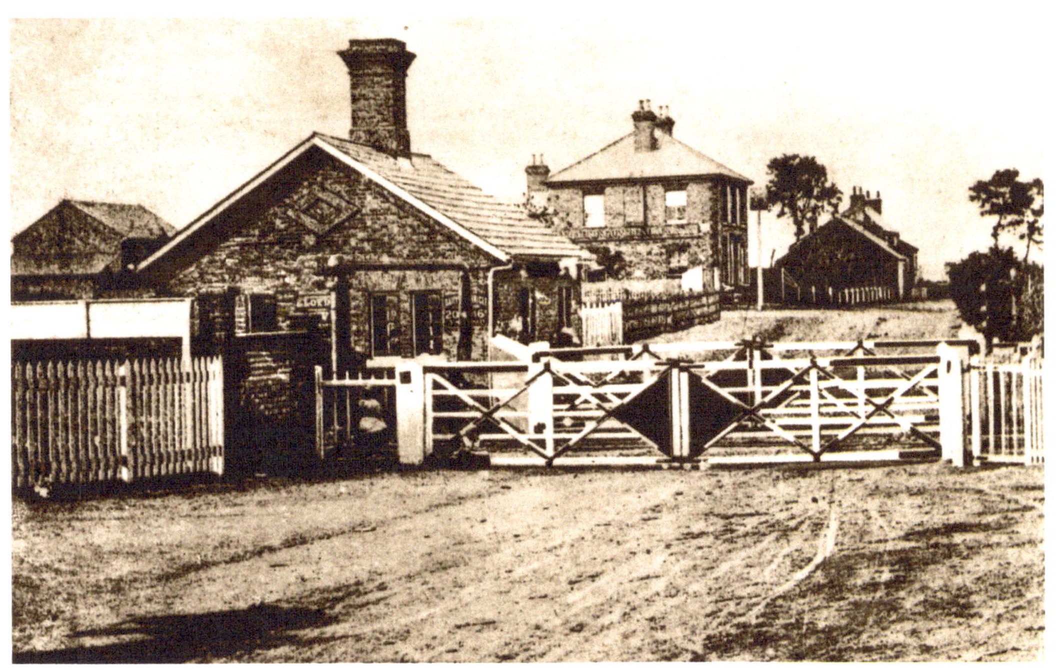

Level Crossing

The level crossing in Ripple Road was still in use until relatively recently. It has now been replaced by a bridge, although it survived much longer than the town's other level crossings.

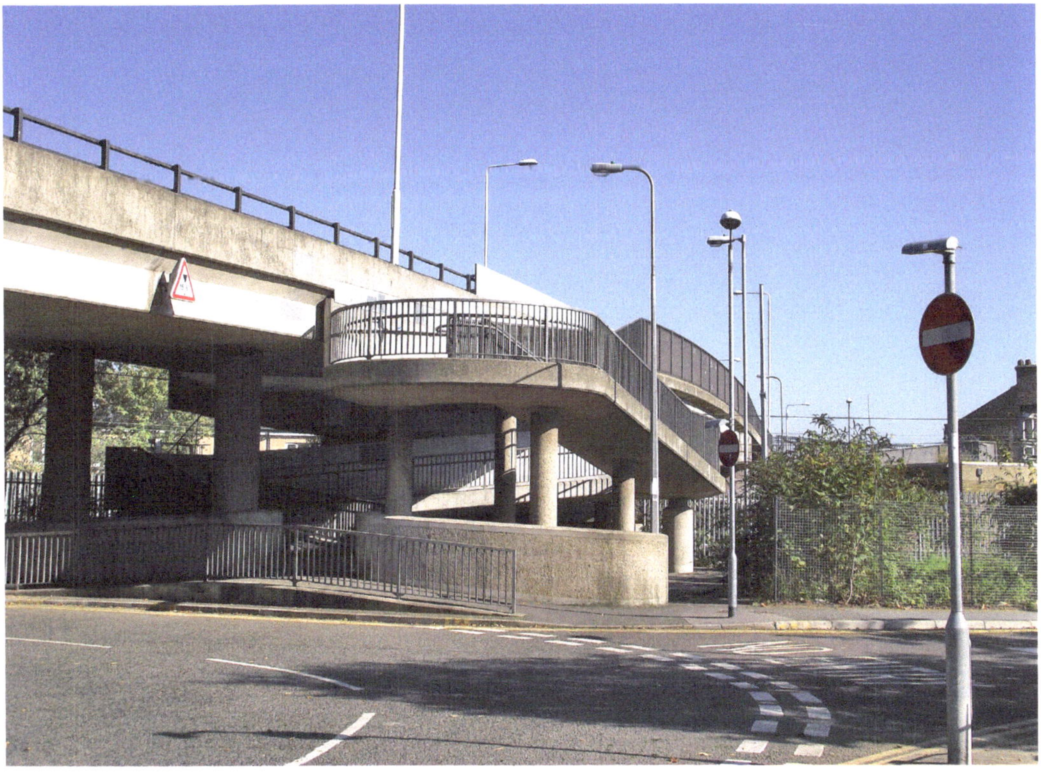

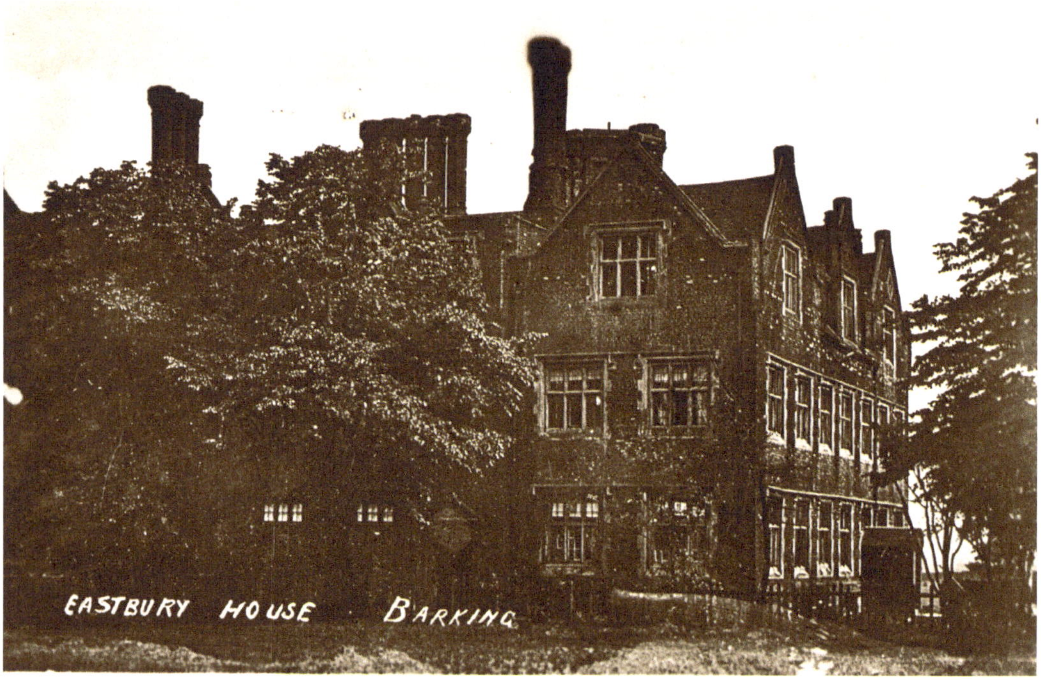

Eastbury House

Eastbury House dates back to the sixteenth century. It is often wrongly attributed to playing a part in the gunpowder plot of Guy Fawkes. The building was left to fall into disrepair in the early twentieth century but has since been restored and is now open to the public.

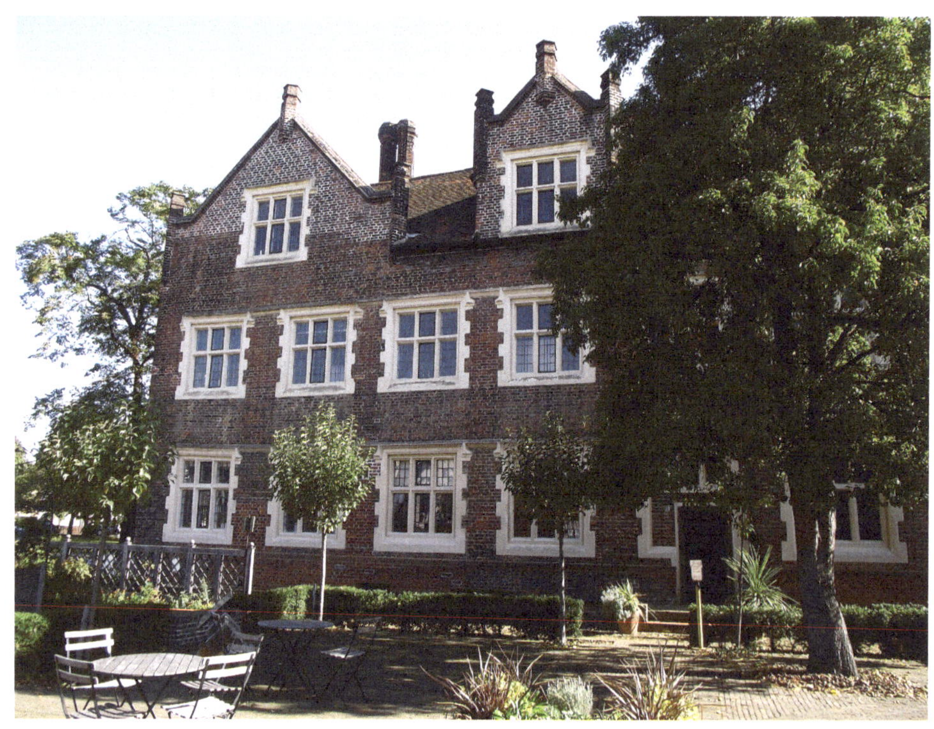

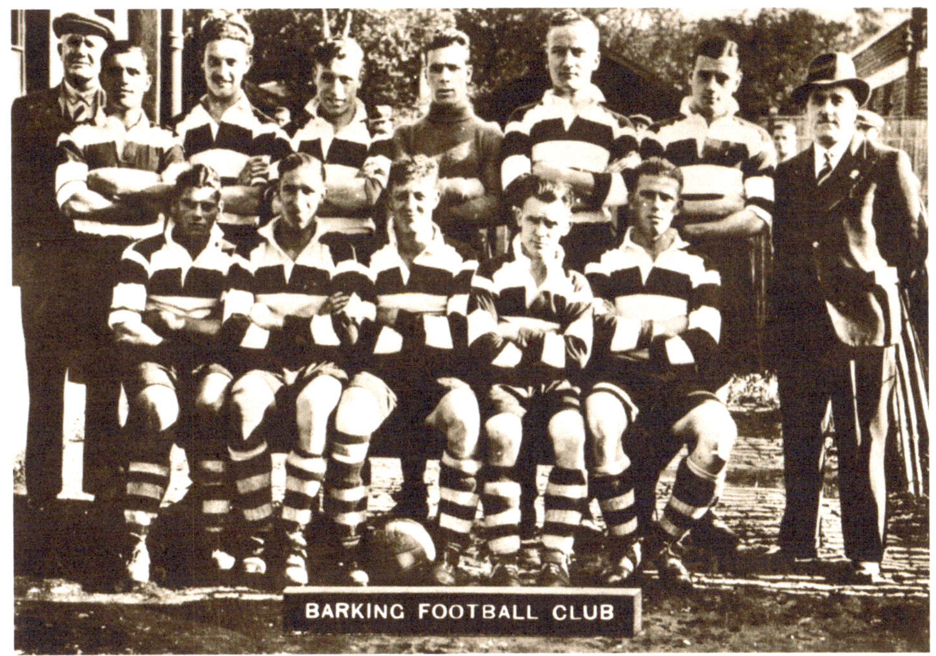

Barking FC

Barking Football Club once had a large ground alongside the railway line opposite the station. At the time, the team was also one of the top local amateur teams in the area. They were winners of both the London Senior Cup and the Essex Senior Cup. The ground now lies beneath Vicarage Fields Shopping Centre and a less illustrious Barking team now play in Maysbrook Park, Lodge Avenue.

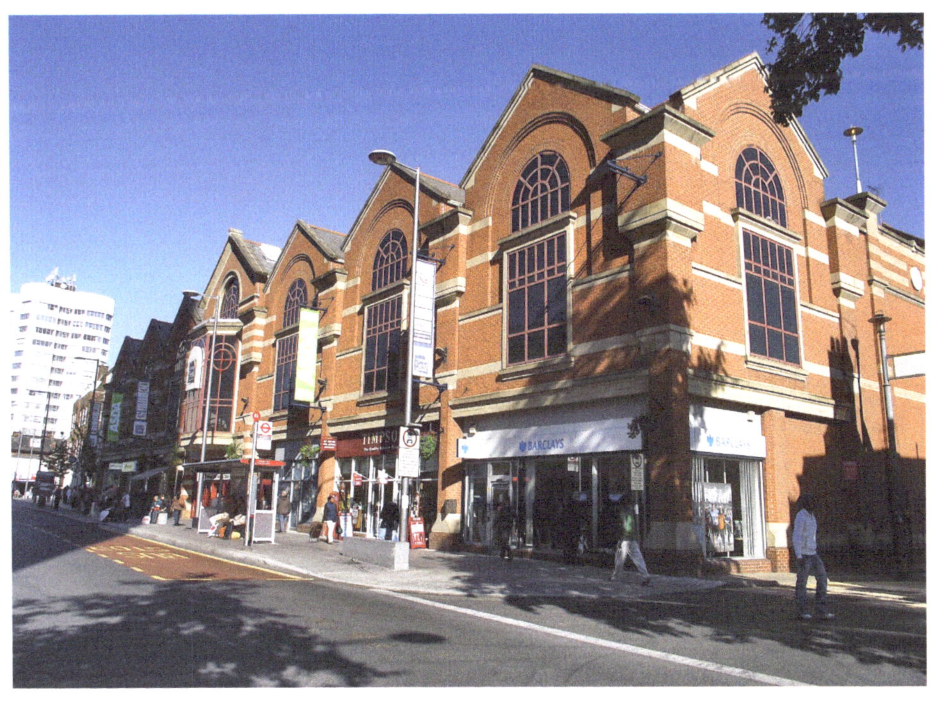

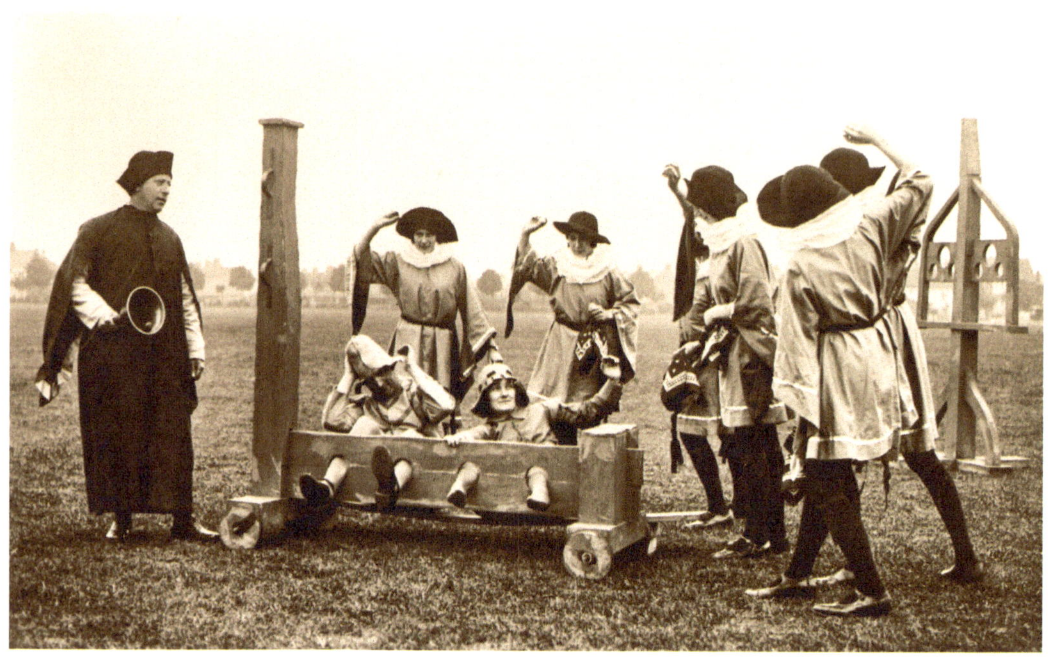

Barking Pageant

Barking Pageant was held to commemorate the town becoming a borough. It was a well-organised event that went on for some time. The old image with the stocks is labelled as Barking Fair. A very new kind of fair is shown in Barking Park in 2010.

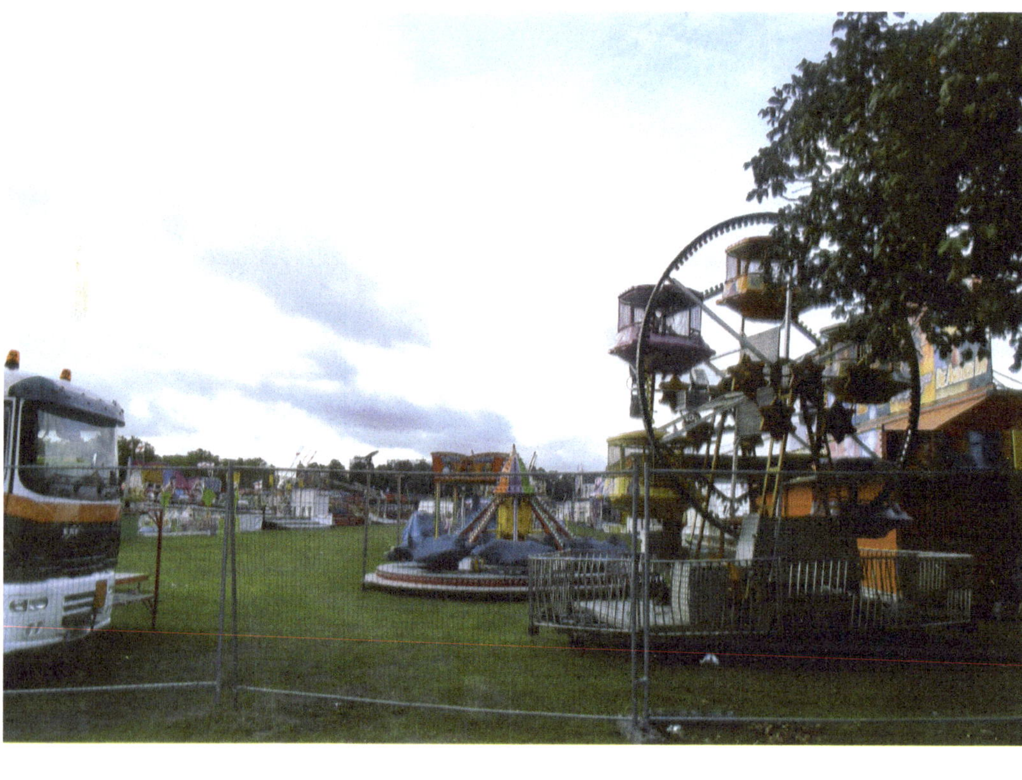

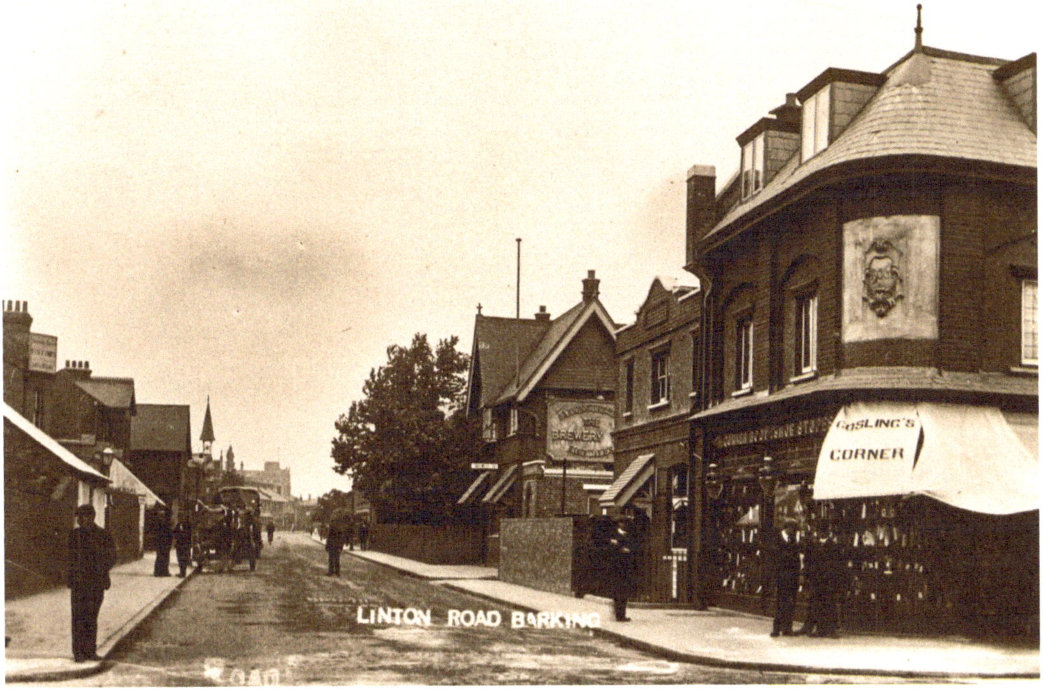

Linton Road

The Brewery Tap public house is one of the few original buildings still standing in Linton Road. Glenny's Brewery used to stand behind it. Much of the rest of the road is now large office buildings and even the large residential Lintons flats have now been demolished. (*Footsteps*)

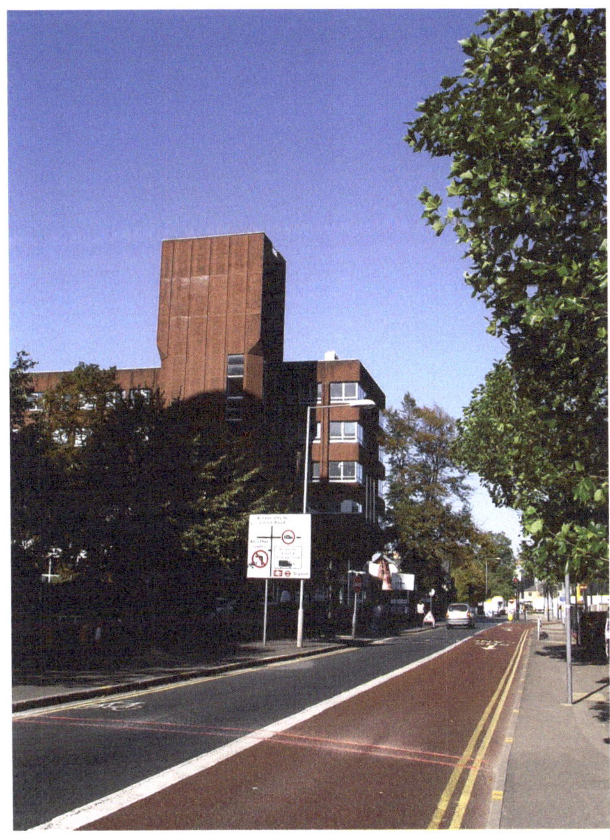

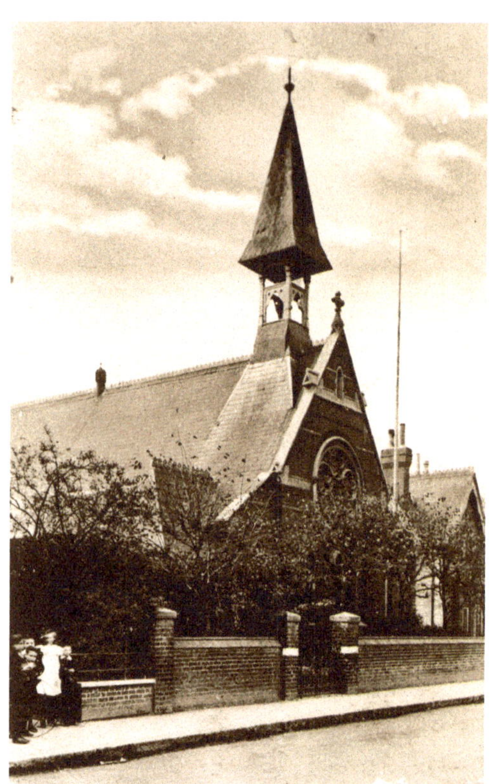

Roman Catholic Church

Strangely, the original Roman Catholic services in Barking were held in the rear of the Red Lion pub, which was actually a church in Linton Road. Services were then held in the Roman Catholic school from 1863 until the original St Ethelburgas church was built in 1869. This has now been replaced by the present building.

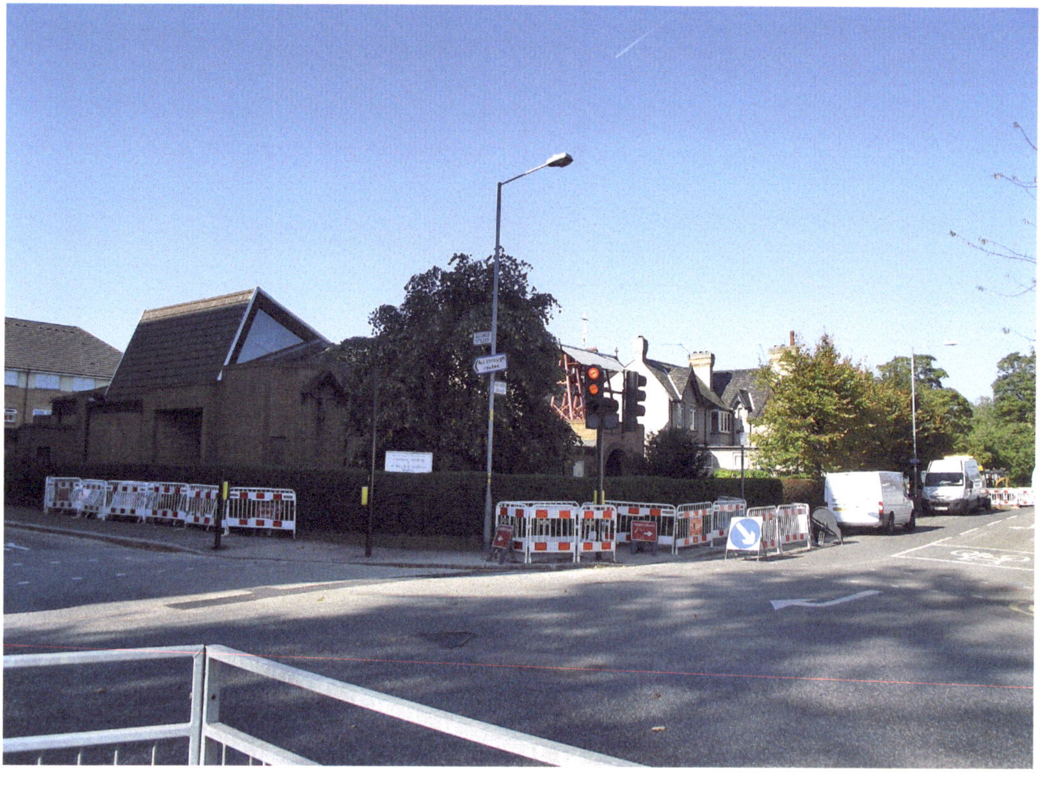

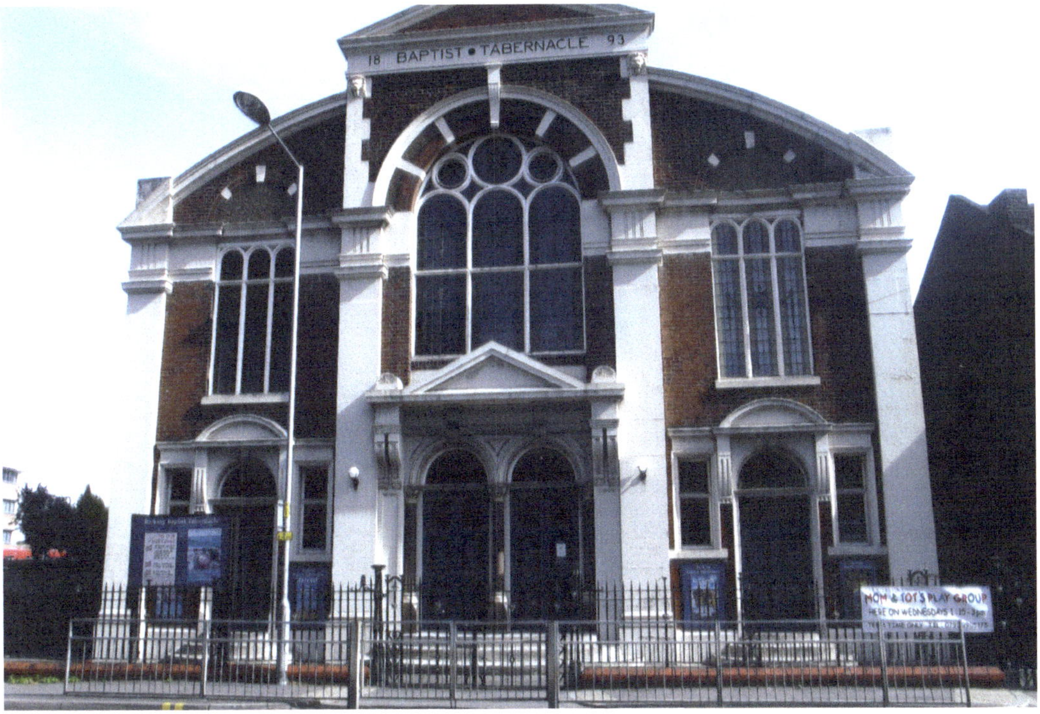

Baptist Tabernacle

The Baptists in Barking were connected with those of Ilford in the nineteenth century. Together with the Ilford branch, a church was erected in Queen's Road in 1851. This was replaced by the Tabernacle in Linton Road in 1893.

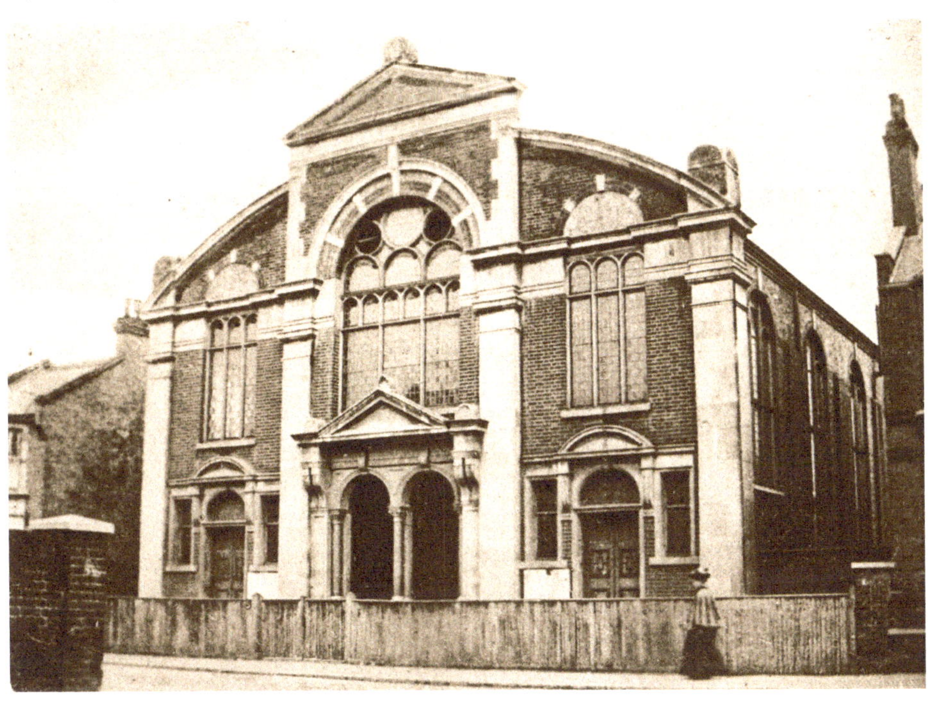

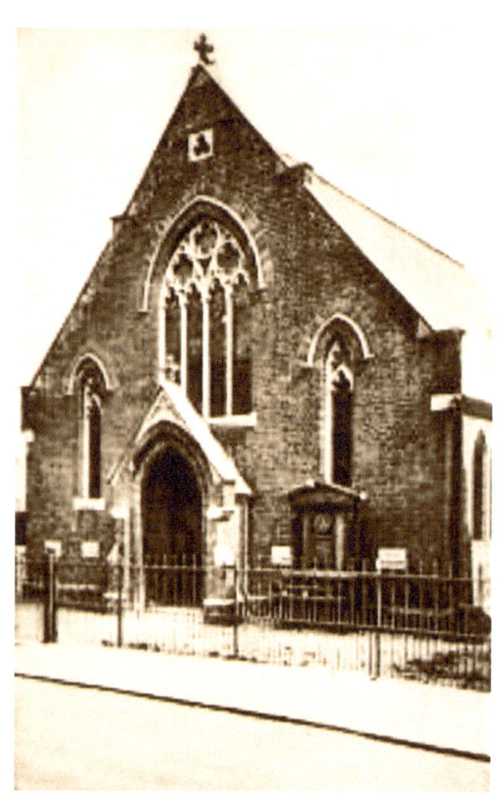

Wesleyan Church

A wooden chapel was the first Methodist church in the town, built in Bull Street. This was later replaced by a new Central Hall in East Street in 1928. This seems to have been on the site of what later became the Capitol Cinema in 1933. The Methodist church now stands in London Road.

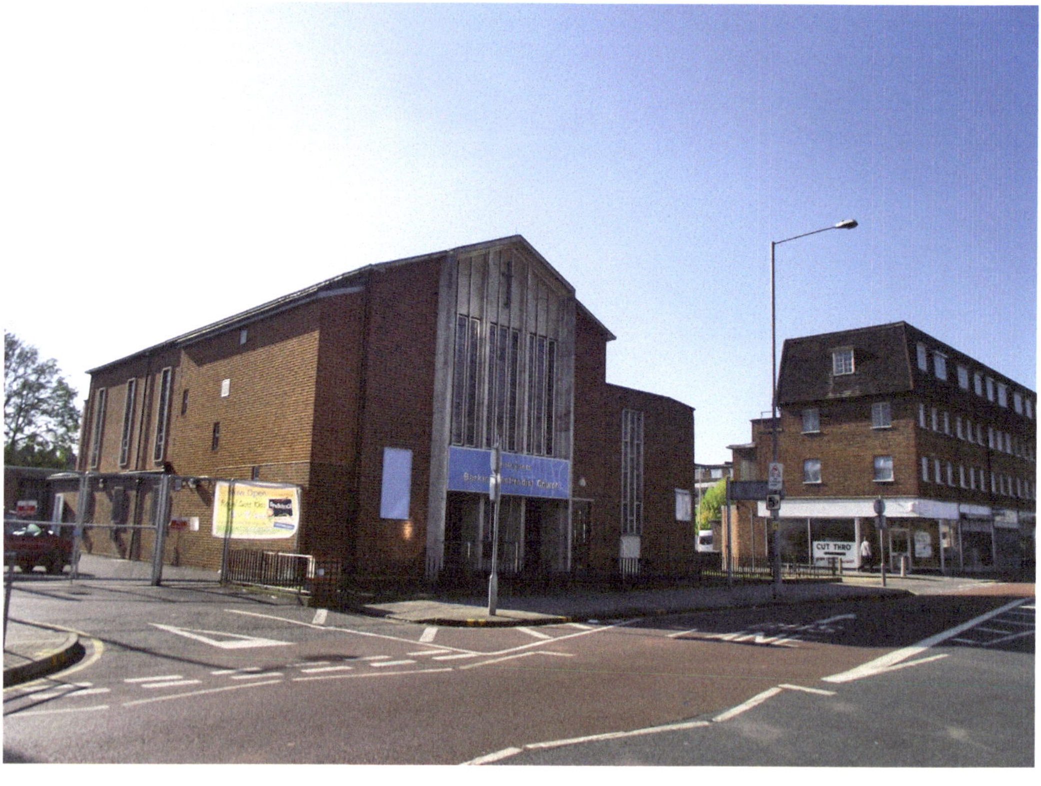

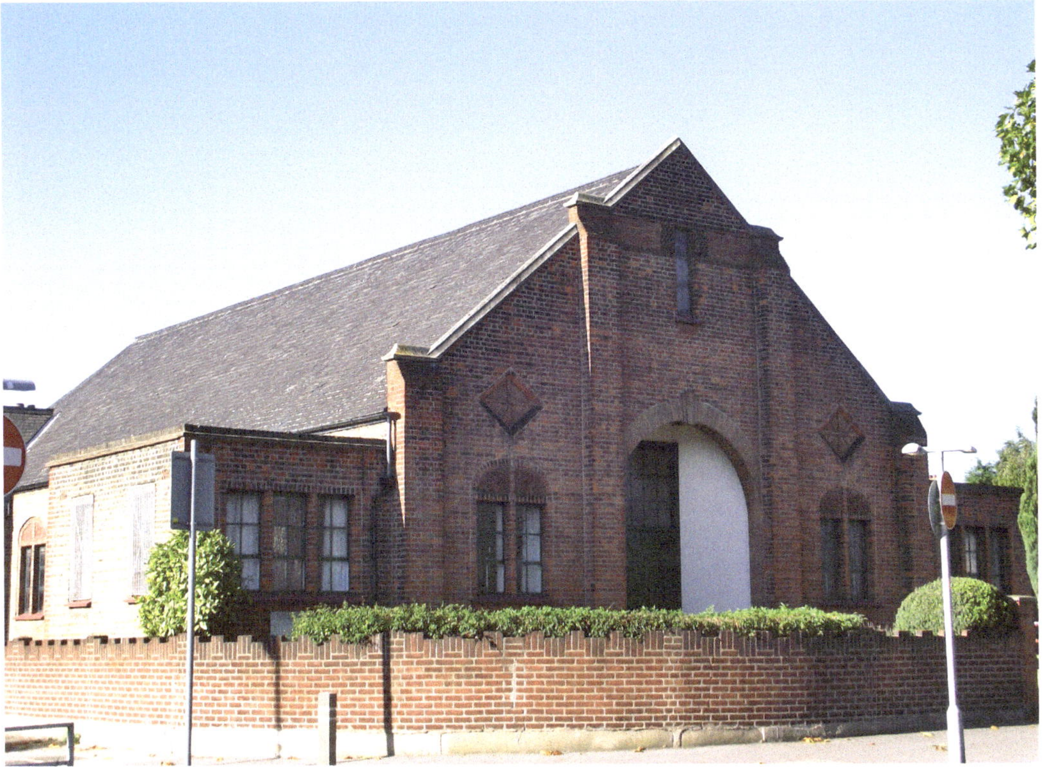

Congregational Church

Congregational meetings were held in a house in Barking from the late eighteenth century. Their first church was built in the Broadway in 1785. It was rebuilt in 1824 and again in 1864. The church in the old photograph was the one that stood in the Broadway until 1929. It was then sold and a new one built in Upney Lane.

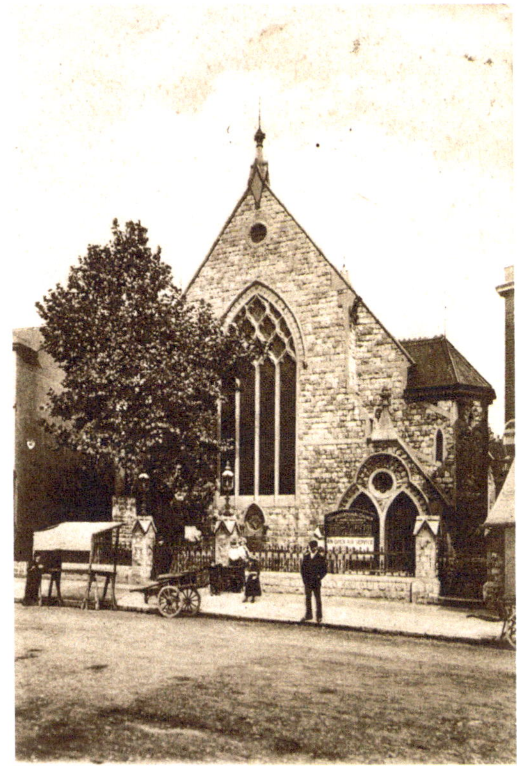

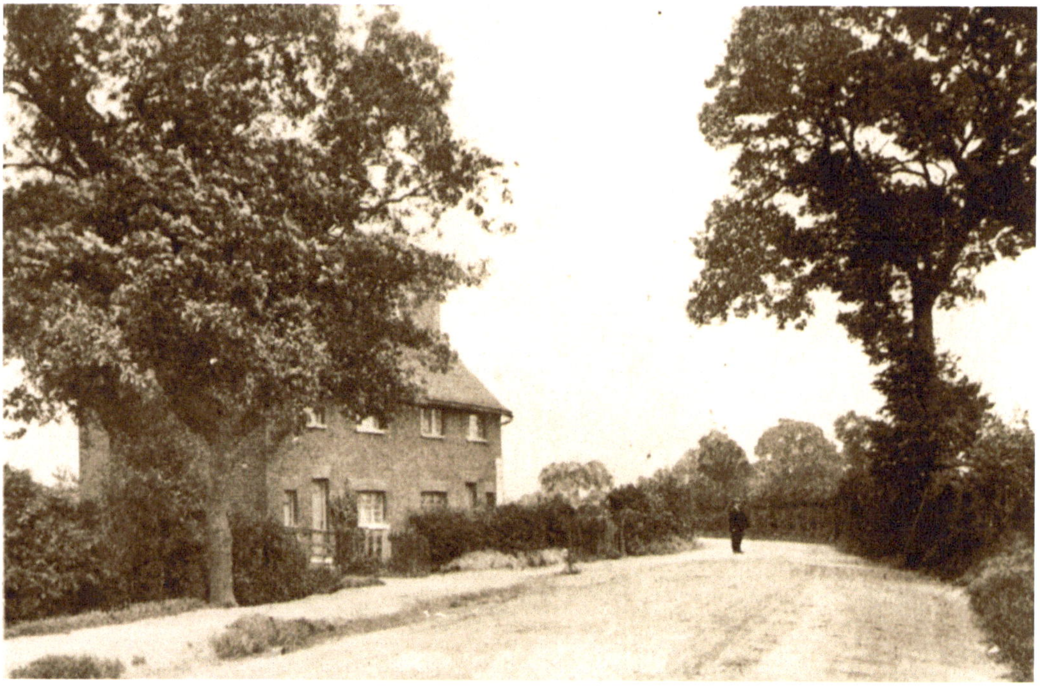

Longbridge Road

Although very rural in the old photograph, the area along Longbridge Road is now very built up. Houses began to spread along the road from Barking in the 1920s. Part of it also is the front of Barking Park and the old technical school that became part of the University of London and is now being converted to homes.

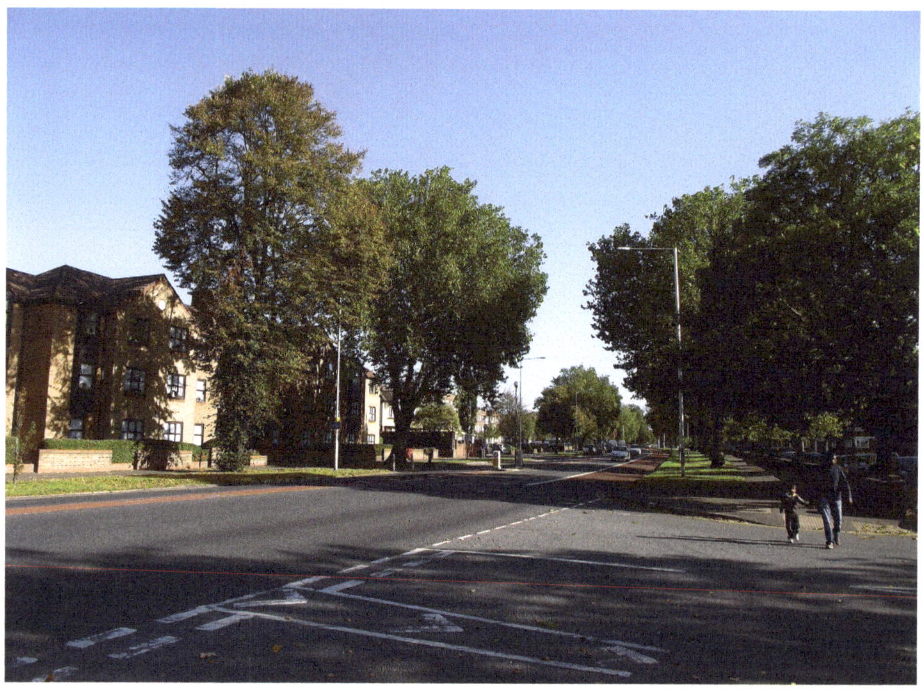

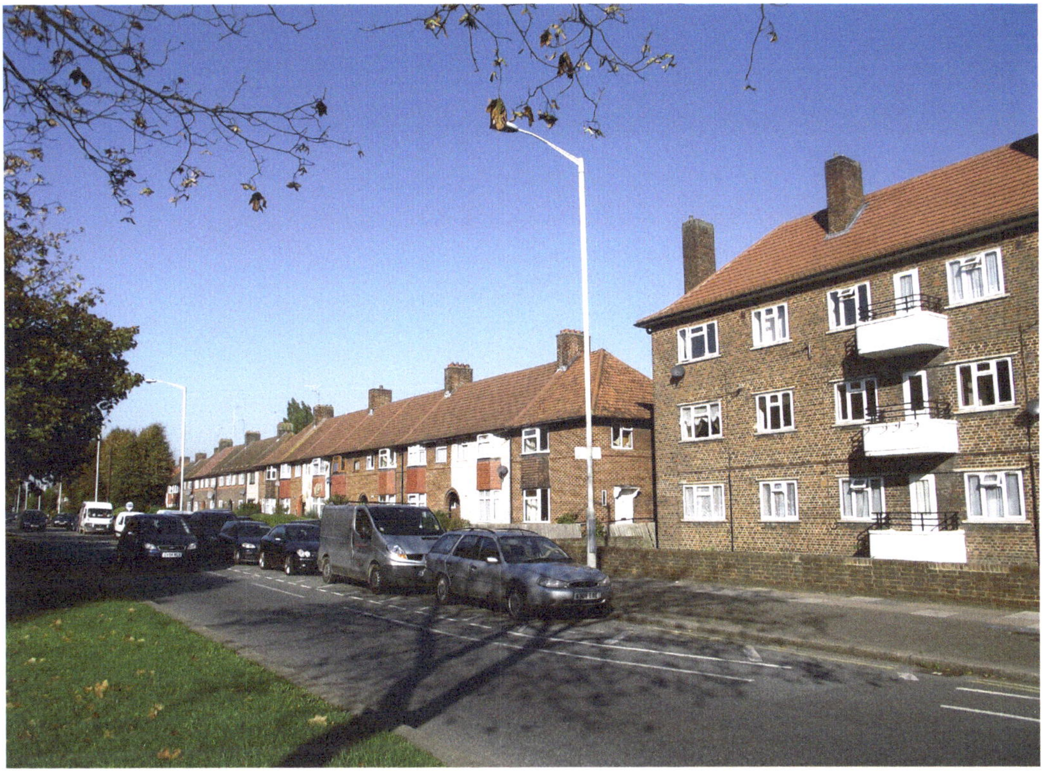

Rural Isolation

The rural aspect of this part of the town was shown in 1734 when six armed men broke into Longbridge Farm and spent hours ransacking the house knowing they would not be disturbed due to its isolation. The Dagenham end of Longbridge Road began to change from its rural past with the coming of the Becontree estate after the First World War.

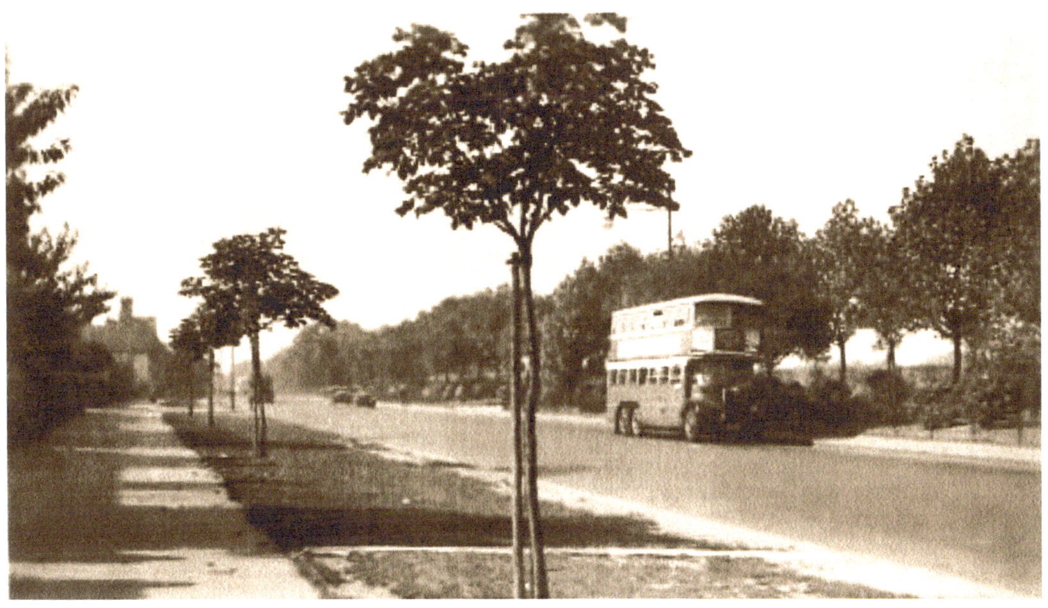

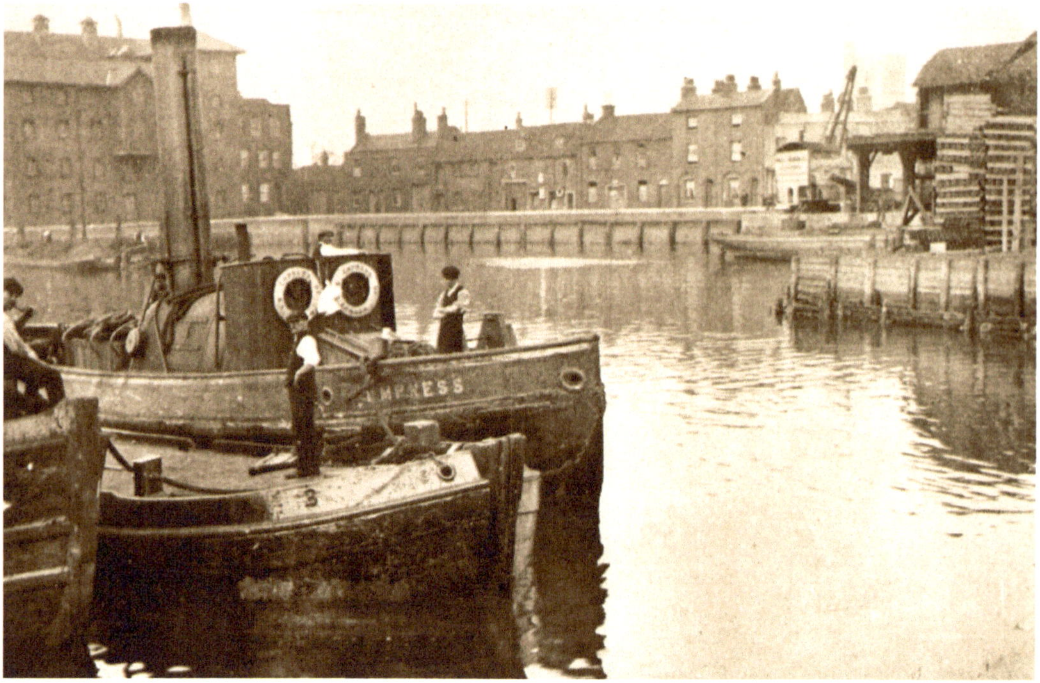

Town Quay

The town quay was once the centre of a thriving fishing industry on which the success of the town was built. It declined in the mid-nineteenth century when the main Short Blue fleet moved to the east coast. The area around the quay then became the centre of early industry.

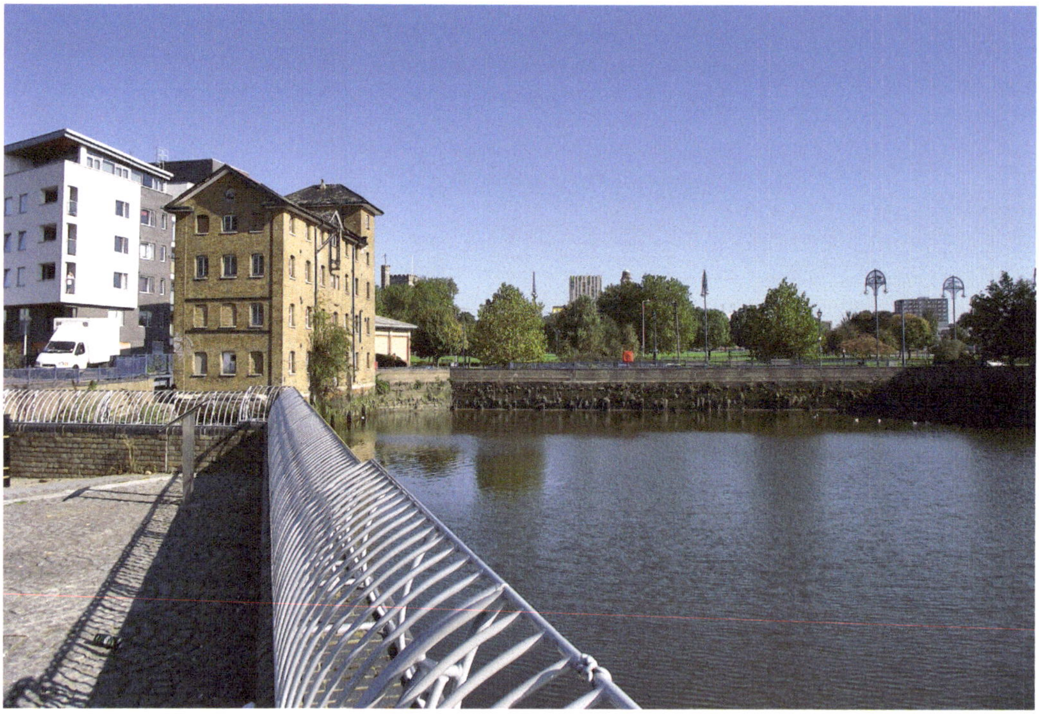

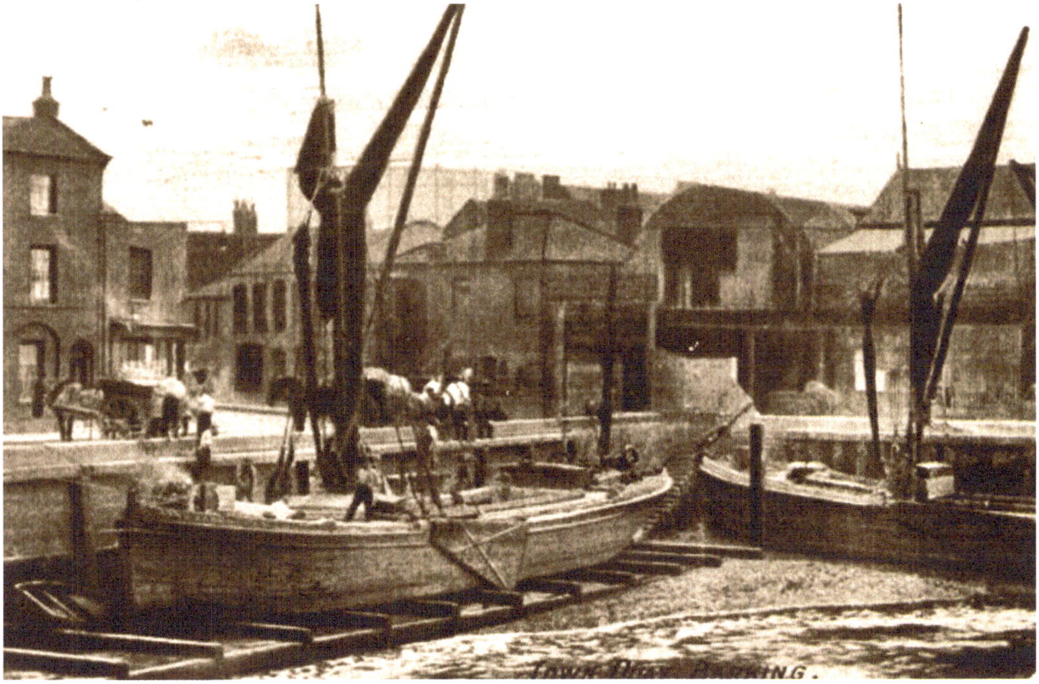

TOWN QUAY, BARKING.

Barges

The early factories around the quay used the river as the main source of transport for both bringing in raw materials and sending out finished goods. Barges could travel as far upriver as Ilford where other factories stood along its banks.

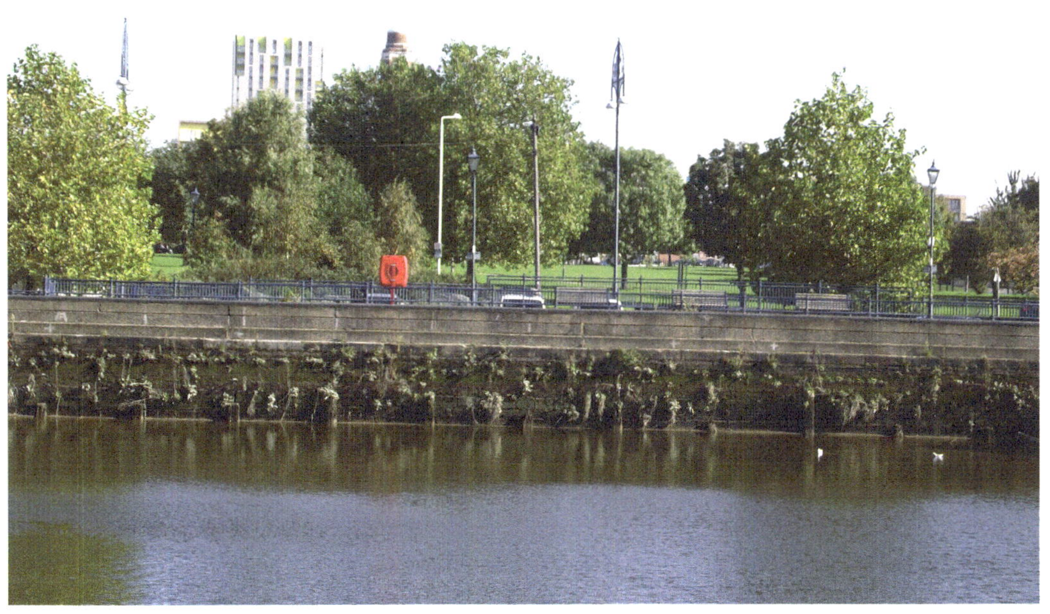

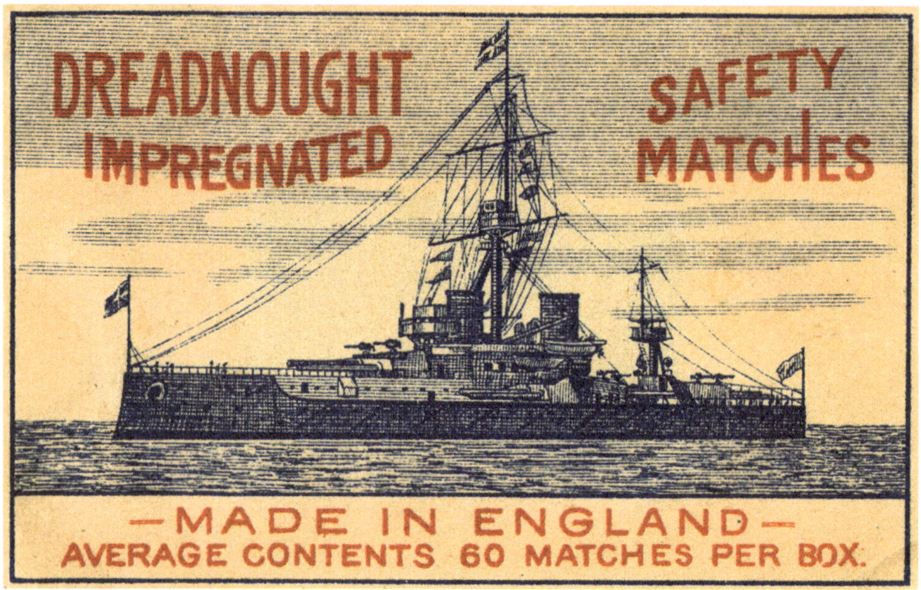

Abbey Match Works

The Abbey Match Works stood in Barking from the turn of the twentieth century when it was known as the Vulcan Match Company. They produced numerous labels that were well known to collectors of matchbox labels. Although nothing of the factory remains, its name is remembered in part of Maysbrook Park known to local residents as Matchstick Island, supposedly due to a train load of matches that overturned there at some time in the past.

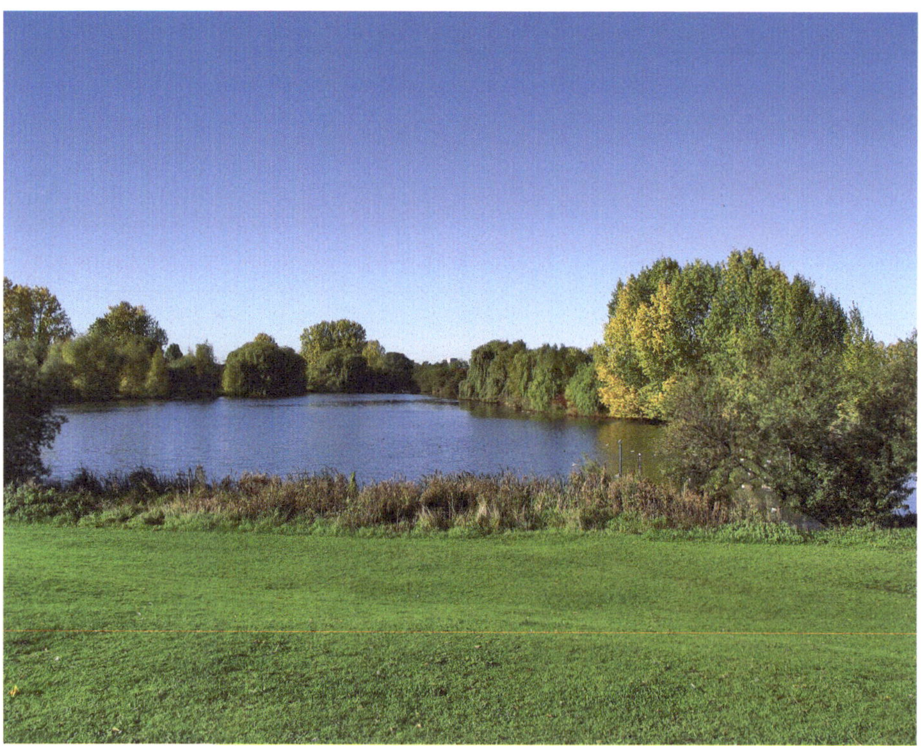

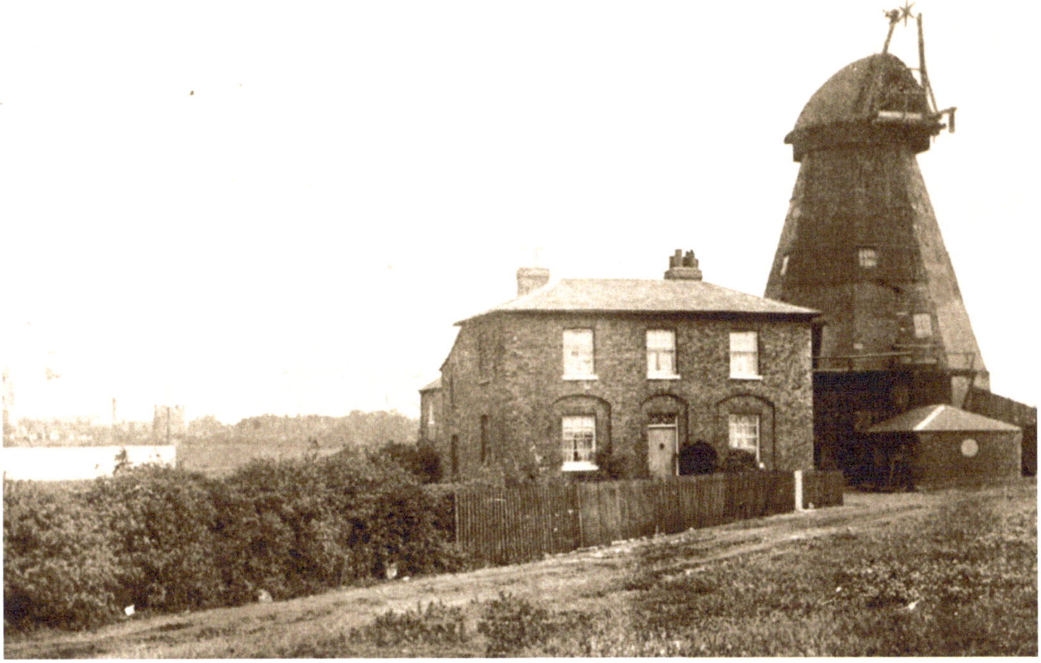

Windmill

The windmill in Barking was known as Wellington Mill and was built in 1815, the year that the Battle of Waterloo took place. There was also a large house and around half an acre of land that went with the mill. It stood on the bank of the Rover Roding, east of London Road. It was demolished in 1926 and today the area is covered by a large retail park.

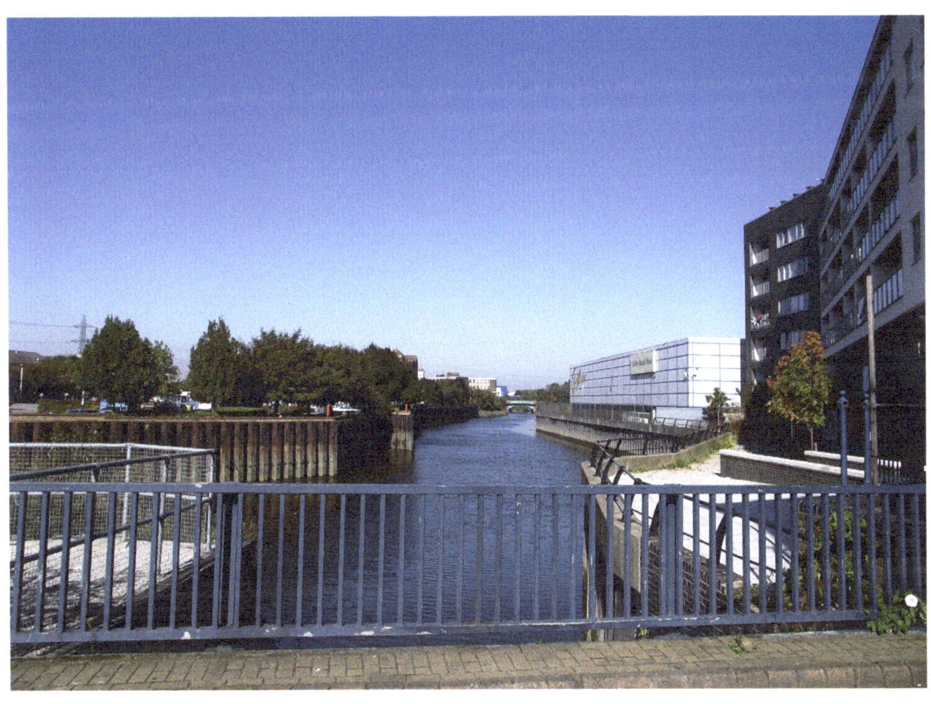

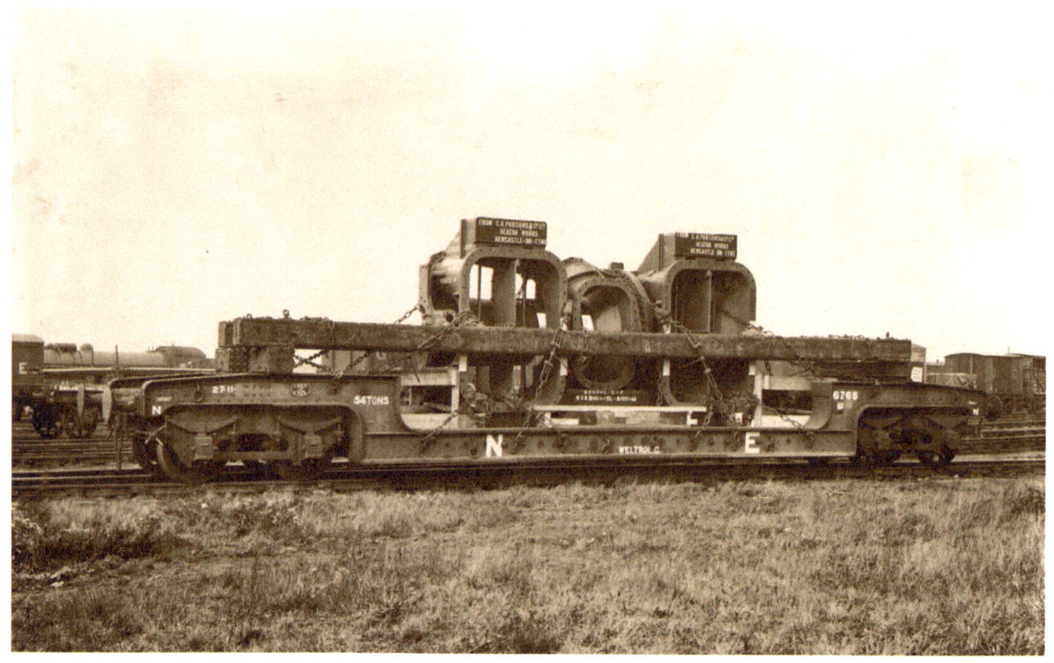

Barking Power Station

The power station was opened in 1925 with a visit from Queen Mary and King George V. It was built by the County of London Electricity Supply Company. The old photograph shows a part being carried by rail in 1928. The power station had its own jetty to take delivery of coal from ships on the Thames. It closed in 1981 after the use of coal-powered electricity declined. The area is now used as Dagenham Sunday Market which moved from its old site in Chequers Lane.

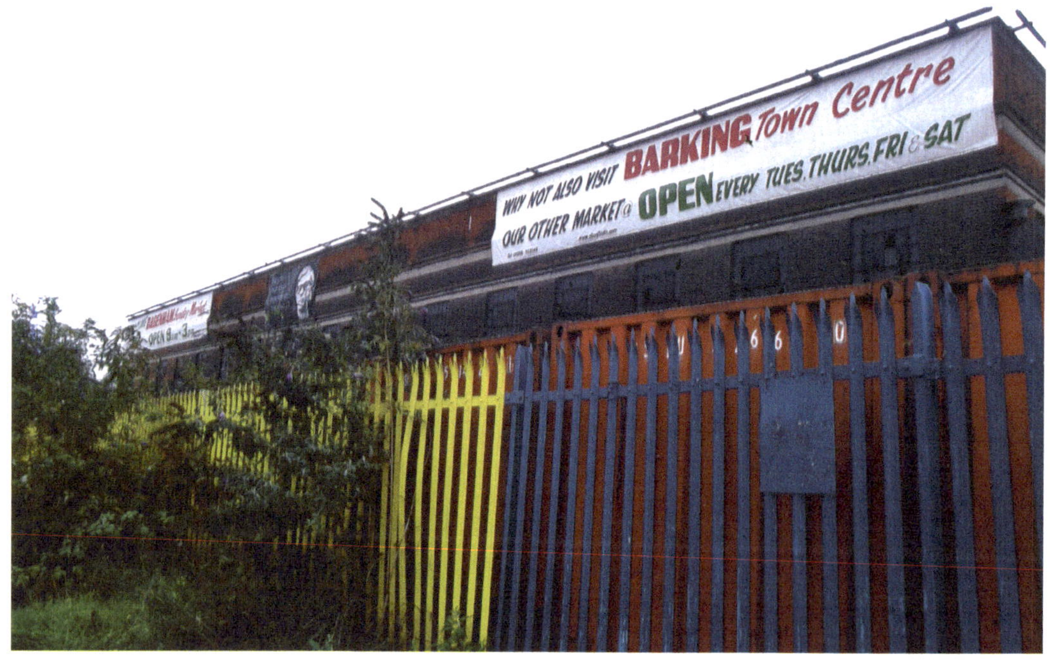

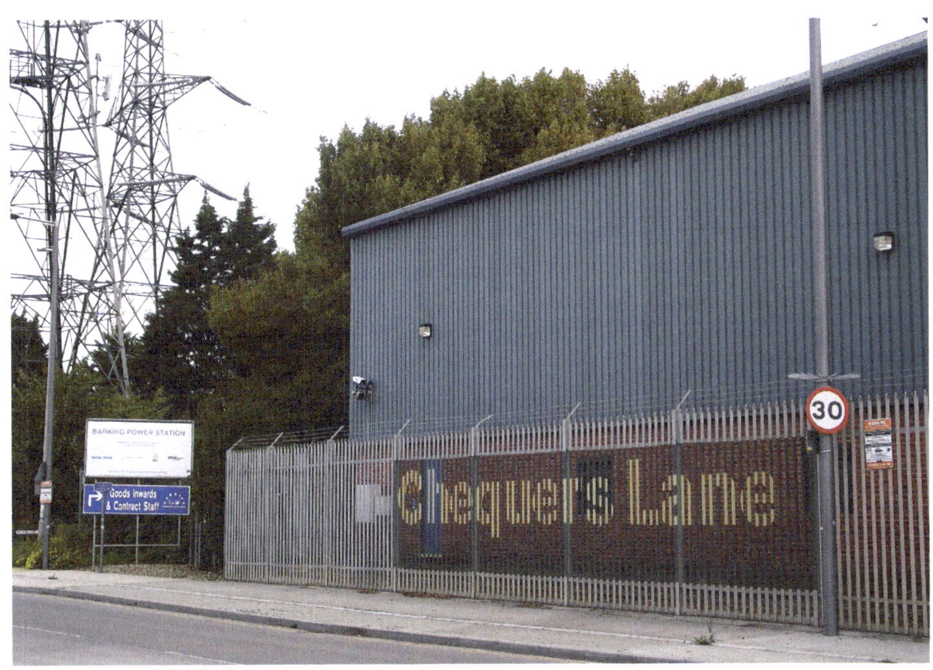

Parts for Industry

Another view of a part being carried to the power station. There was a row of cottages on the corner of River Road and Ripple Road across from the Volunteer public house that were for the use of power station employees. They were knocked down along with the Volunteer when the A13 road was widened. A new power station opened in Chequers Lane in 1995 which replaced the Sunday market held there which moved to the old power station site.

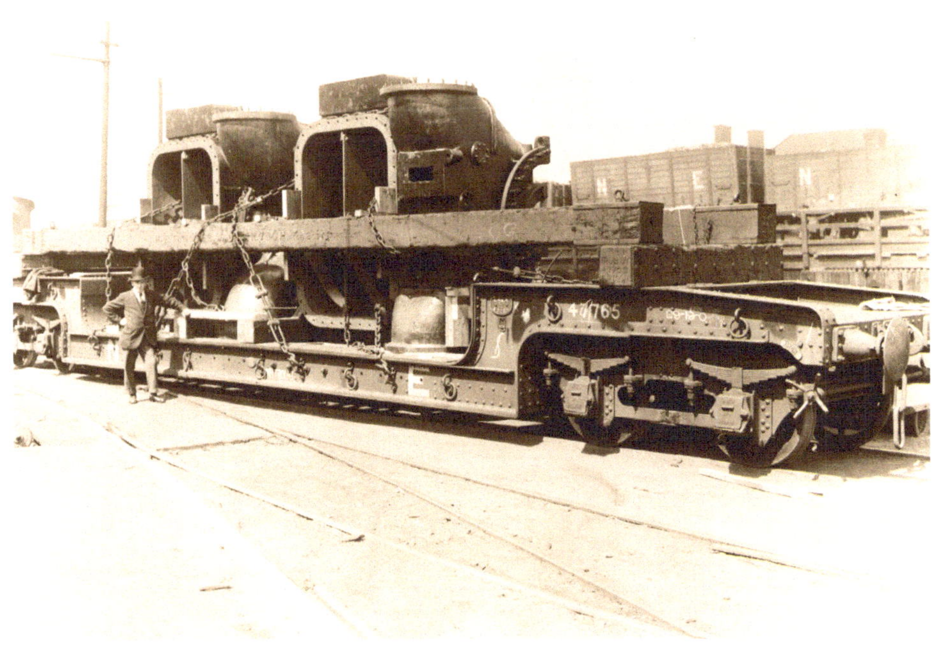

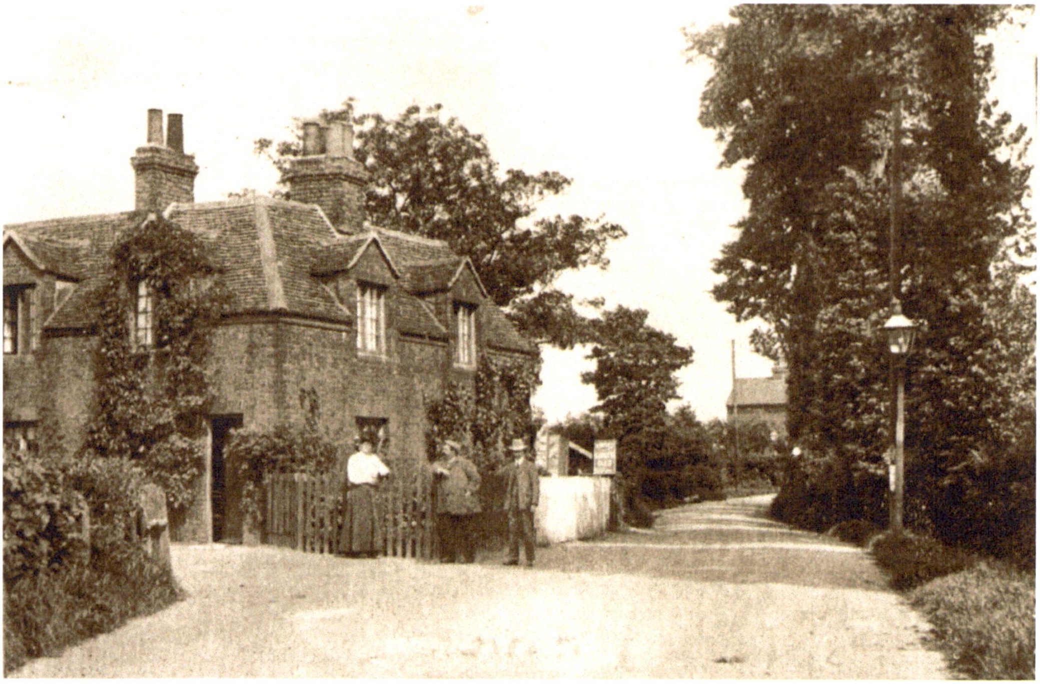

Upney Lane

Upney Lane was once a small hamlet which was separate from Barking. Since the old photograph was taken, Barking has spread eastwards to engulf the old area with more modern buildings and Barking Hospital, although this is now much reduced in size to what it once was.

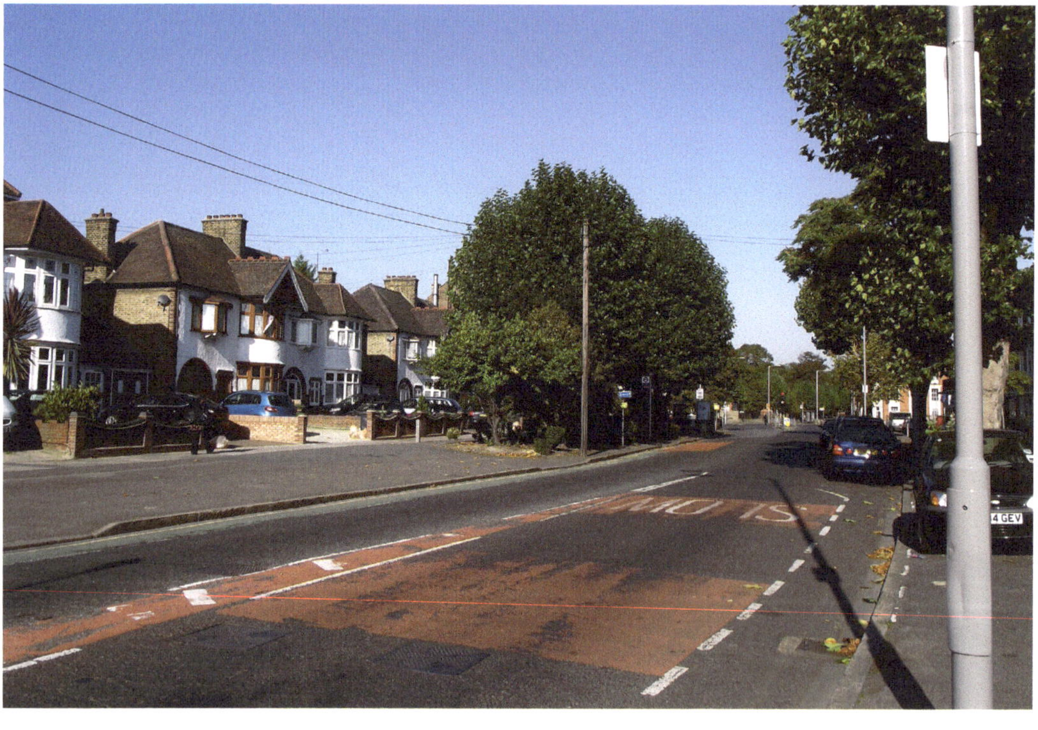

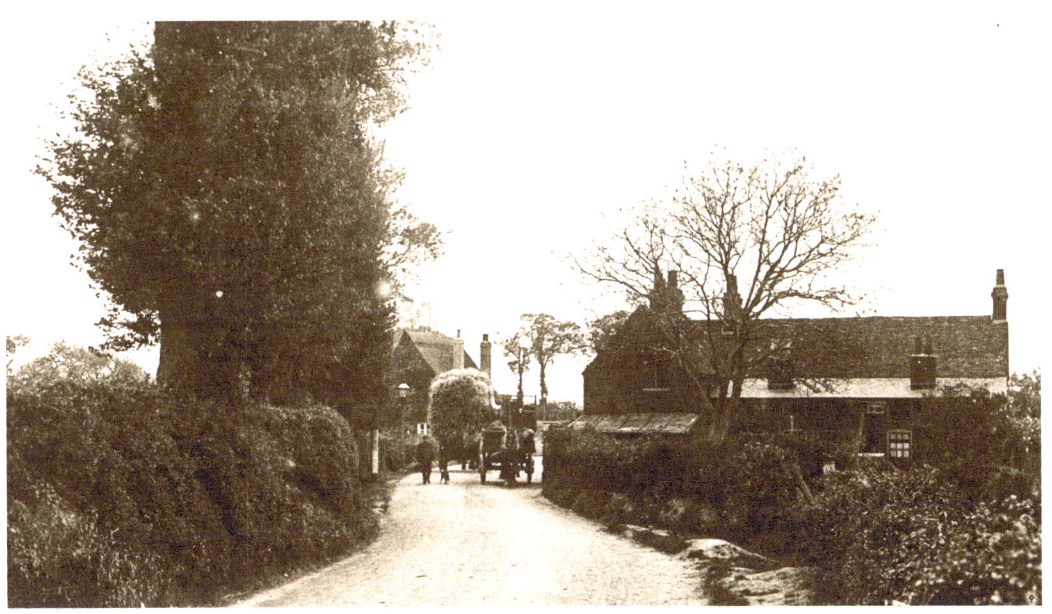

The Underground

The transformation of Upney Lane from a rural Hamlet to a thriving local area is shown by it having its own underground station. It opened in 1932 when the electrified line was extended from Barking to Upminster. It was around this time that a number of council houses were built in the area.

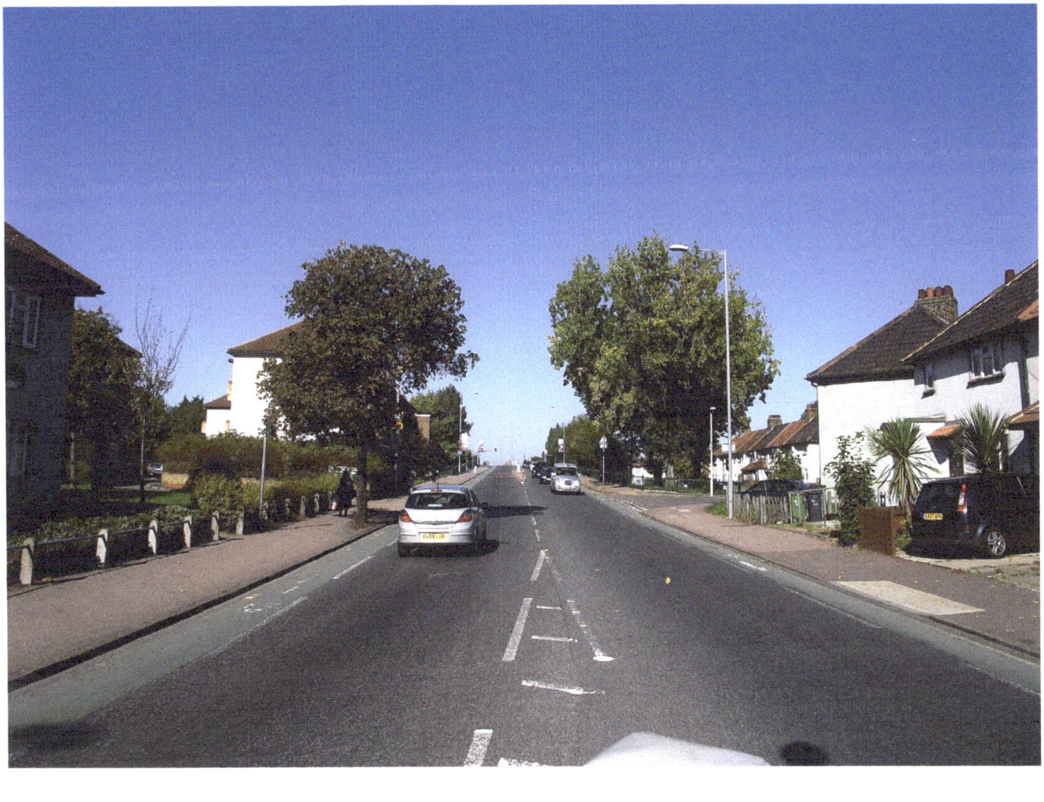

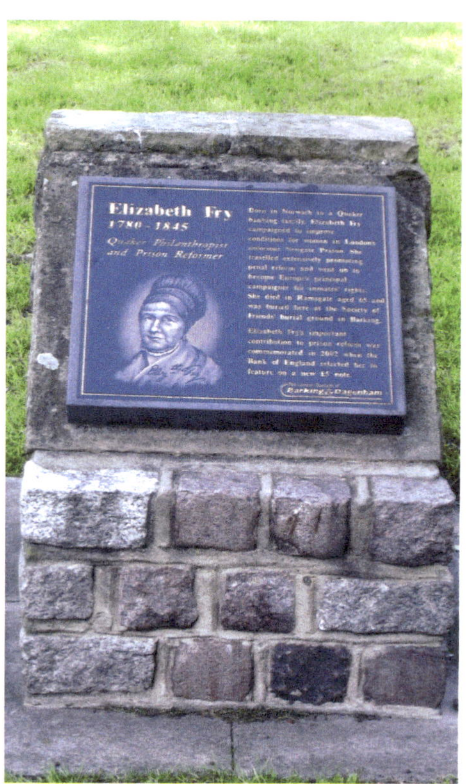

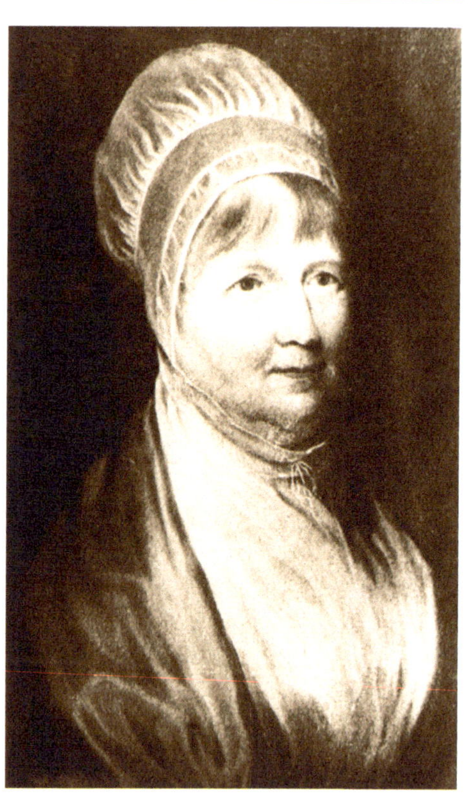

Elizabeth Fry

Elizabeth Fry was one of the most famous prison reformers in history. She became known to the royal families of a number of nations. Fry and her family used to holiday at a cottage at Dagenham Breach. She was a Quaker and was buried in the Quaker burial ground in North Street. This became a garden when the old meeting house became a Sikh Gudwara in the 1980s. A memorial to Fry was placed in the garden in 2003.

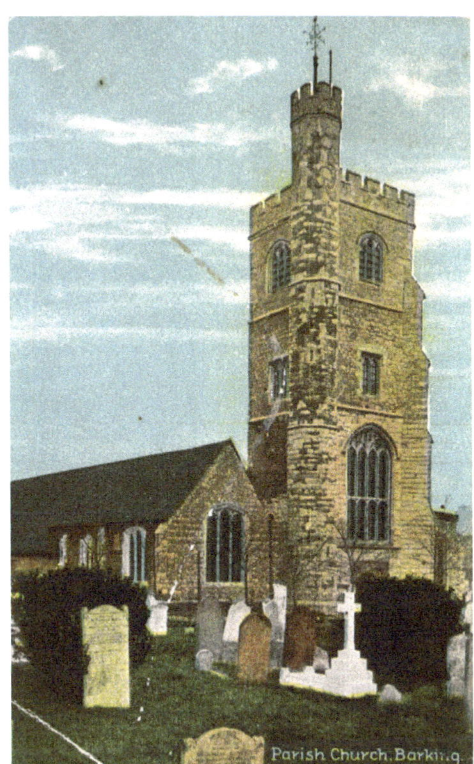

St Margaret's

The parish Church of St Margaret's was originally a chapel associated with the abbey. Much of the present building dates from the fifteenth and sixteenth centuries but has been added to since then. Although the building may not have changed since the old image was taken, the trees have obviously grown.

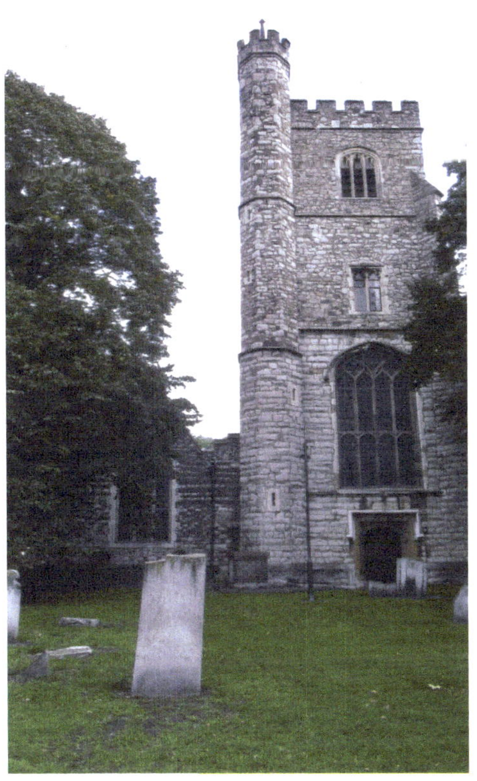

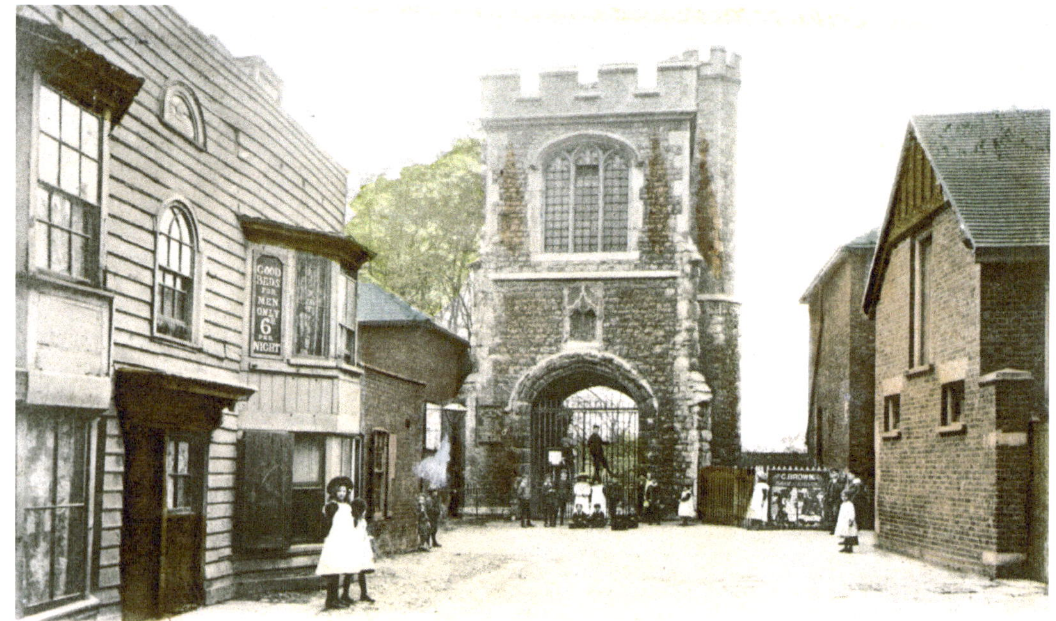

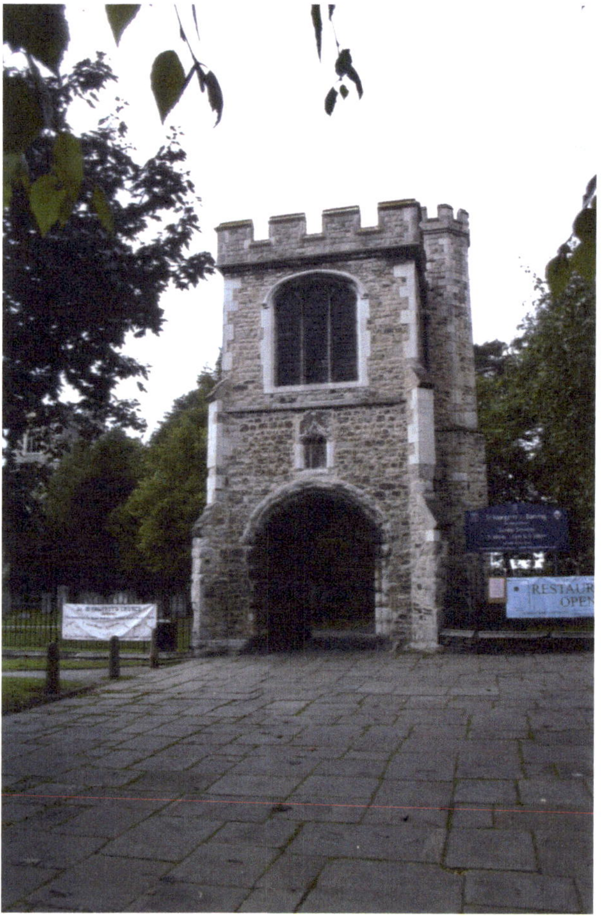

Curfew Tower

The Curfew Tower and some ruins are all that remain of Barking Abbey, which dated back to the seventh century and was the owner of much of the land around both Barking and Dagenham. In the eleventh century, William the Conqueror stayed at the Abbey while the Tower of London was built. The abbey was demolished in the sixteenth century. The old image shows how buildings once stood right up to the tower.

Health and Safety

The old image shows the Curfew Tower from inside the churchyard. The railings have since been removed and no doubt due to the present climate of public safety a notice states beware of the uneven pathway.

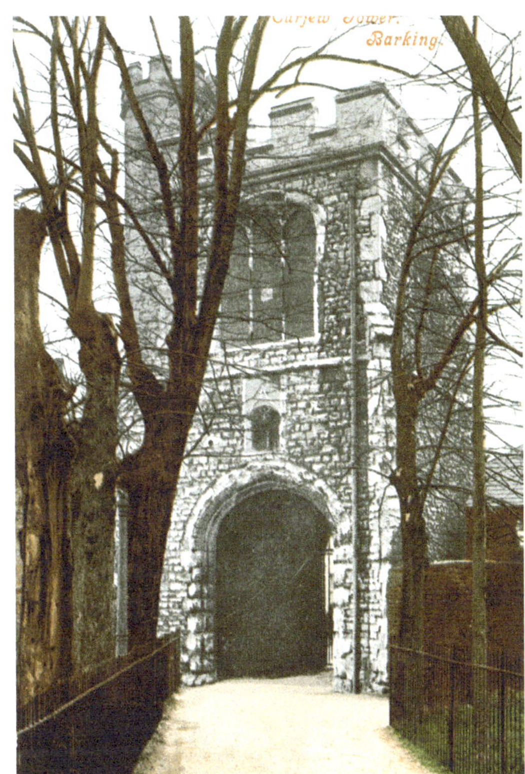

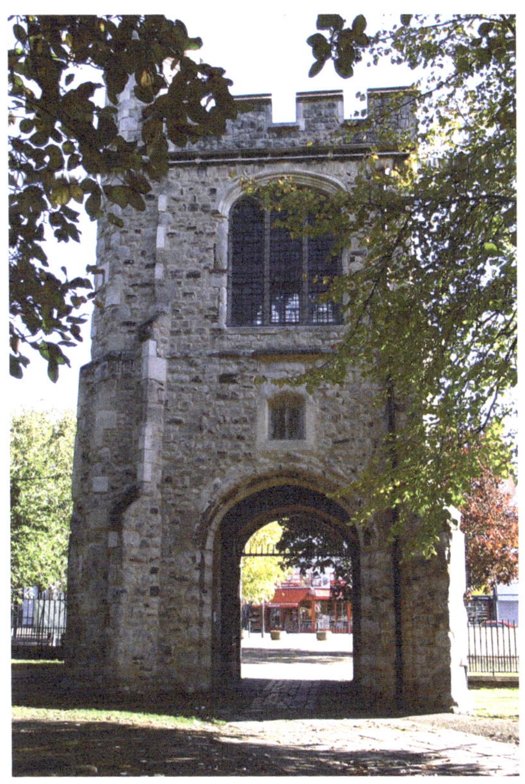

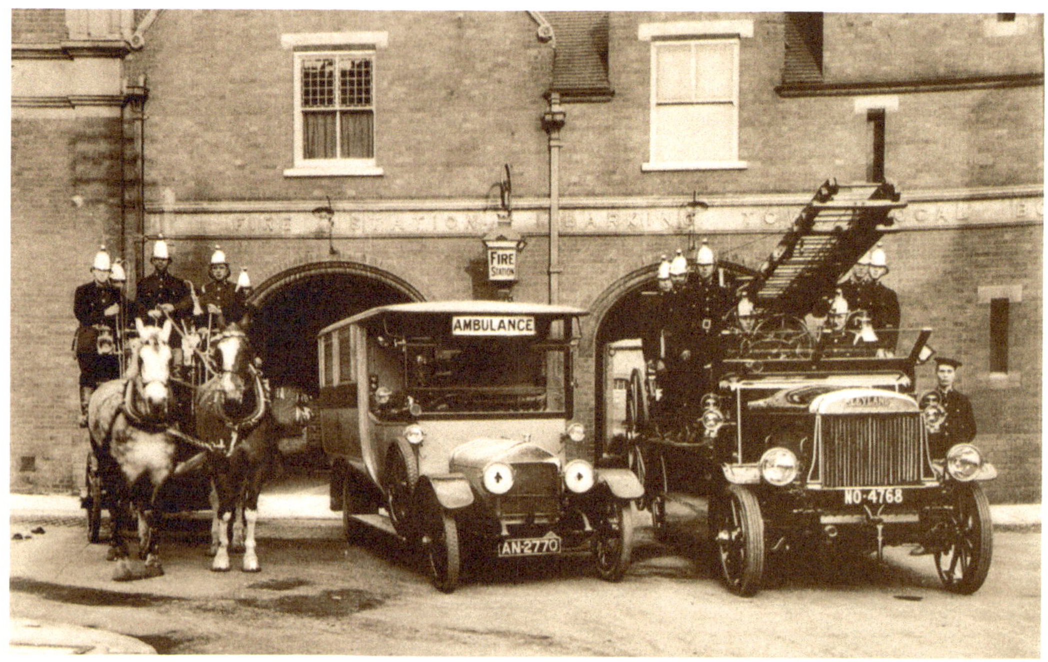

Fire Station

Barking first had a volunteer fire brigade in 1886. In 1897, the council bought a steam fire engine. A fire station was built in East Street. The old image shows the fire brigade in 1925. The modern fire station now stands at the A13 Alfred's Way and dates from the 1930s.

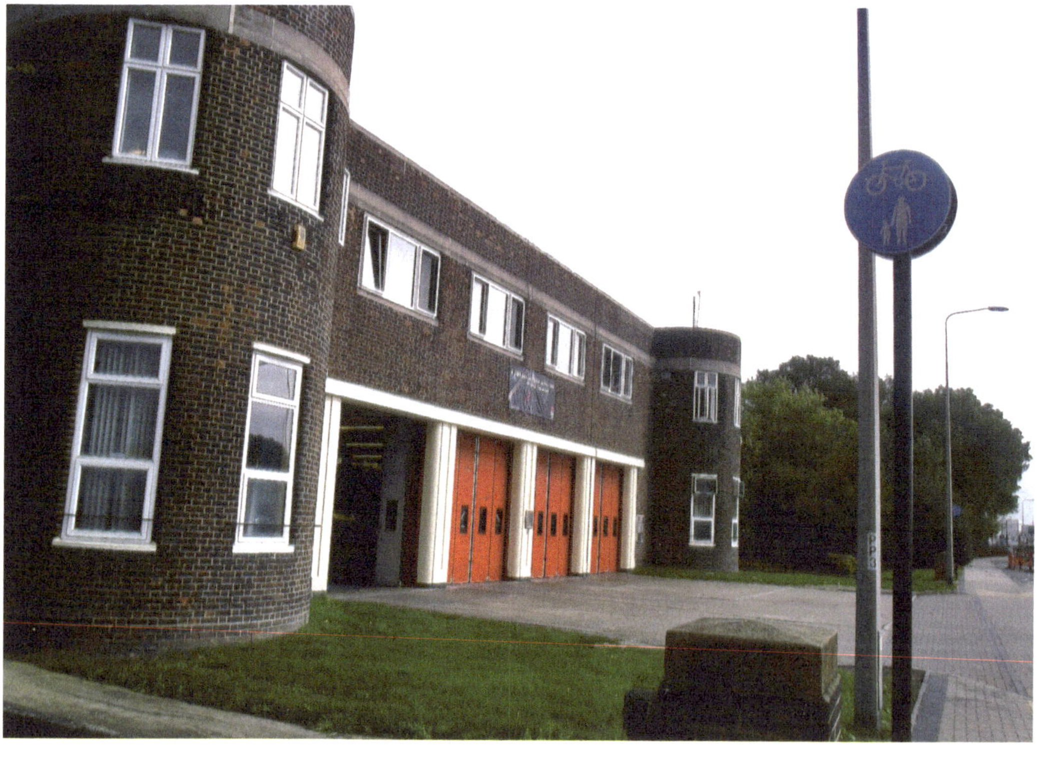

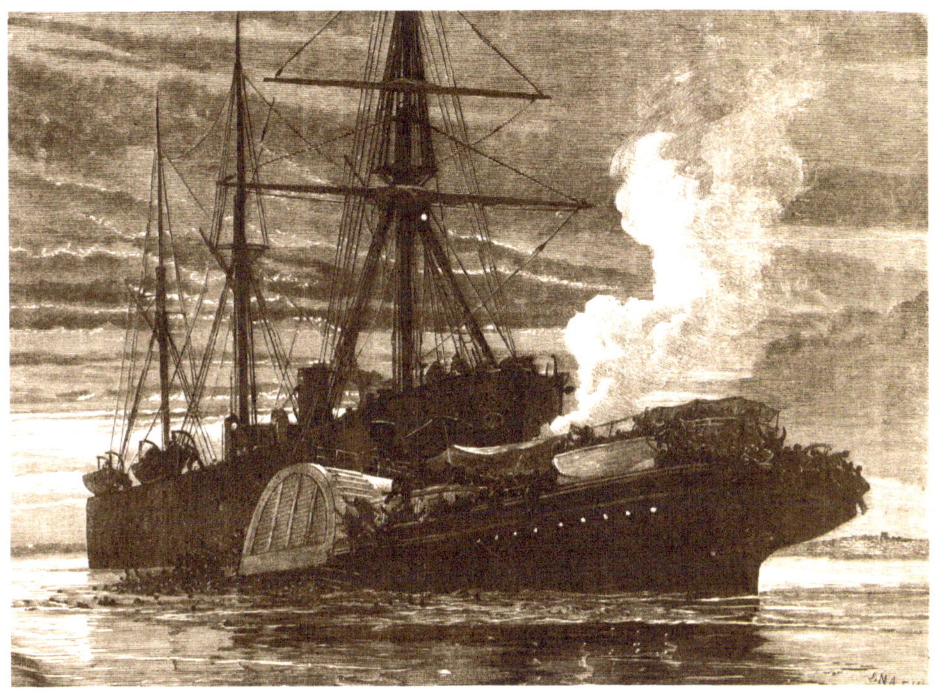

Princess Alice

The *Princess Alice* was a pleasure steamer that was involved in a collision near Barking Creek on the Thames in 1878. It still remains the cause of the largest loss of life on any inland waterway accident in the history of the country. Many of the survivors and some of the fatalities were taken to the hamlet of Creekmouth. Now all that remains is the pub and a small open space with a memorial to the disaster.

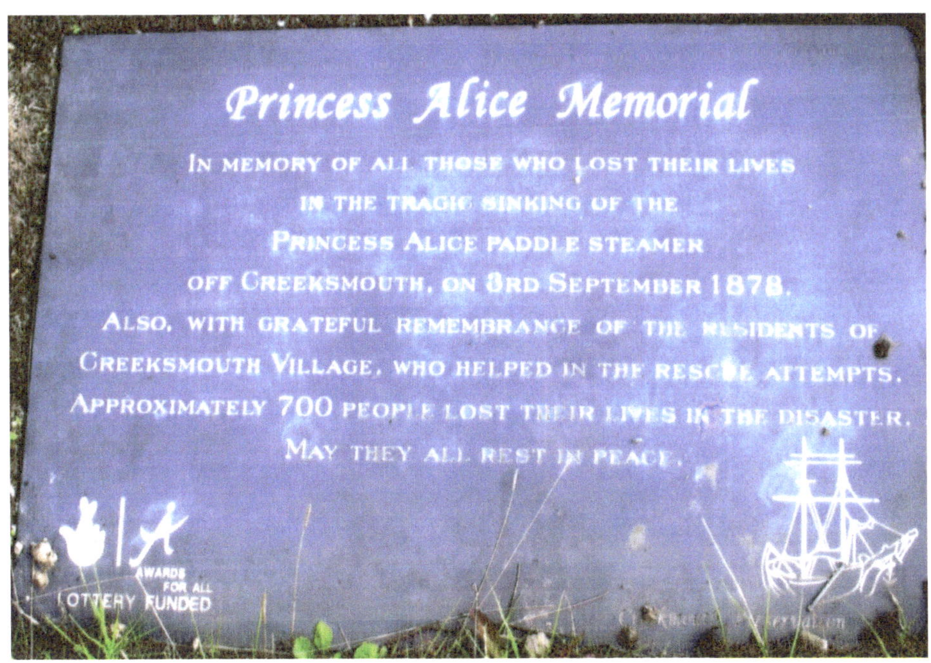

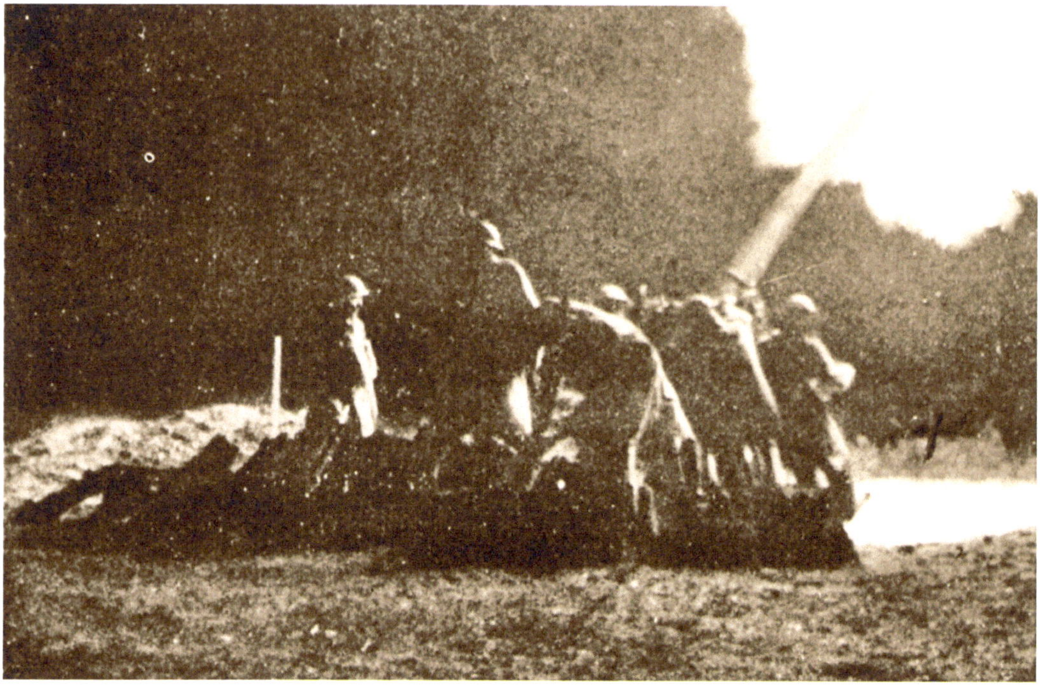

Barking Artillery

The old photograph is of the 156th (Barking) AA battery Royal Artillery. It was made into a Christmas card in 1939. Written in the card was 'Us in action.' I am not sure where the gun was positioned but one relic of the Second World War in the area is the pillbox opposite Dagenham East Station.

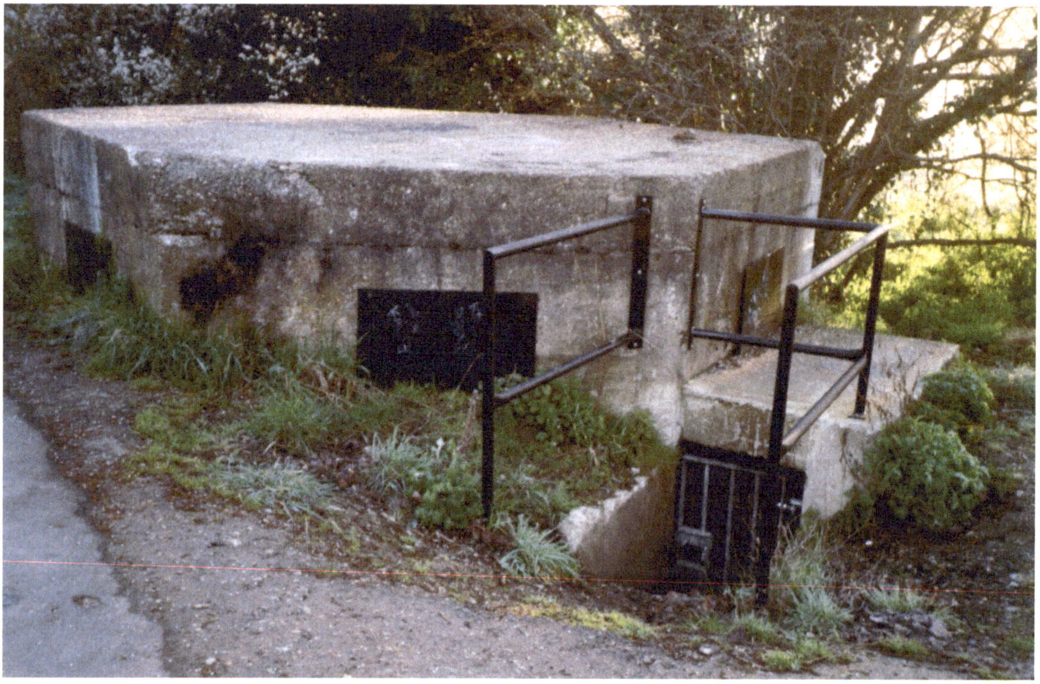

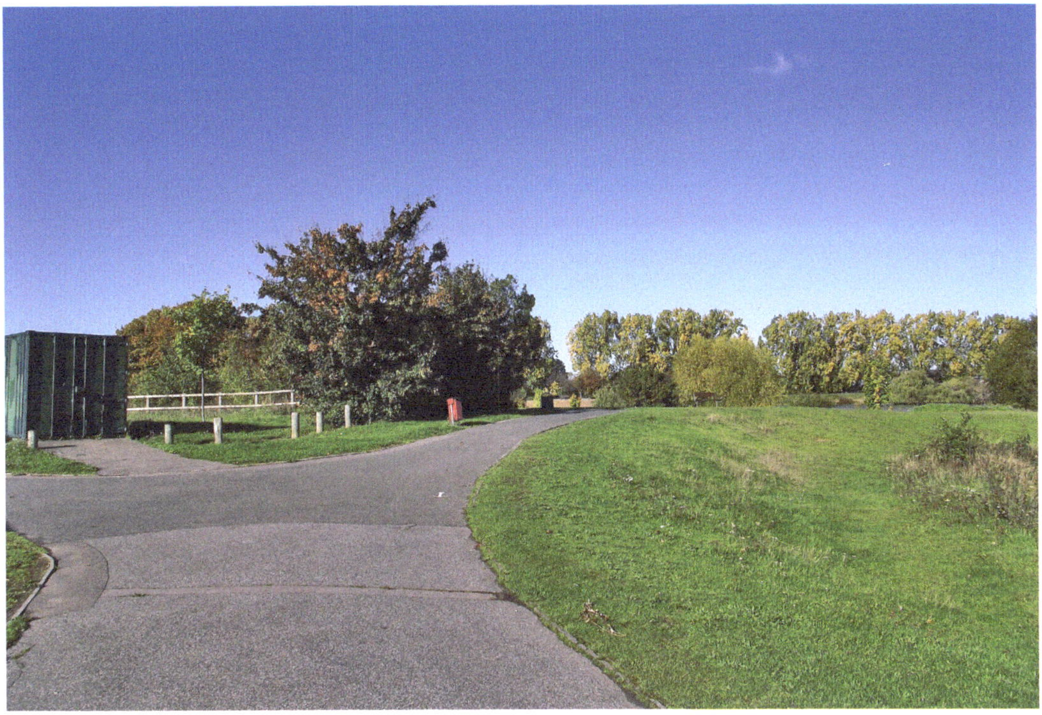

Maysbrook Park

The park has great sporting connections as it was a training area for the Essex Beagles athletics club. It is also now the site of Barking FC's grounds. The lake was also used for boating by a number of local schools.

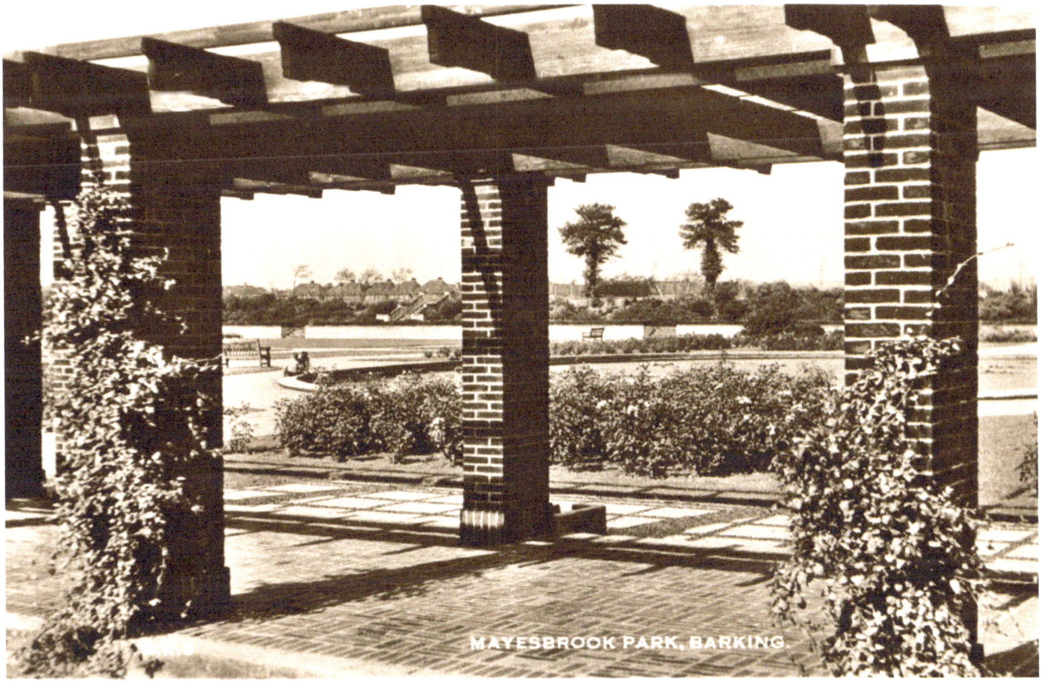

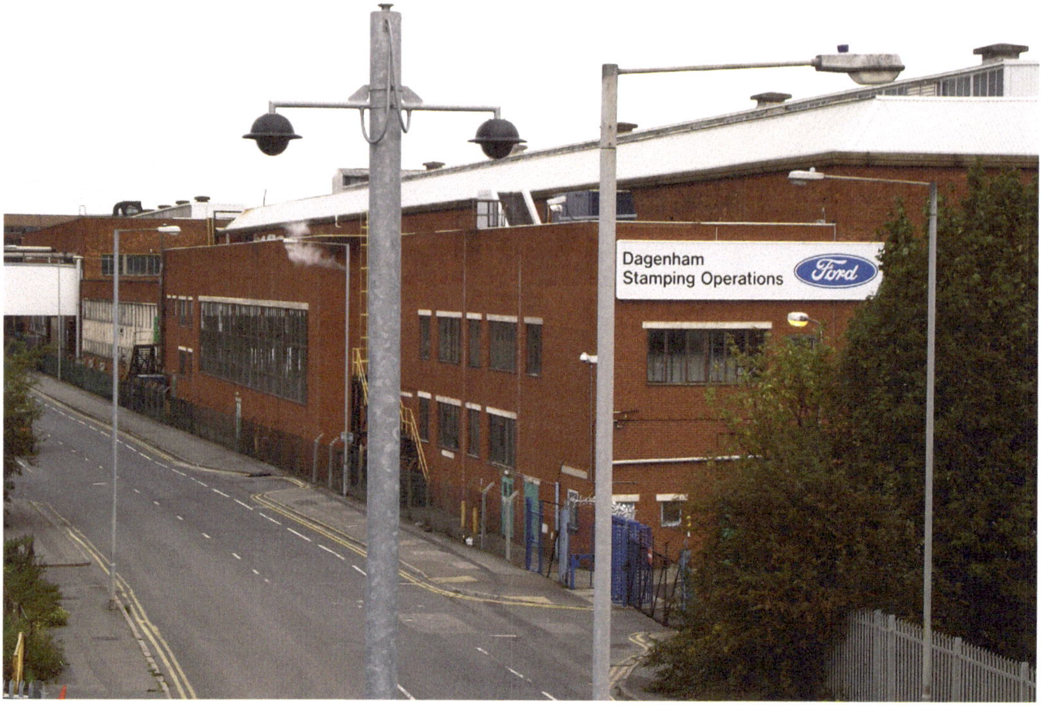

Ford's

The Ford factory in Dagenham was built in the 1930s. The old image shows men working on its construction. It went on to become one of the area's largest employers for a number of years. The modern image shows part of Ford's today.

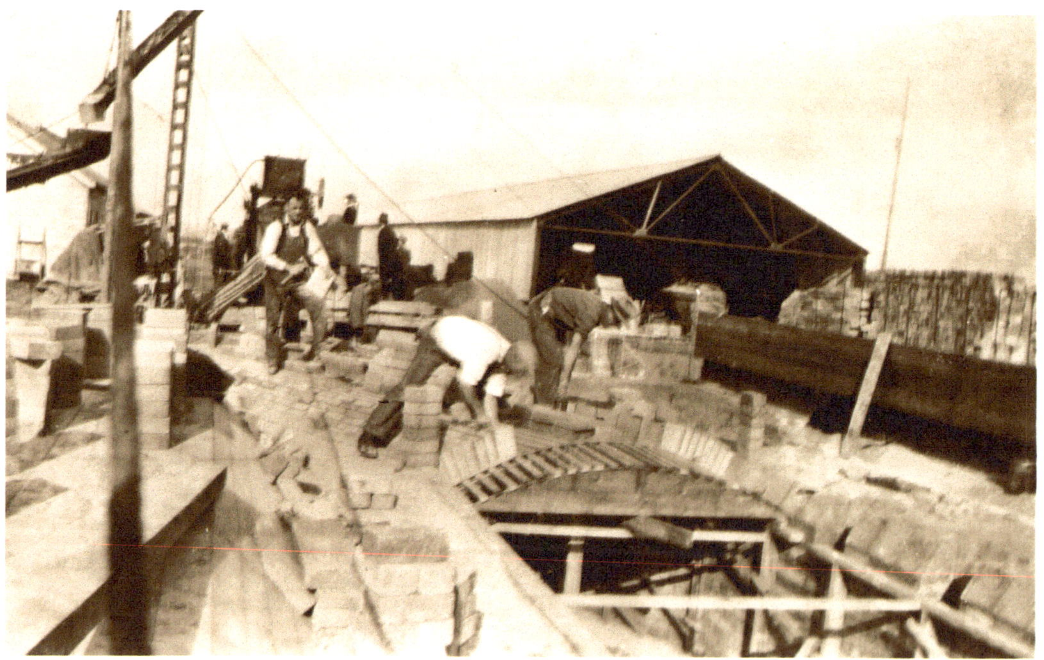

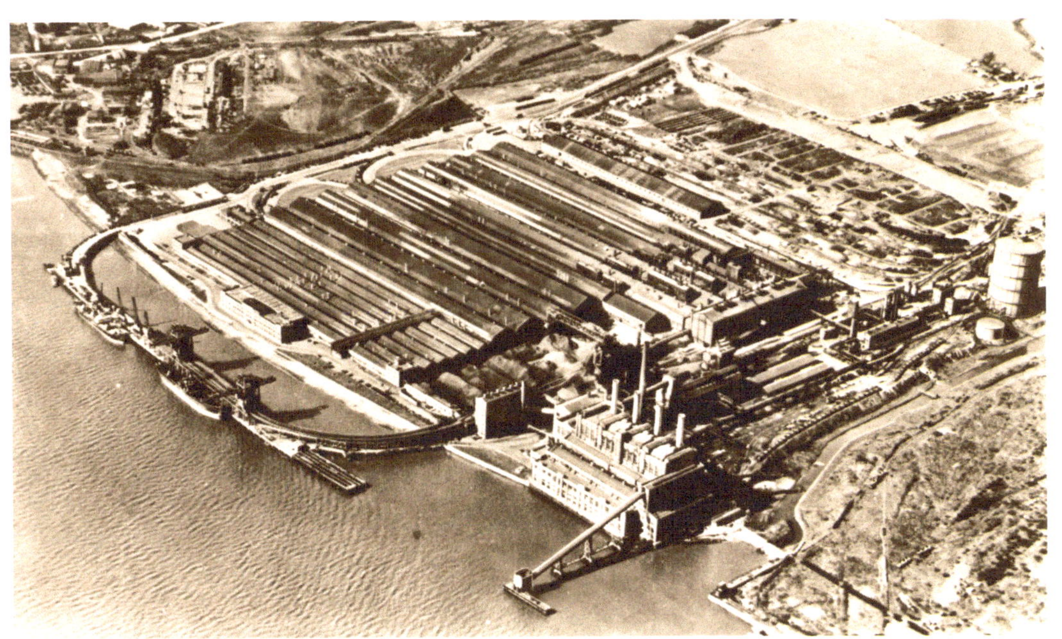

Industrial Dagenham

The Ford Motor Company began to build their large Dagenham factory in 1929 after buying 244 acres of riverside land from Samuel Williams in 1924. The first vehicles were built in 1931. The works then went on to cover much of the area of Dagenham's river frontage. The Ford works today are divided by the Channel Tunnel rail link and the new A13 Road. (*Ford Motor Company*)

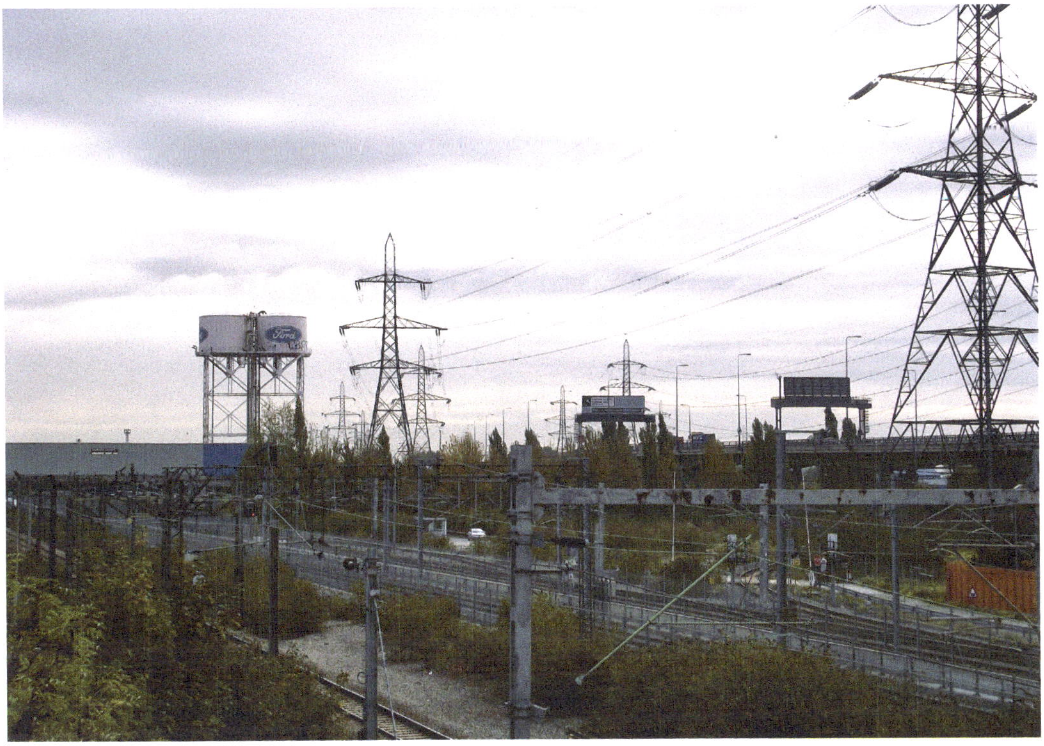

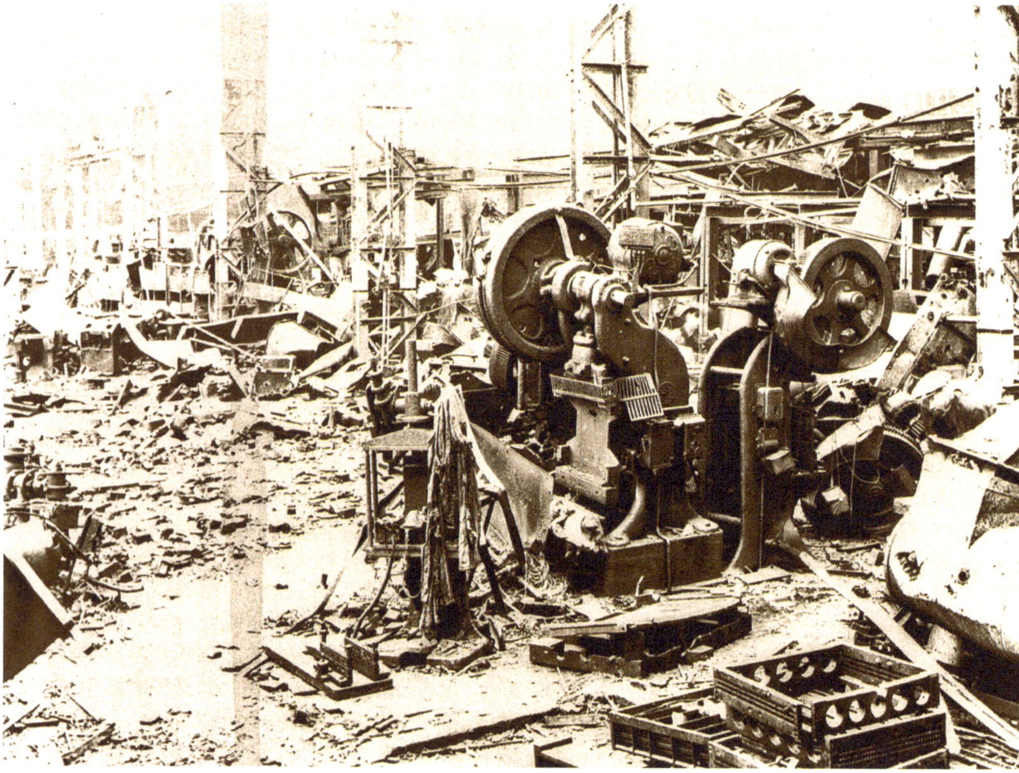

War Damage

Being situated on the river made the Ford factory an obvious target for German bombers. For this reason war contracts were at first withheld from the company. As the old photograph shows, it was often damaged by bombing but production soon restarted. Below is another modern view of the factory. (*Ford Motor Company*)

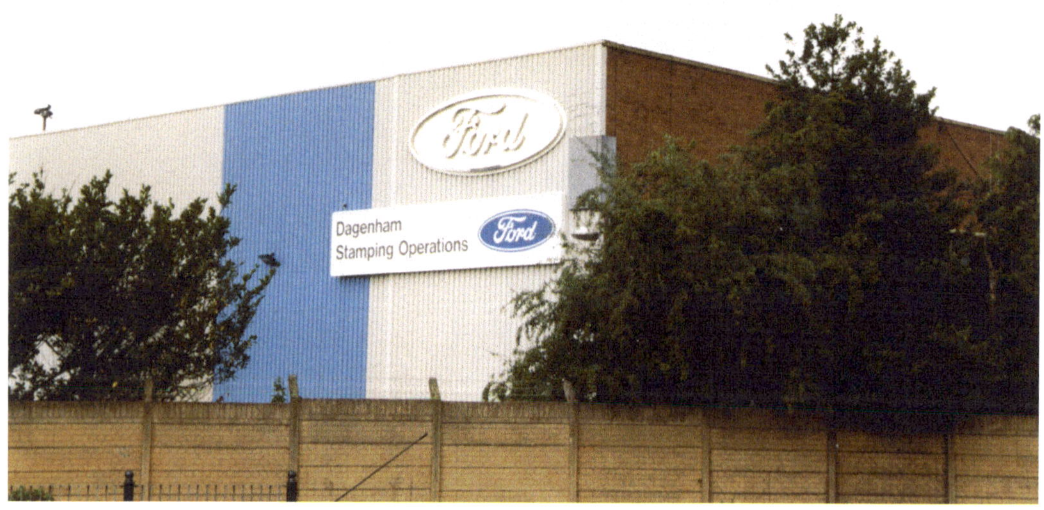

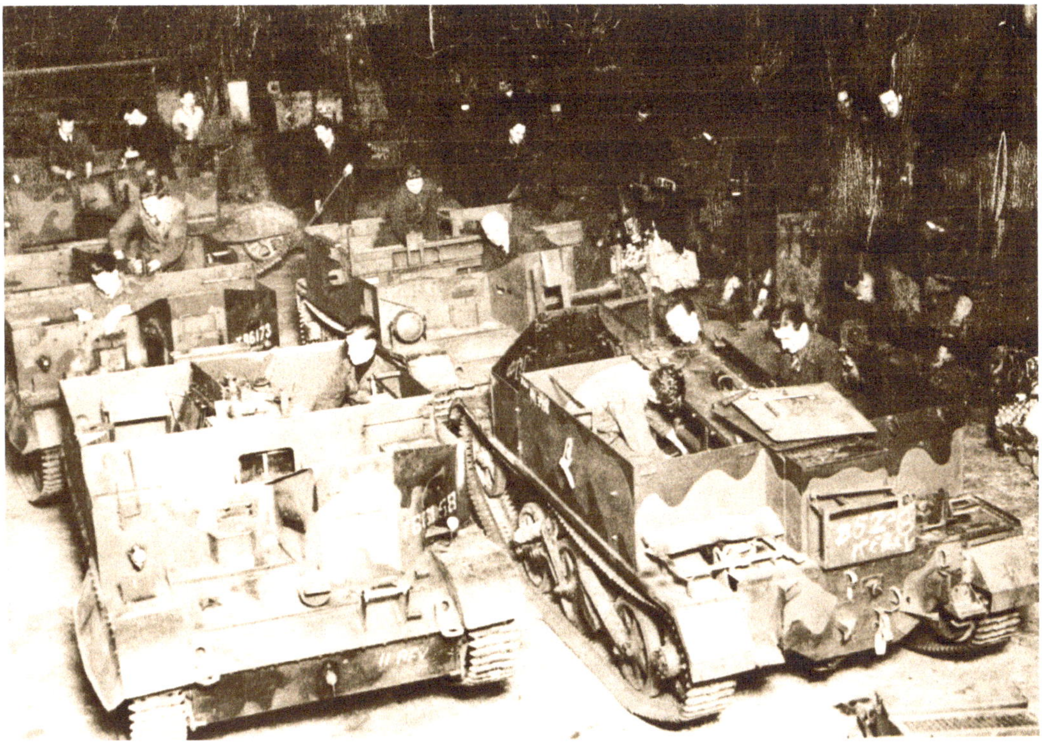

Messages to the Front

The messages scrawled on the Bren Gun Carriers in production show how the men working on the production lines felt about the machines they were making and what they hoped they would achieve. Production of complete cars unfortunately ended at Dagenham in 2001. (*Ford Motor Company*)

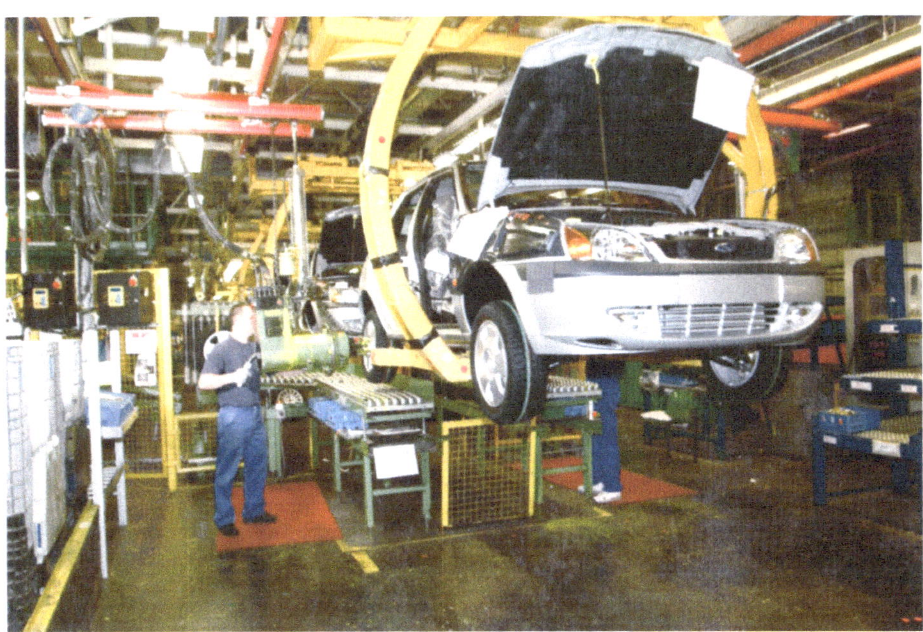

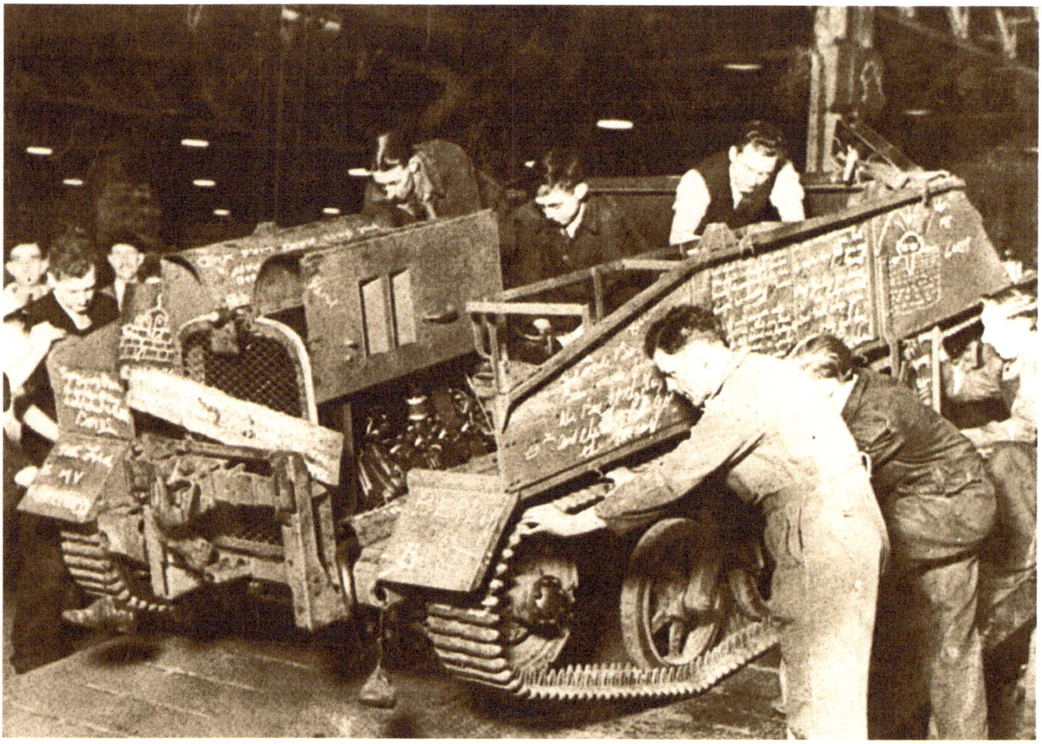

The War Effort

The type of vehicles made during the war was obviously very different to those produced in peacetime as the old photograph shows. It also shows how labour intensive old production methods were compared with more modern working practices. (*Ford Motor Company*)

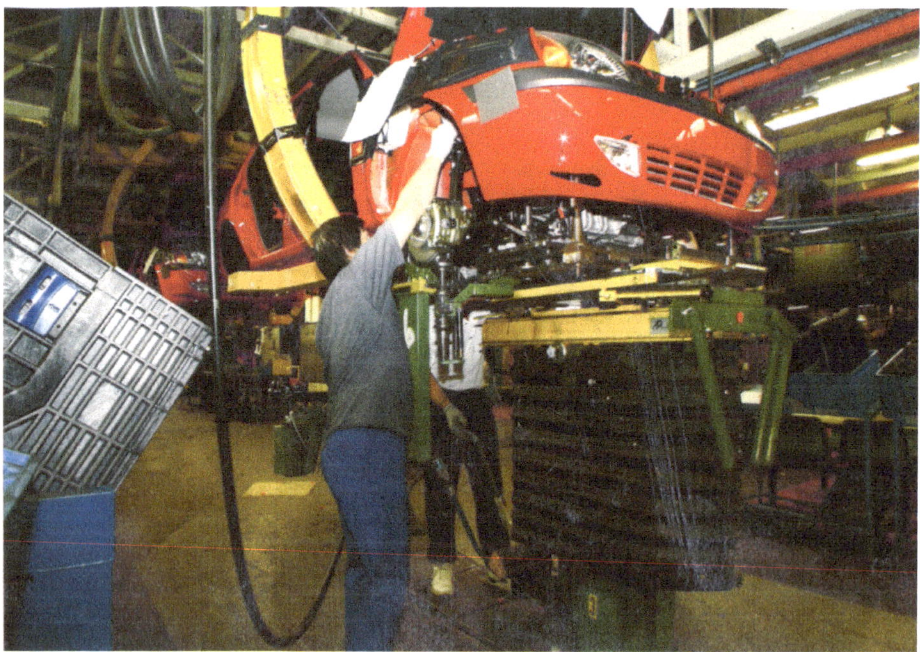

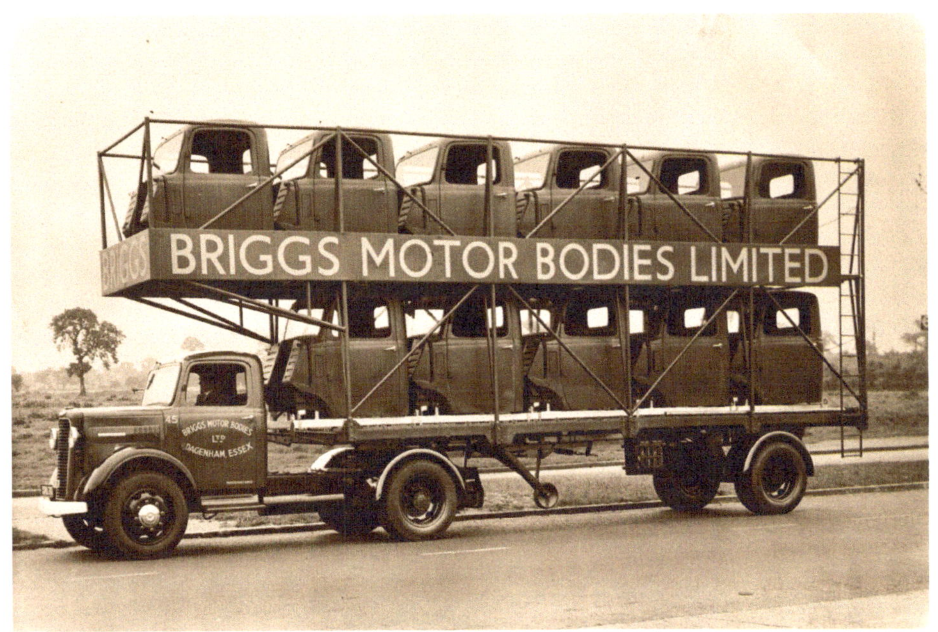

Briggs Bodies

Briggs Bodies was an American company that supplied Ford Motor Company with bodies for their vehicles. When the Ford Dagenham plant opened, Briggs also opened their own factory next to Ford's. As with other employers in the area, Briggs had a thriving social club and their football team, Briggs Motor Bodies FC played in the London league between 1935-51. They played at Victoria Road, now the home of Dagenham and Redbridge, until 1955 when they amalgamated with Ford United at Rush Green. The factory was bought by Ford in the 1950s. Below is another modern view of Ford's.

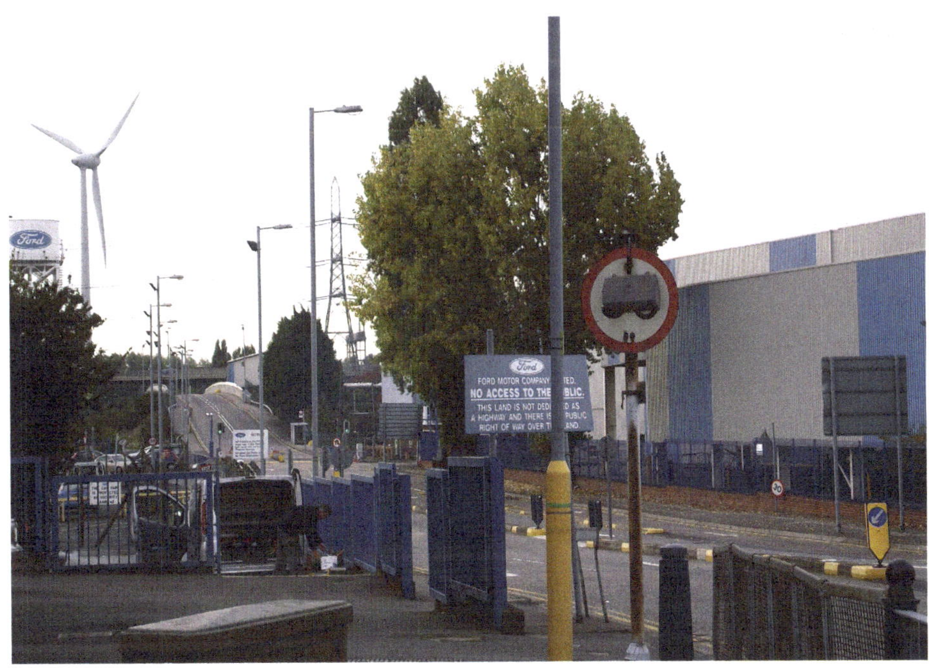

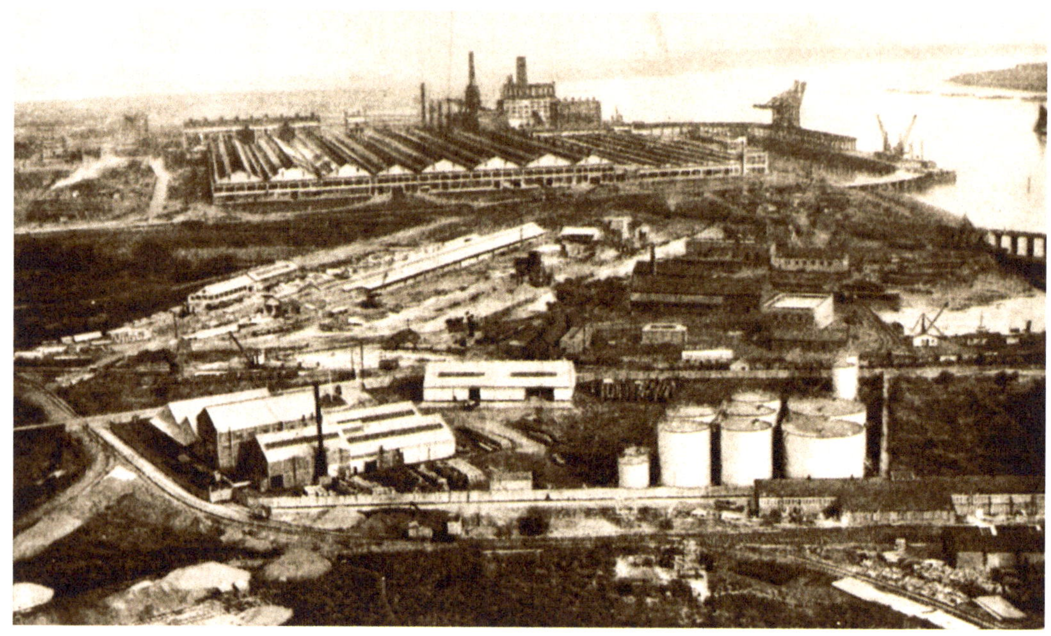

Samuel Williams

Samuel Williams bought thirty acres of land on the Thames at Dagenham in 1887 and built Dagenham Dock and a rail line to serve it. He then filled in the marshland surrounding the area and built an industrial estate. The company eventually developed its own shipping company. It closed in 1985. The modern photograph shows the docks today.

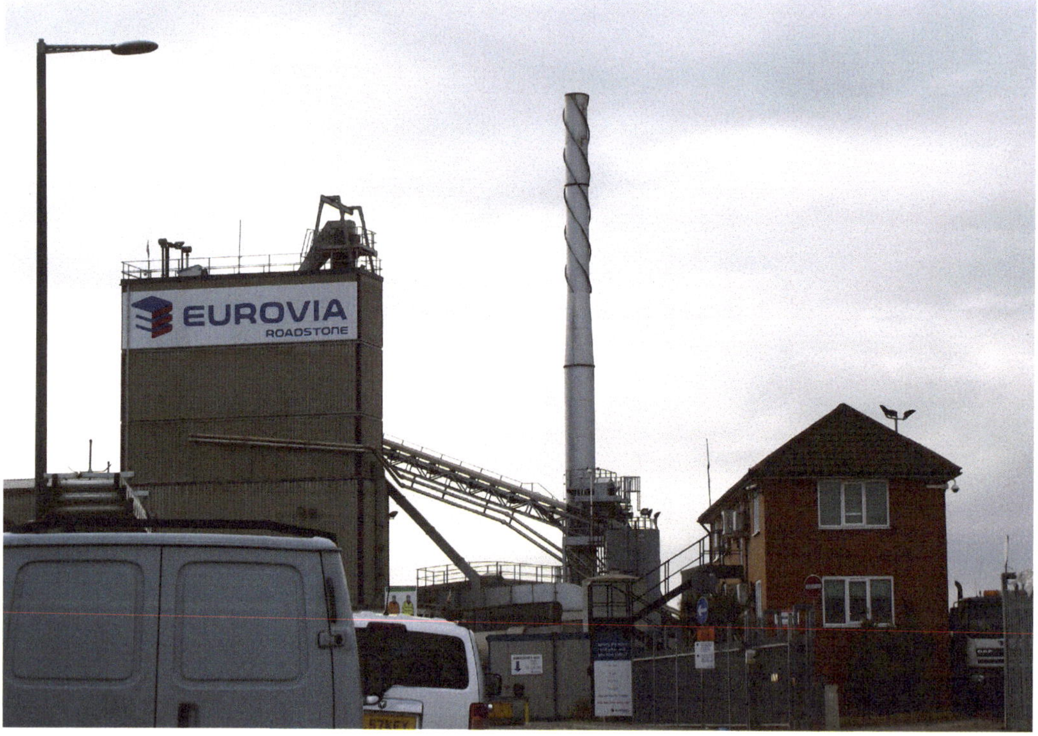

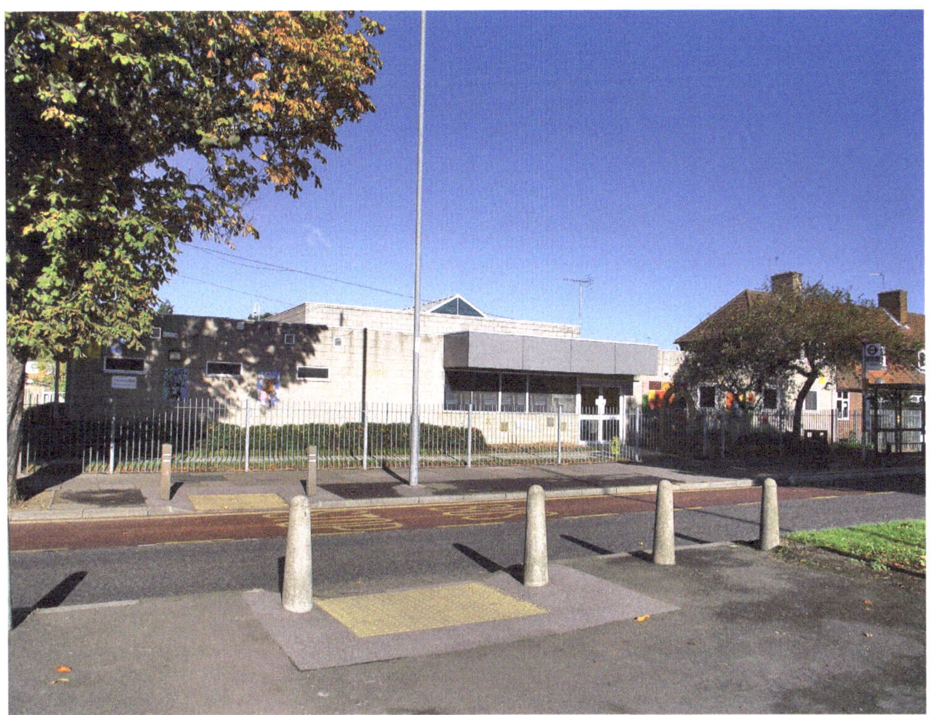

Boys' Club

Up until the late 1960s and early 1970s there were numerous youth clubs in Dagenham. Most senior schools seemed to have their own. These then began to close down leaving only a few unconnected with schools or school premises. The modern photograph shows the Beacon Youth Centre in Becontree Avenue.

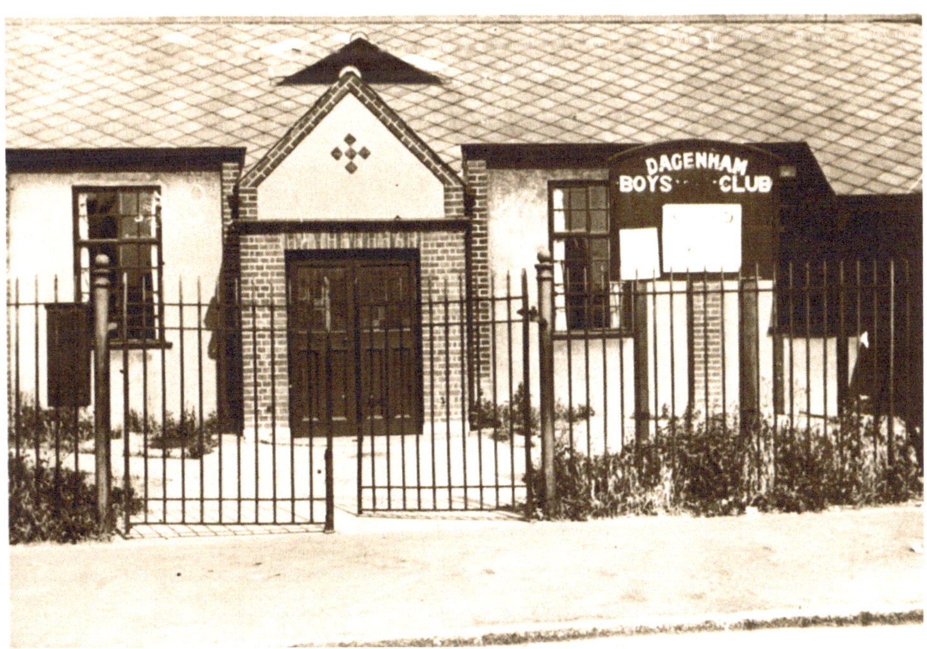

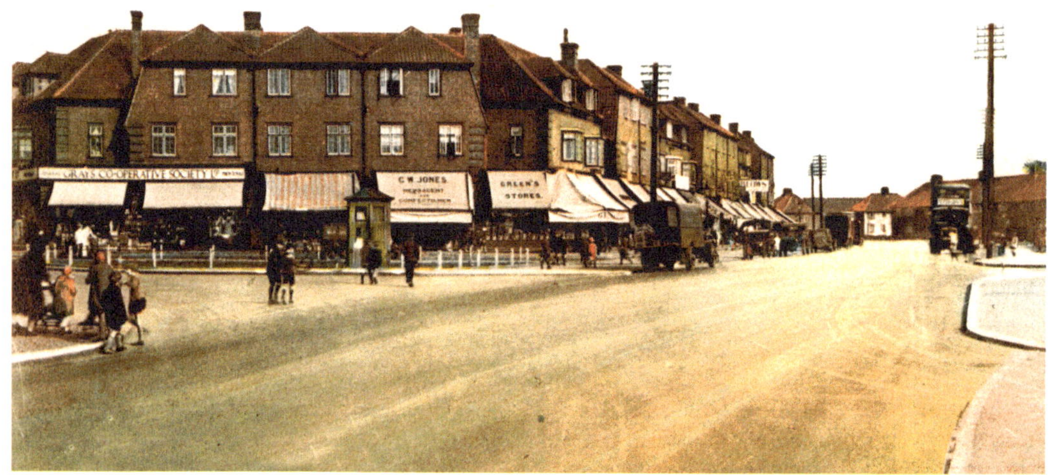

Five Elms

Five Elms is one of the small parades of shops that were built to provide shopping facilities for the newcomers to the Becontree estate. These areas usually provided all a family's needs before the arrival of supermarkets. As with other parades of shops, some now stand empty.

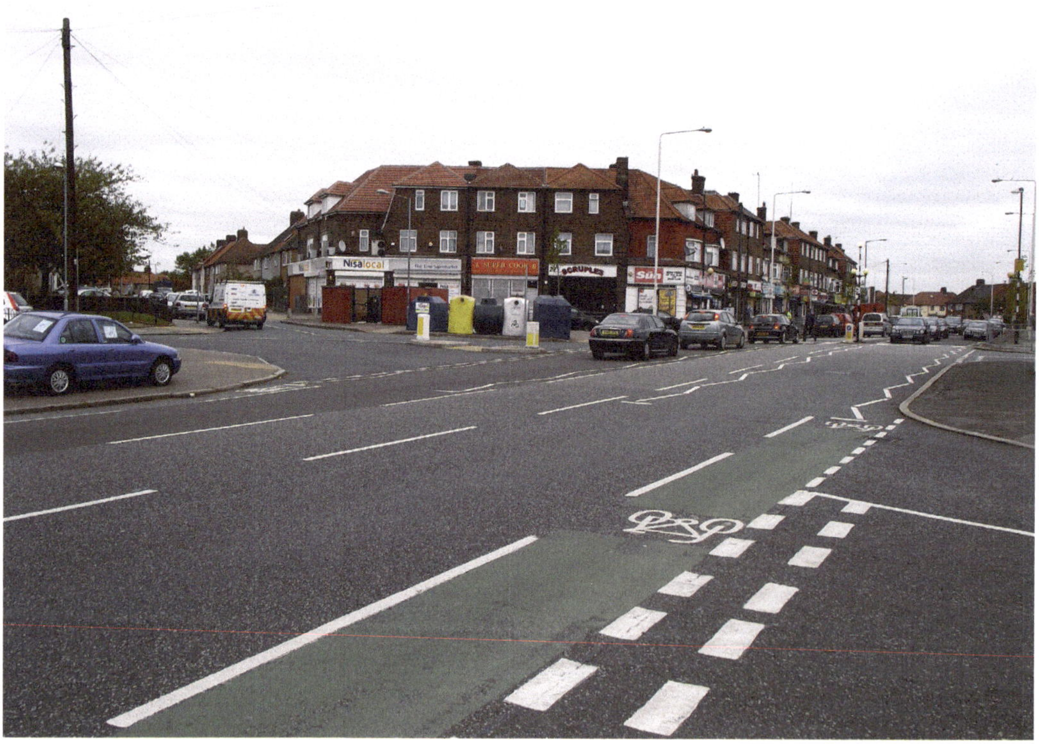

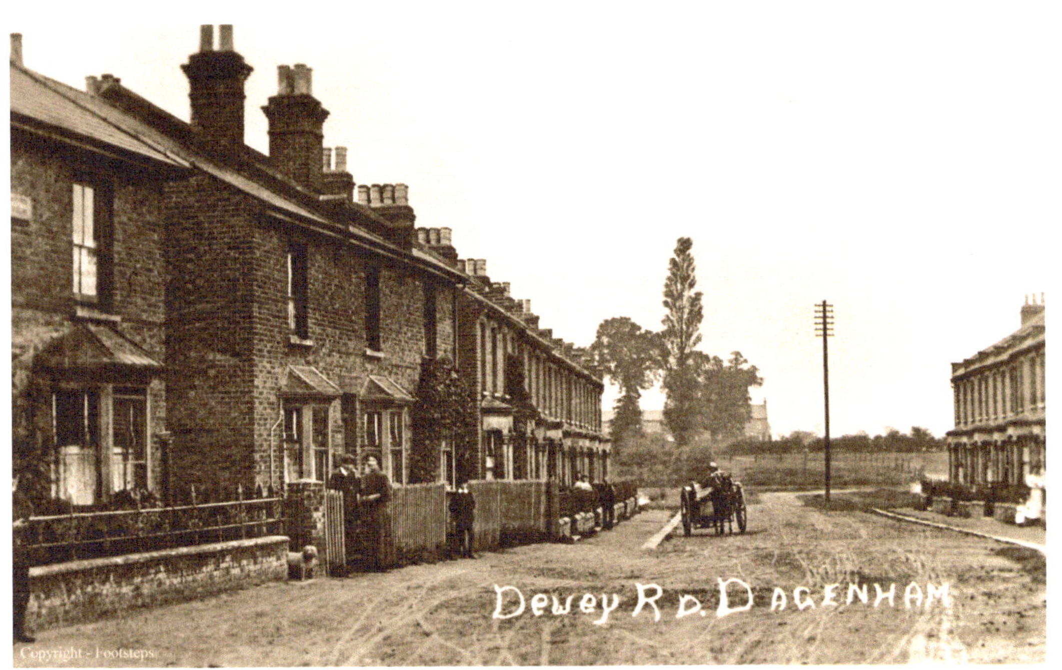

Dewey Road

Dewey Road is situated close to Dagenham East Station. It runs from Rainham Road South down to Exeter Road. The far end is close to where the old village was situated and the houses shown in the old image must be those shown in the modern photograph as the rest of the houses in the road look much more modern.

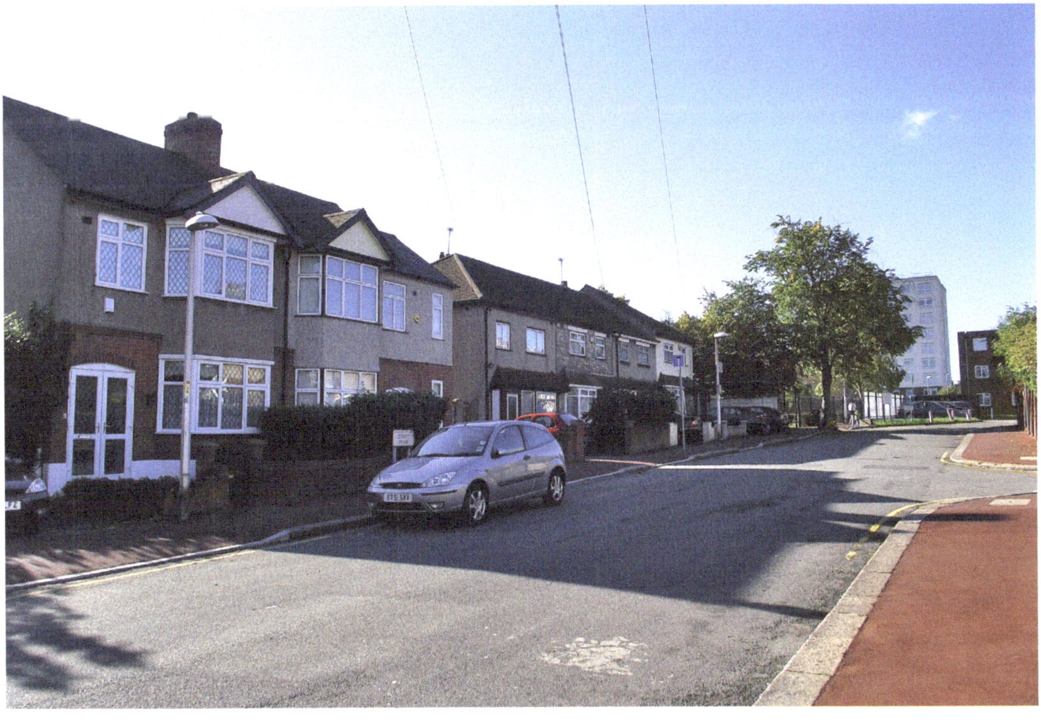

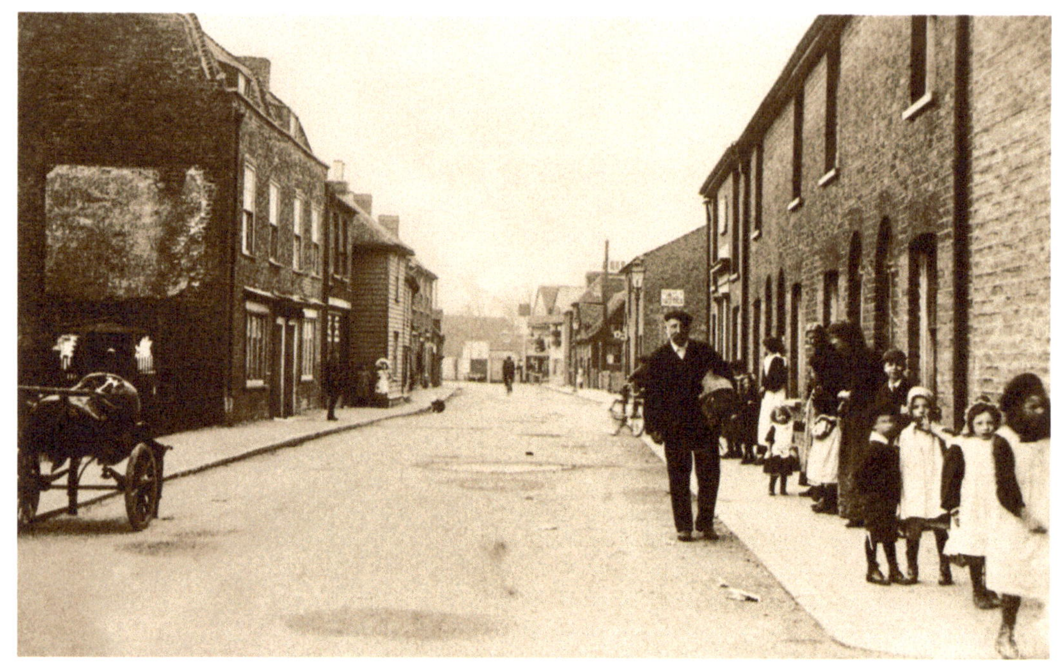

Bull Street

Bull Street was originally part of the old Dagenham village. Little of the original buildings still remain although the Bull public house is still there. The first inn on the site dated from the eighteenth century. In the mid-nineteenth century it became a stopping point for the Rainham omnibus. The street is now known as Rainham Road South.

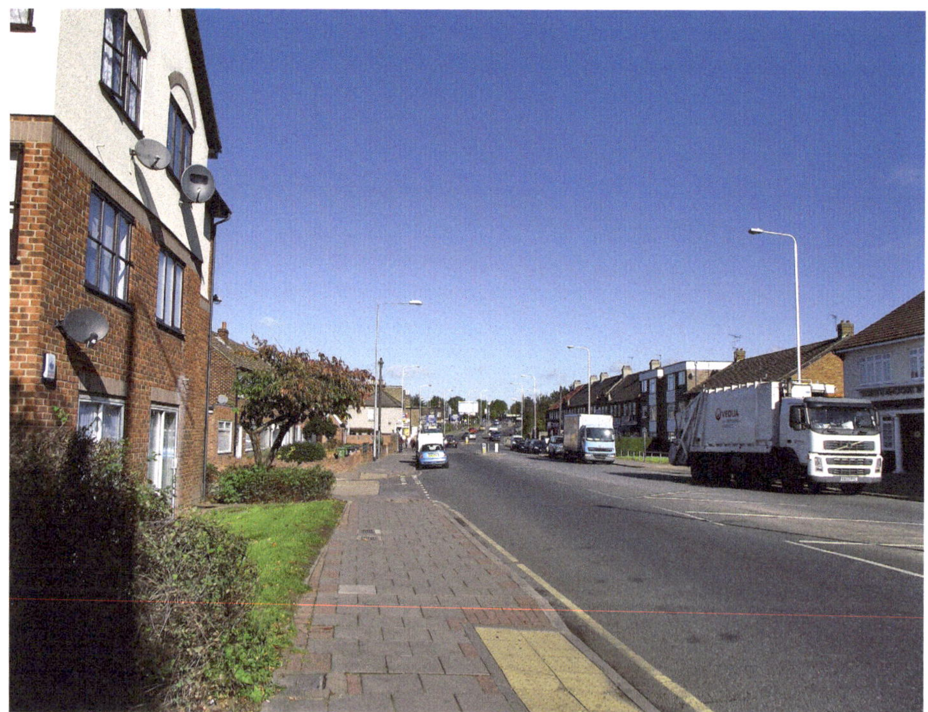

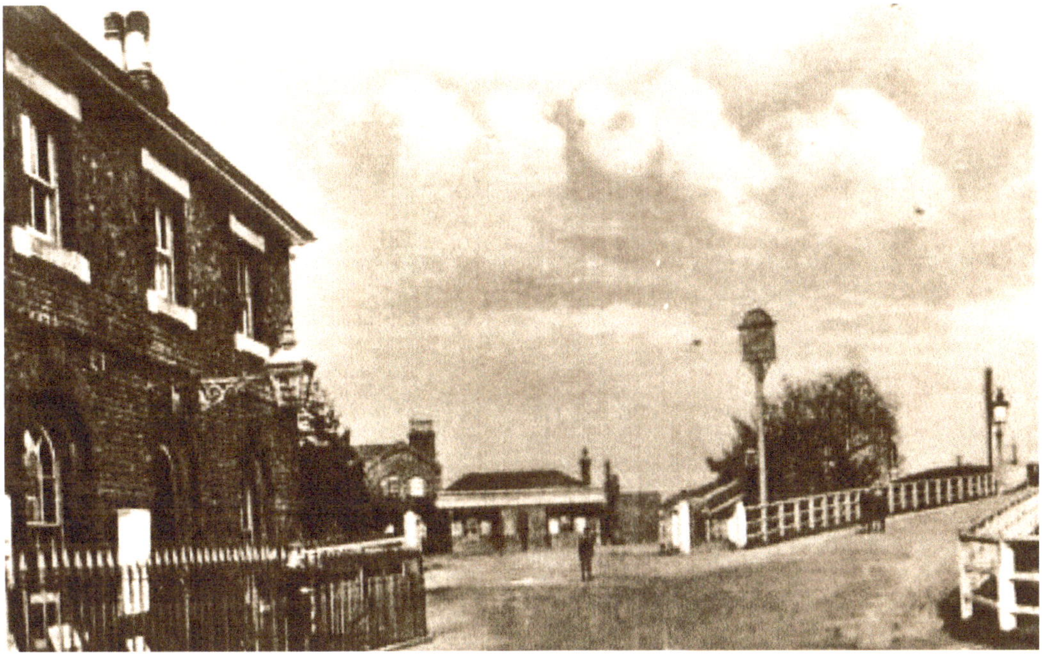

Police Station

The original Dagenham police station was an old wooden building in the village. This was replaced in 1850 with a purpose-built station in Rainham Road South in 1850. It was then replaced by a new station in 1961 further along the same road on the other side of the railway station. The old station is now a Grade II listed building.

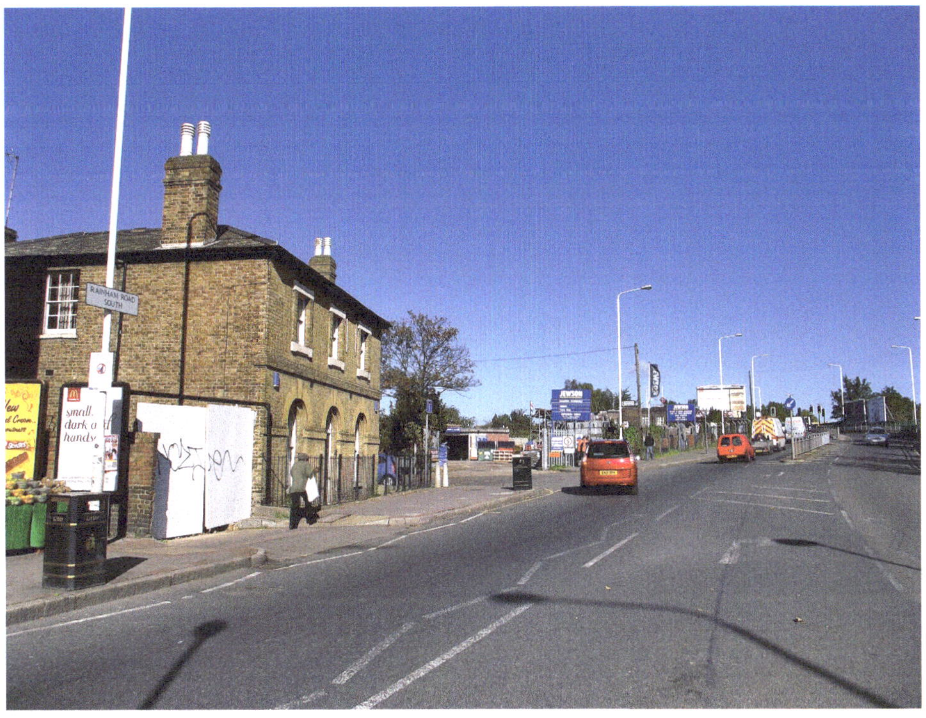

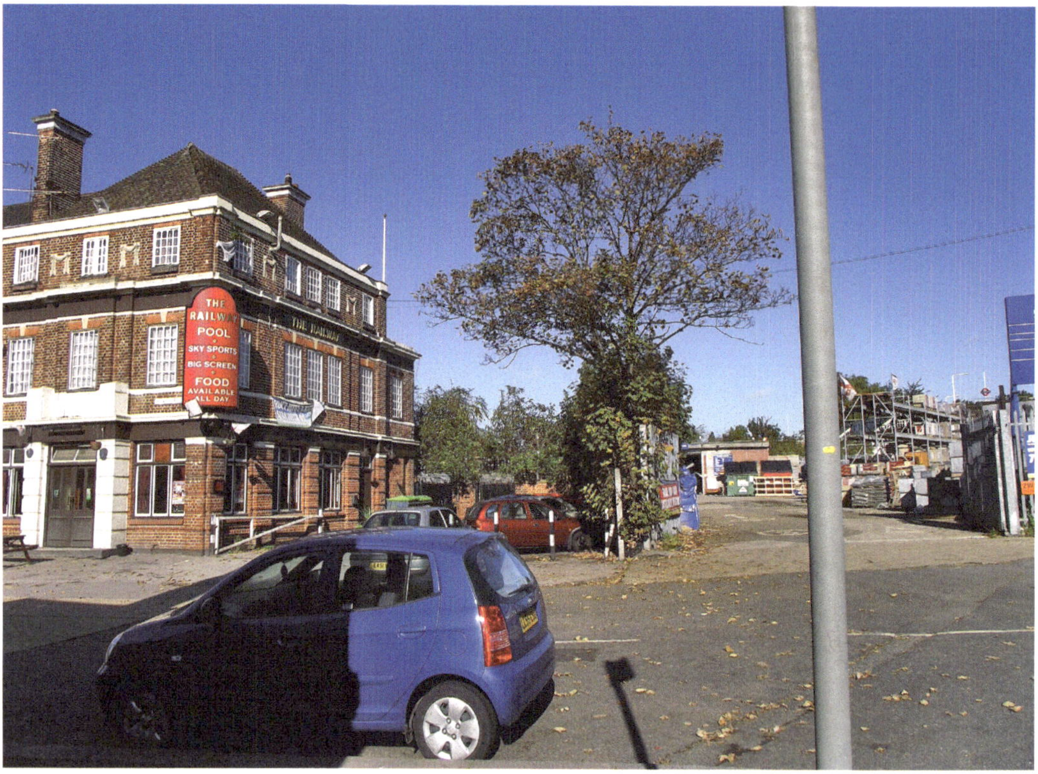

Dagenham East Station

The station was built in 1885 as Dagenham Mainline Station. It was part of the London, Tilbury and Southend Line. It became part of the electrified line from Barking to Upminster in 1932 from when the majority of the present station buildings date. The yard where the men in the old image are standing is now a builders' merchant.

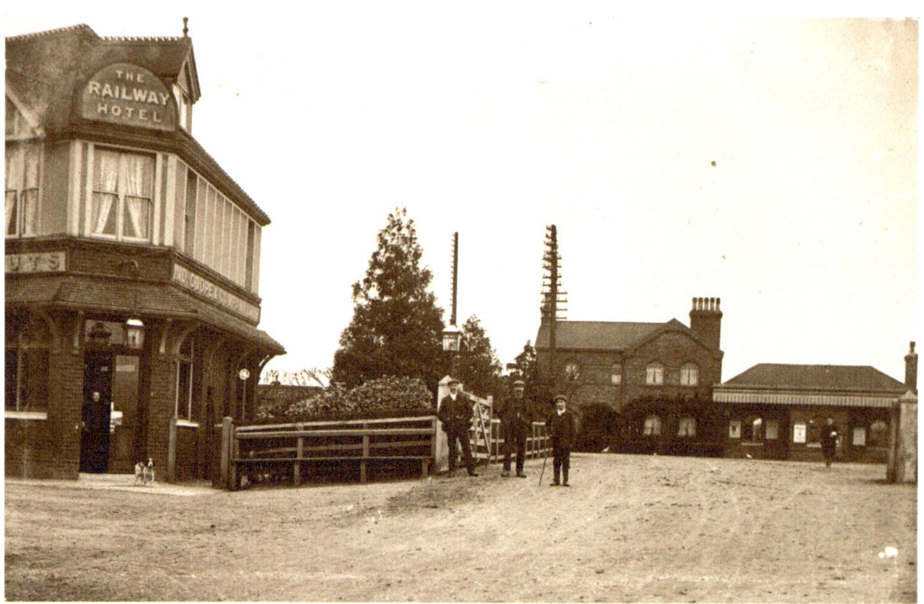

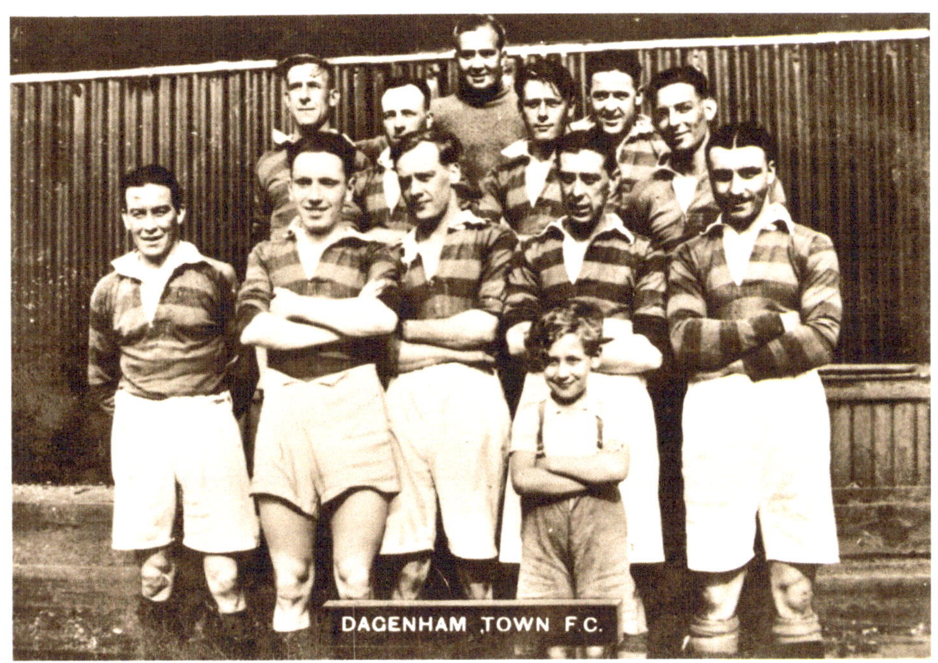

Dagenham Town FC

Dagenham Town FC was the founder of the present Dagenham and Redbridge FC. They moved to their present ground on Victoria Road in 1955 when the Briggs Motor Bodies FC moved to amalgamate with Ford United at Rush Green. Since then Dagenham amalgamated with Redbridge Forest which itself was an amalgamation of several famous old clubs such as Walthamstow Avenue, Ilford, and Leytonstone to become Dagenham and Redbridge.

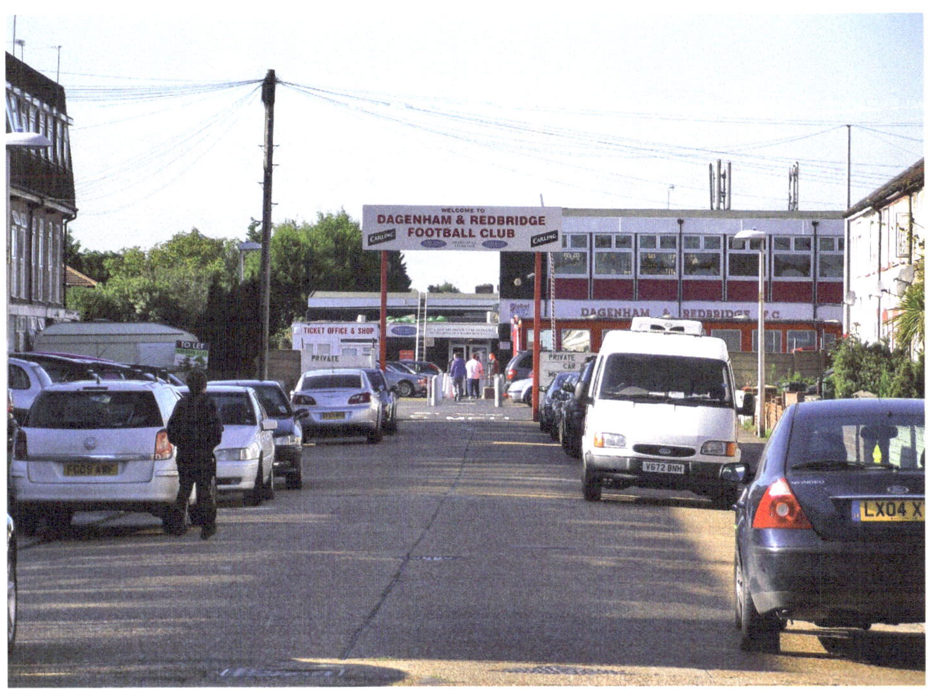

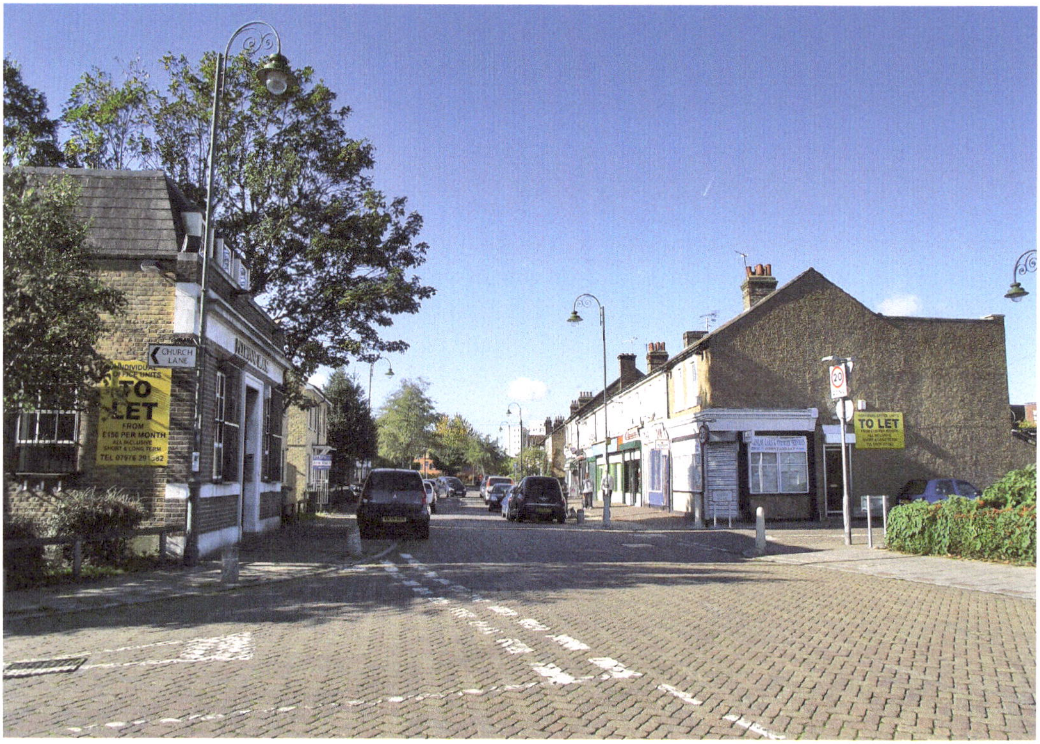

Crown Street

Crown Street was the original road of the old Dagenham village and led to the church. It is unrecognisable today from the old image. The oldest part of the road is where it runs between the church and the Cross Keys Inn.

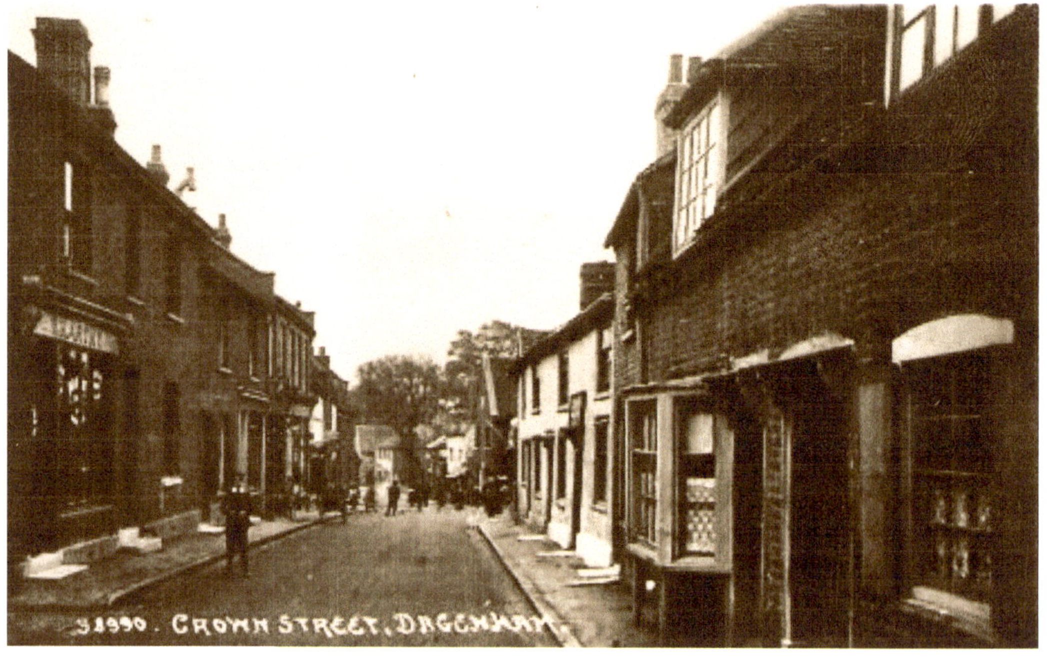

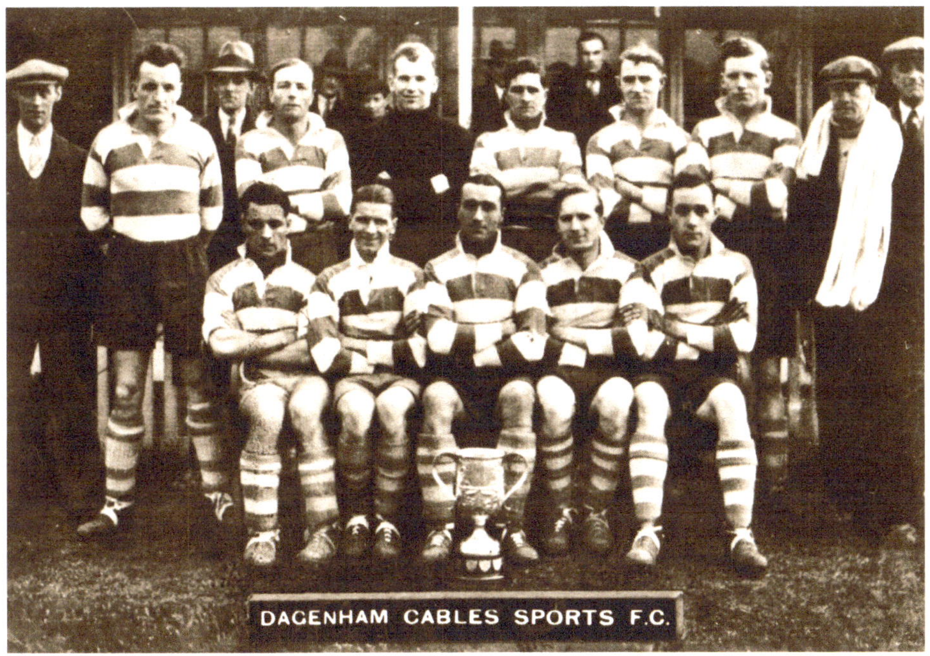

Telephone Cables Football Club

The telephone cables factory was on an 8-acre site in Chequers Lane from 1900 and was one of the town's larger employers. They had a large sports ground behind the Cross Keys public house where well-attended family days were held every year. They also had a successful football team, which for a company team played at a very high level. The sports ground is now covered by blocks of flats.

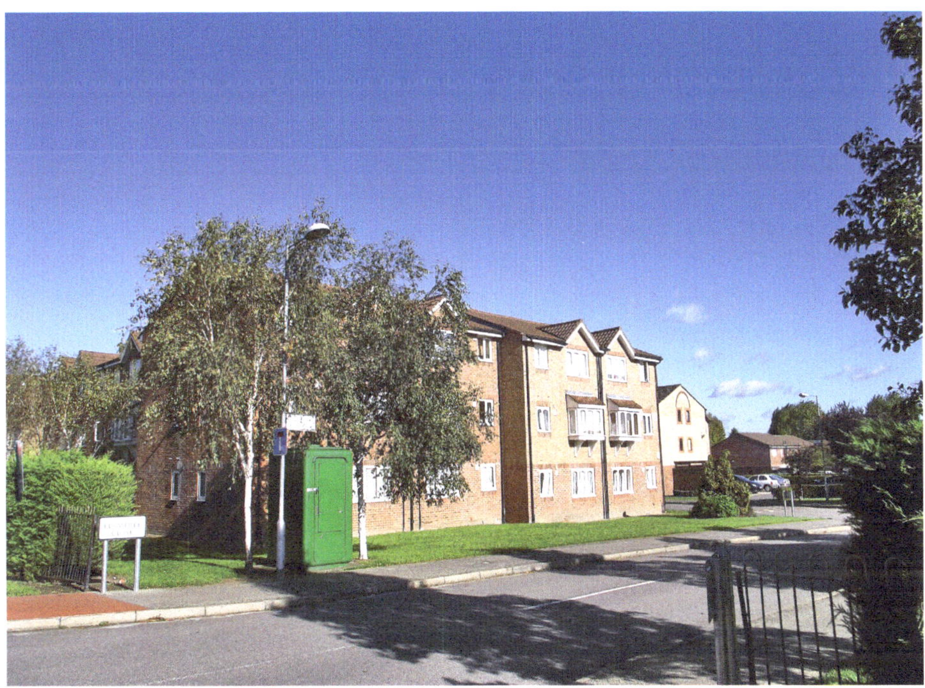

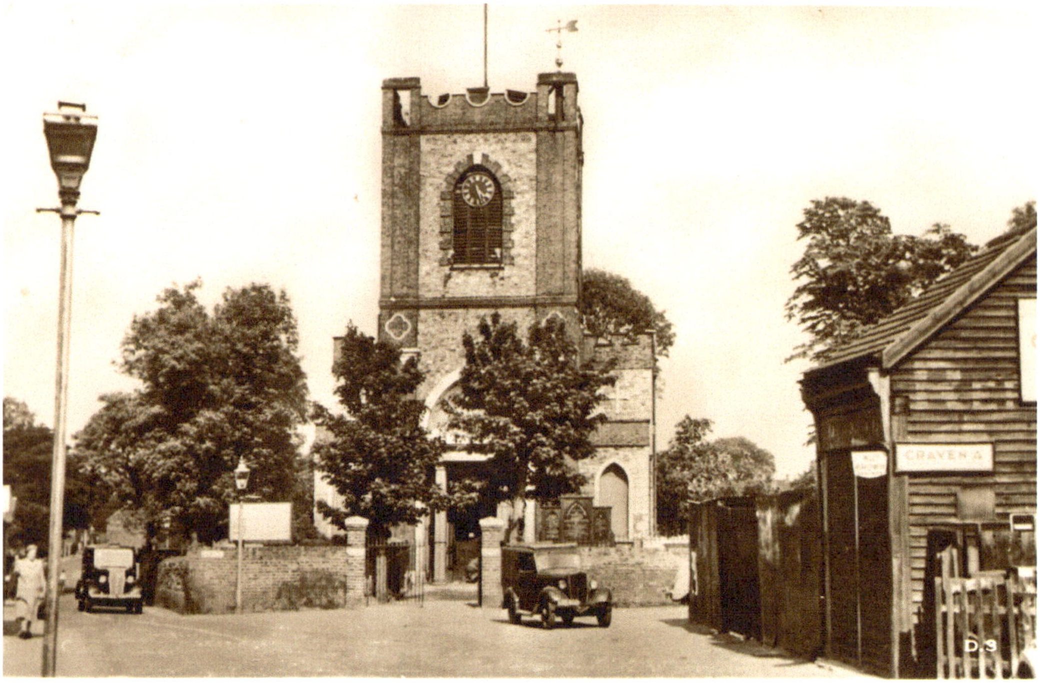

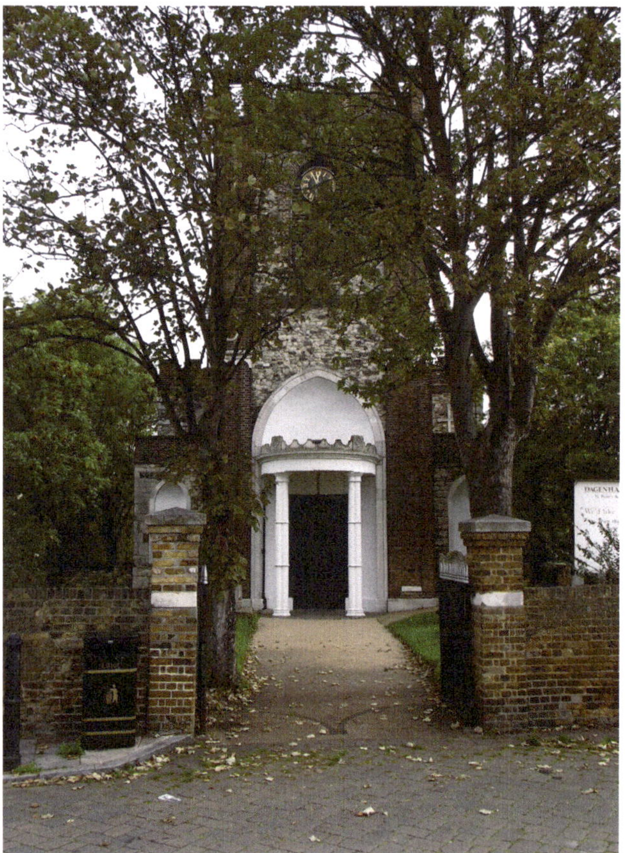

Dagenham Church

The parish Church of St Peter and Paul dates from the thirteenth century, although most of it is much later than this. It stands in what was originally the old village of Dagenham before the huge council estate covered the area. Apart from the nearby Cross Keys Inn little else of the old village remains.

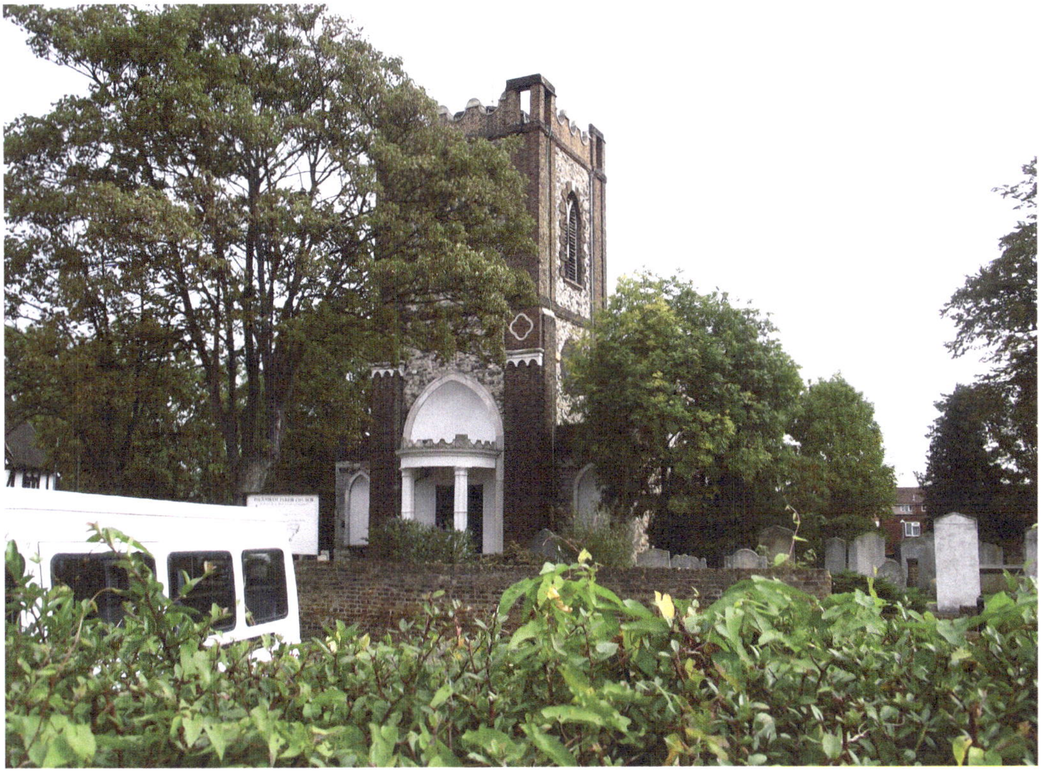

The Church Spire

The second photograph of the church has one big difference to the first one, it has a spire; this was removed in 1921. Little else seems to have changed except the shed on the right has vanished from the previous photograph.

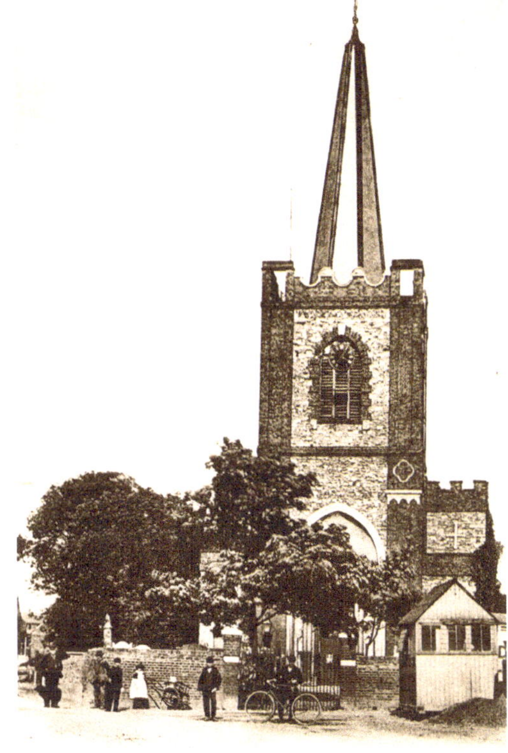

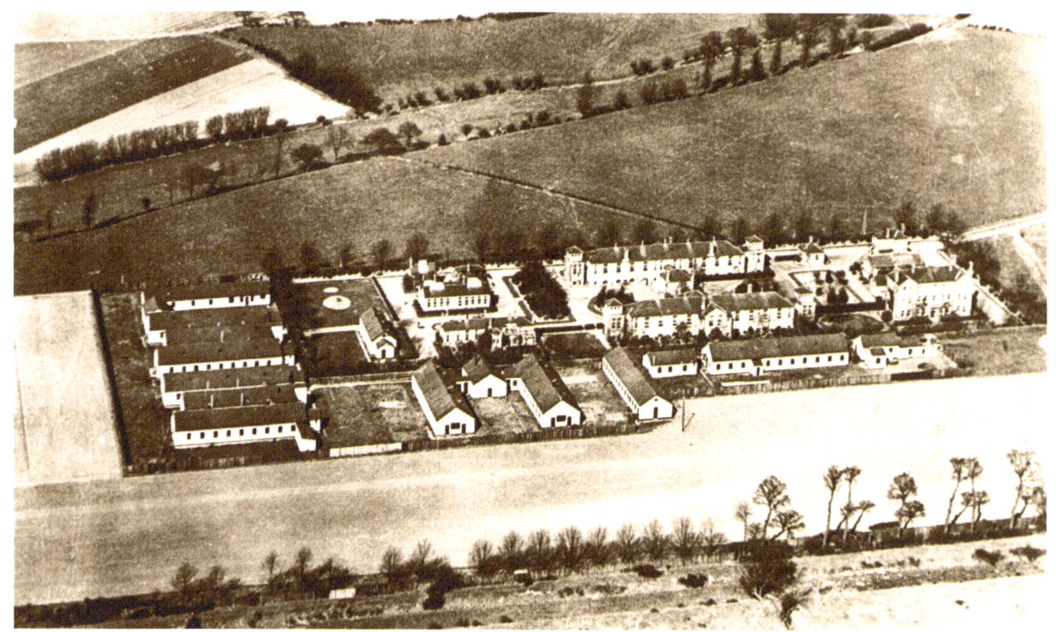

Dagenham Hospital

Dagenham Hospital began life as a smallpox hospital built in 1899 by West Ham Council. It later became a TB sanatorium in 1912. It was built on Rookery Farm near the River Rom. After the Second World War it became Dagenham Hospital and closed in 1986. The buildings are now gone and the land is part of the country park stretching across the east of the town.

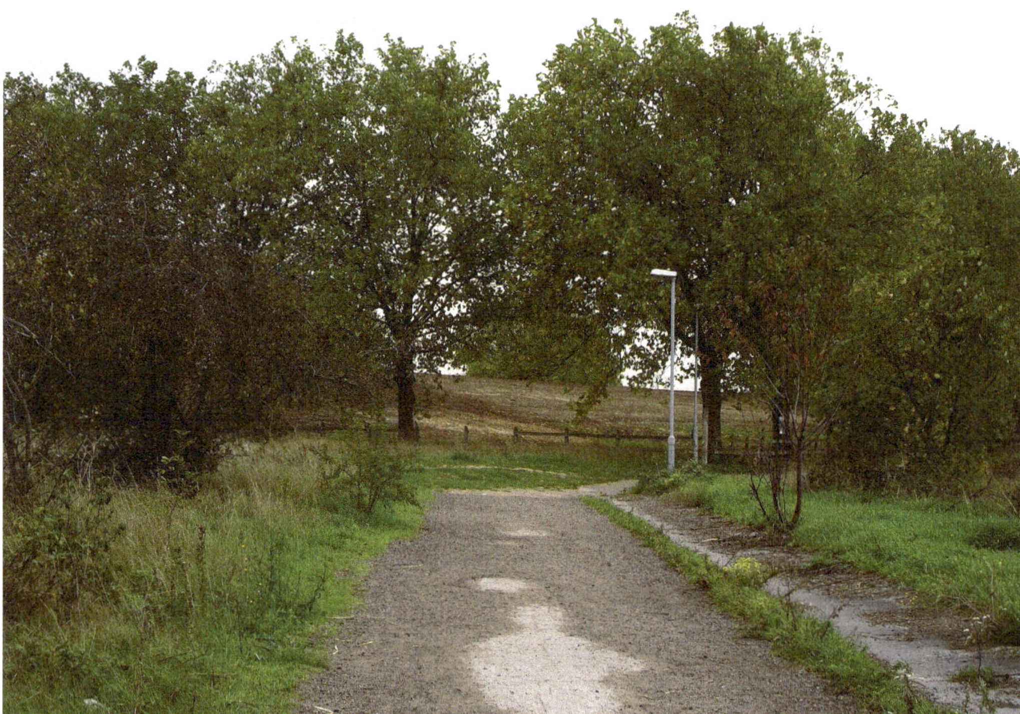

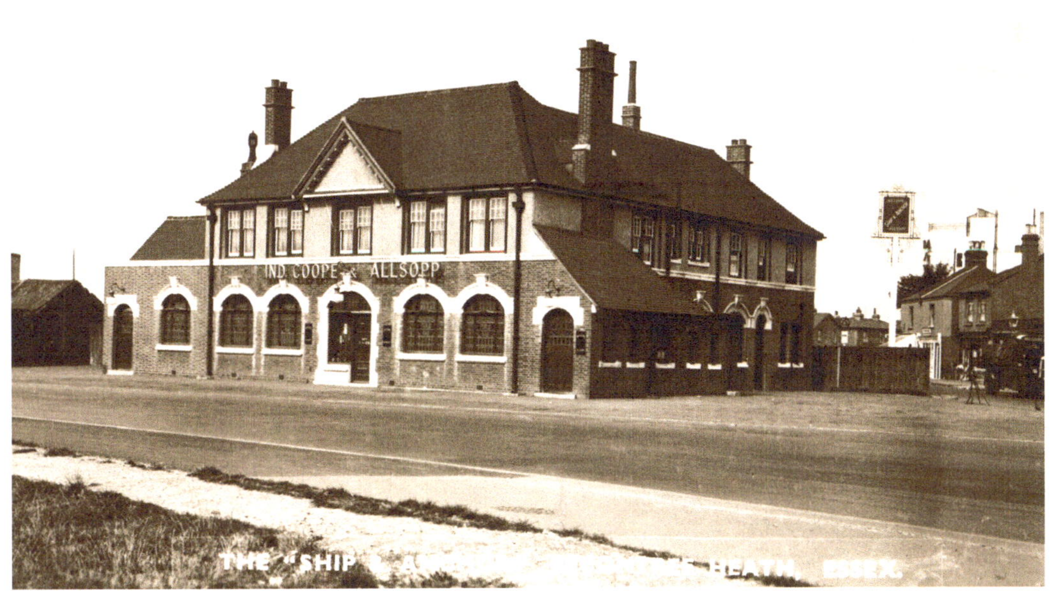

Ship and Anchor

The Ship and Anchor is situated at Becontree Heath and dates back to the mid-nineteenth century, although the present building may be more modern than this. The pub was one of three within a short distance of each other. It is opposite the Three Travellers and was close to the Merry Fiddlers, now the site of a garage.

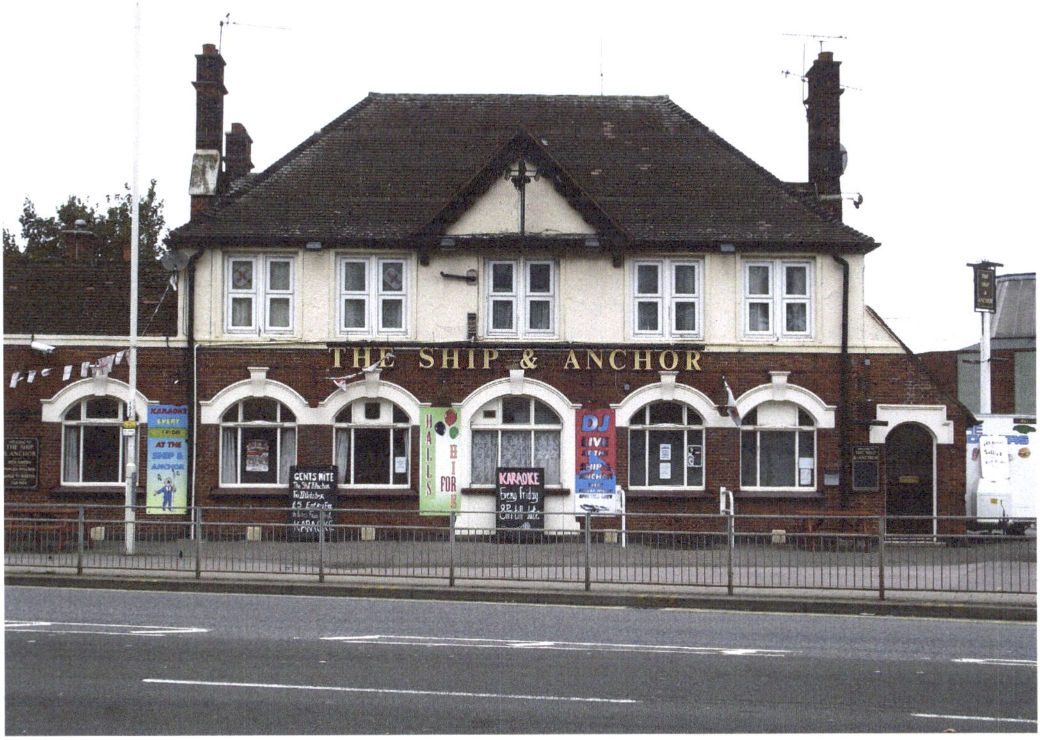

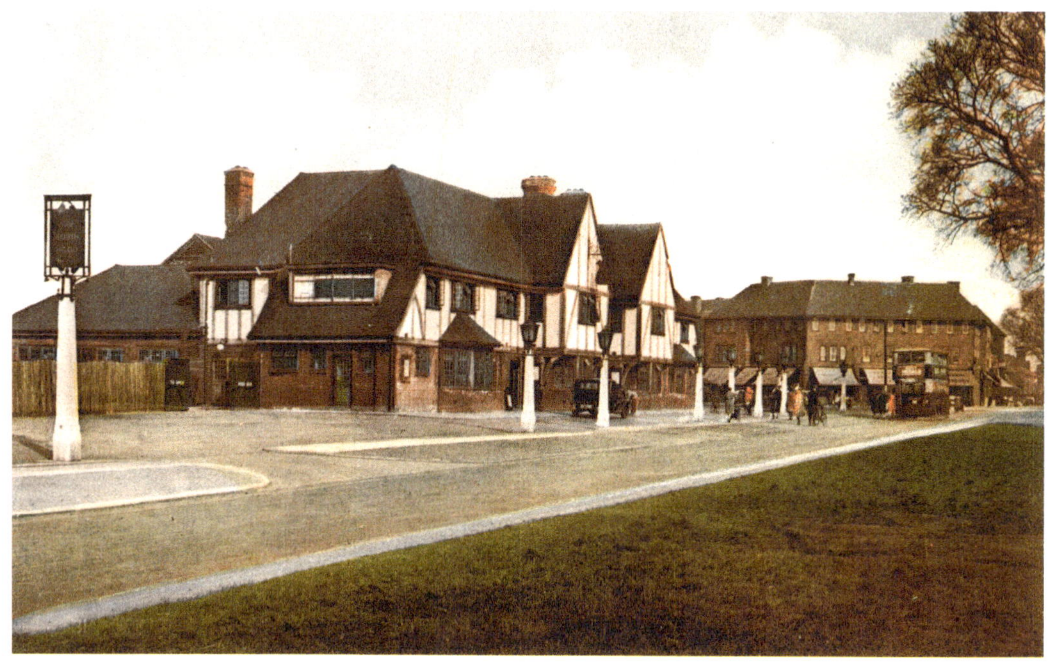

Robin Hood

The original Robin Hood public house stood in Bennett's Castle Lane from the mid-nineteenth century. The building later became the People's Dispensary for Sick Animals. The Robin Hood in Longbridge Road dated from 1930. The site is now a Lidl supermarket.

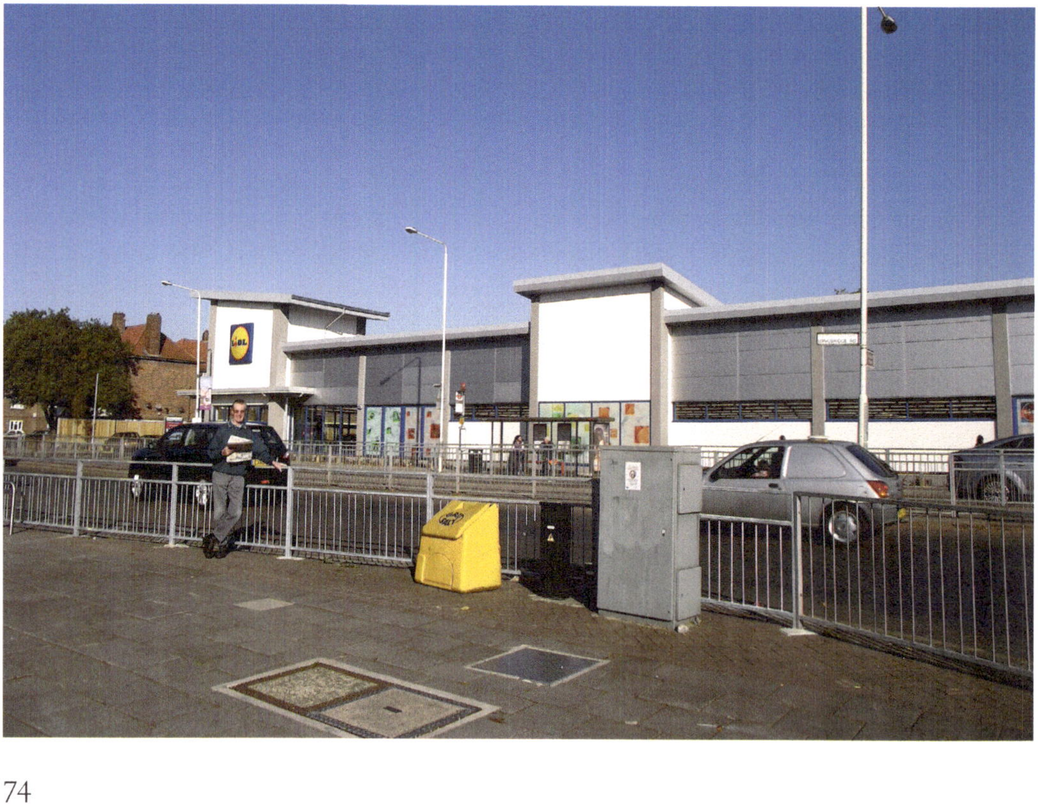

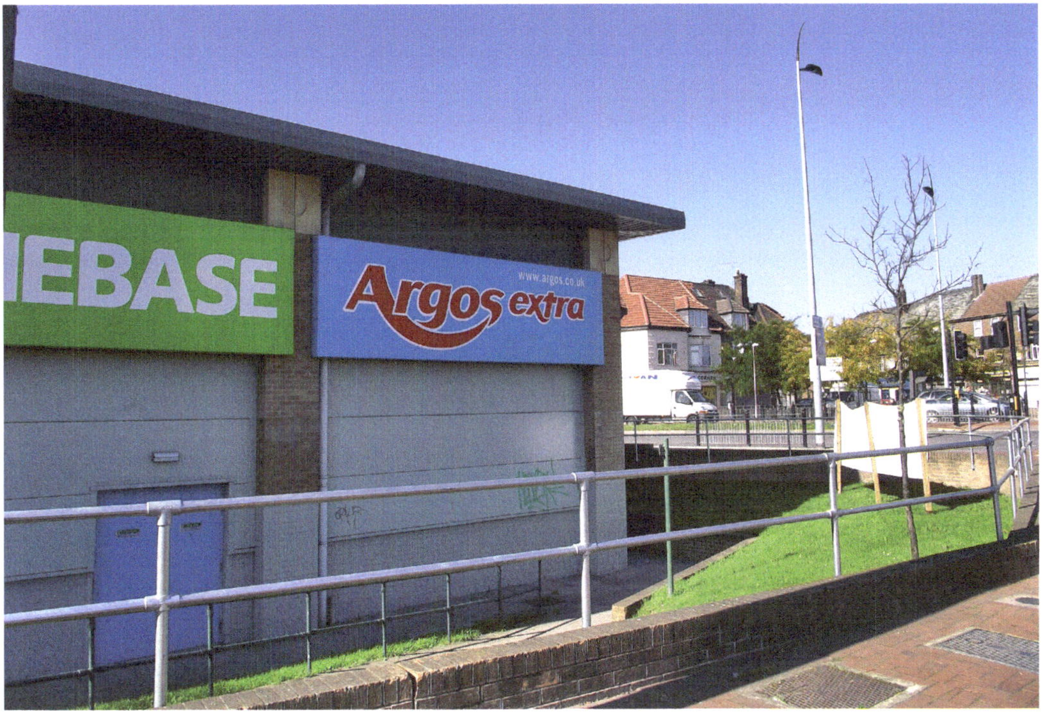

Chequers

The Chequers public house stood at the junction of Chequers Lane and Ripple Road. It was well known in the early days of the twentieth century as a country inn for those on trips out from London. The site of the old building is now part of a retail park but the area is still known as the Chequers to older people.

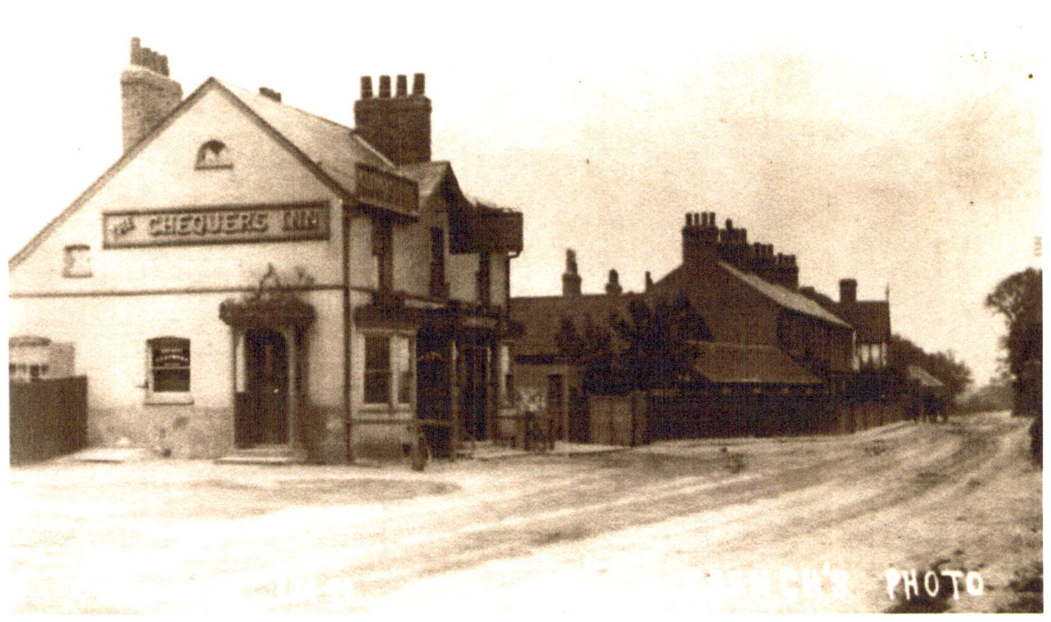

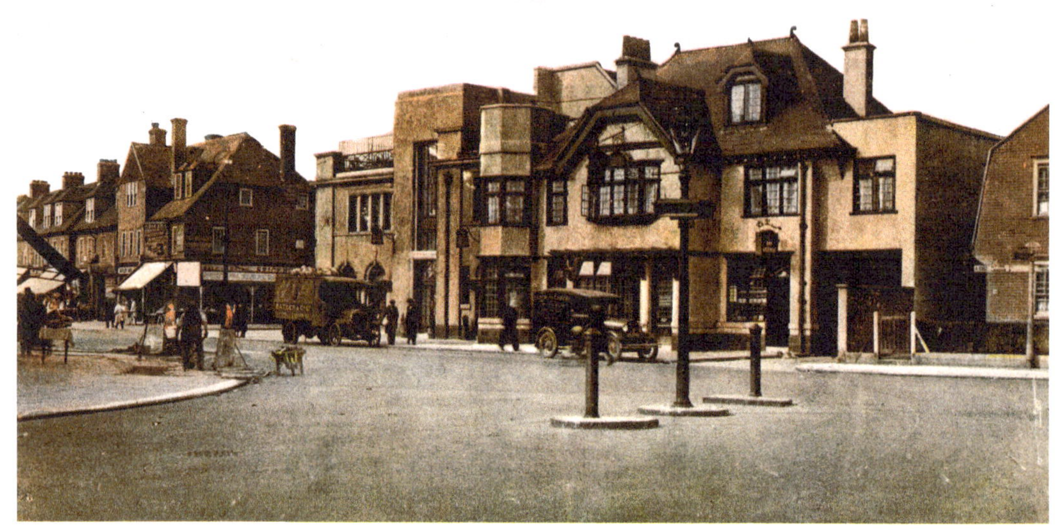

The Royal Oak

This Royal Oak stood in Green Lane. The site originally dates from the mid-eighteenth century but the building in the old photograph seems to be later. The pub had the novel idea of having a stage behind the bar so you could watch groups like the all girl Mission Belles who appeared on *Opportunity Knocks* and were regulars at the venue. The site is now home to a block of flats.

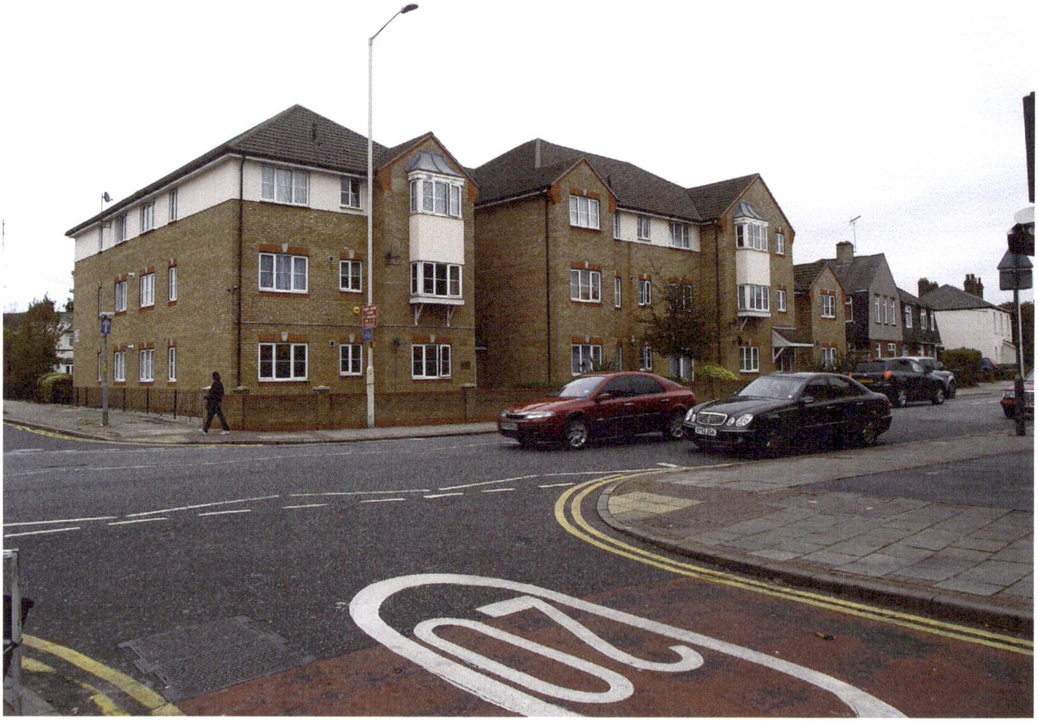

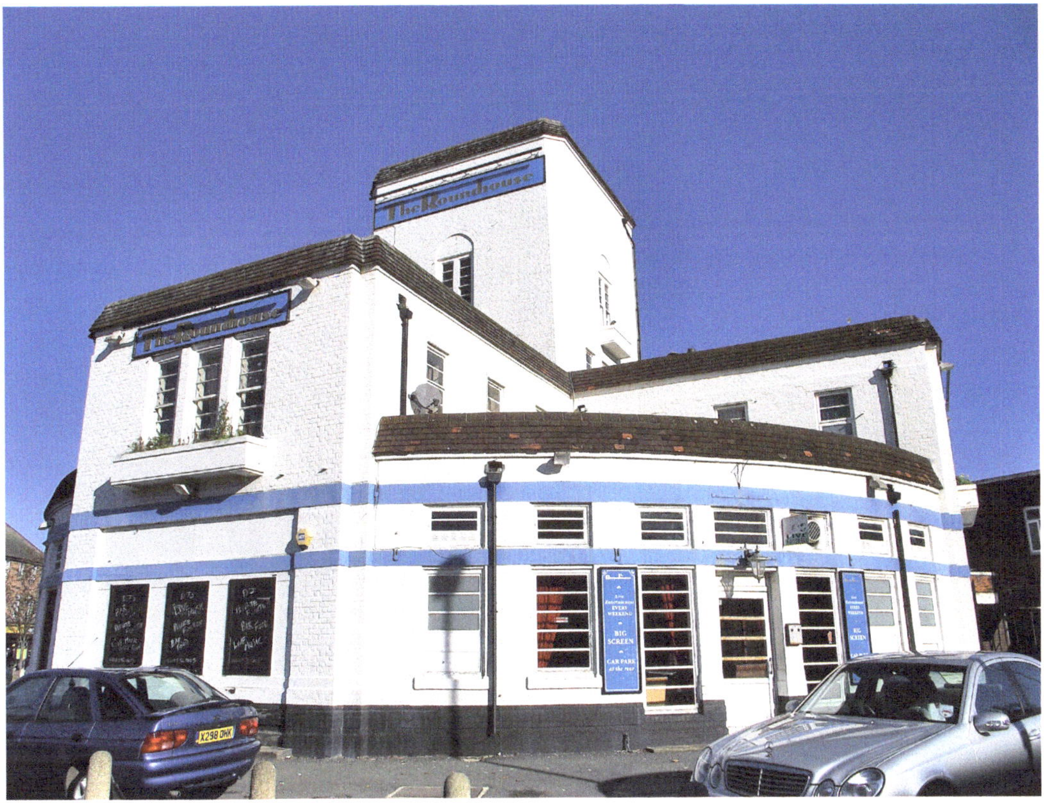

The Round House

The Round House in Lodge Avenue will be best remembered as the Village Blues club, a live music venue which in the 1960s and '70s was one of the leading music venues in London. Most of the big names of the era played there as the poster for T-Rex from 1970 shows.

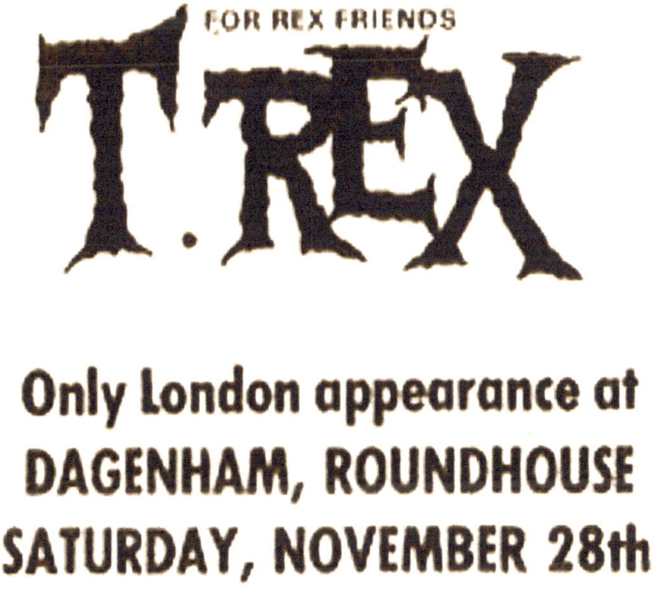

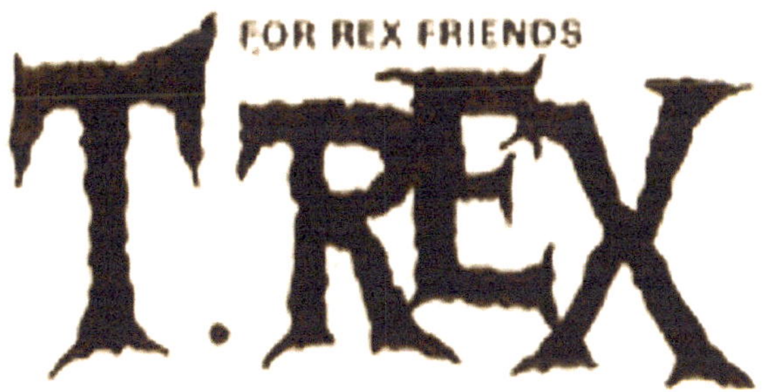

Only London appearance at
DAGENHAM, ROUNDHOUSE
SATURDAY, NOVEMBER 28th

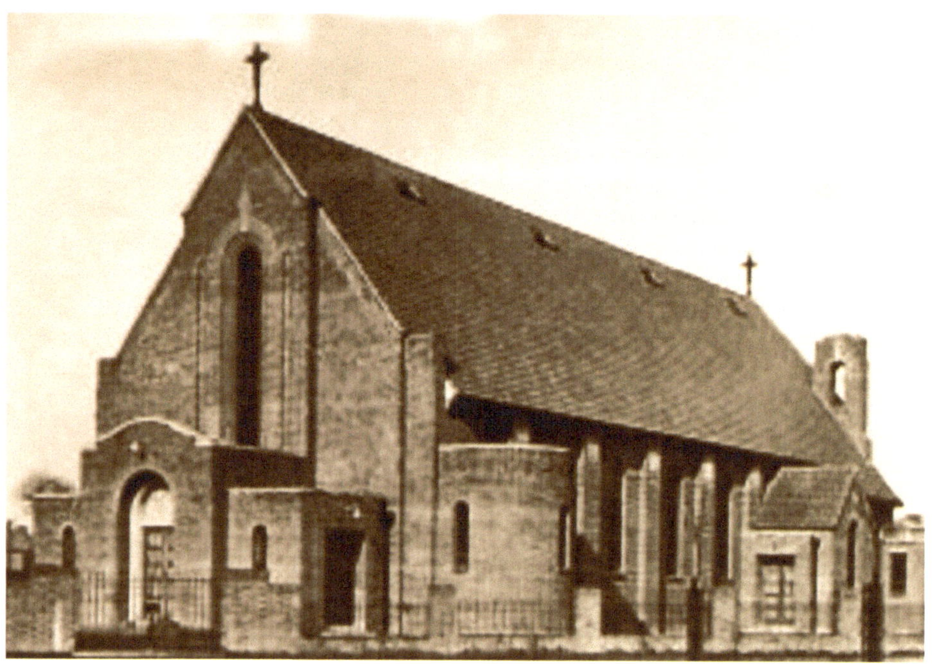

Holy Family

The Holy Family was the third Roman Catholic church built in Dagenham in 1934. There were already two, St Vincent's near Ilford, built in 1926, and St Peter's at Goresbrook Road, also built in 1926. St Joseph's Catholic primary school now stands behind the church.

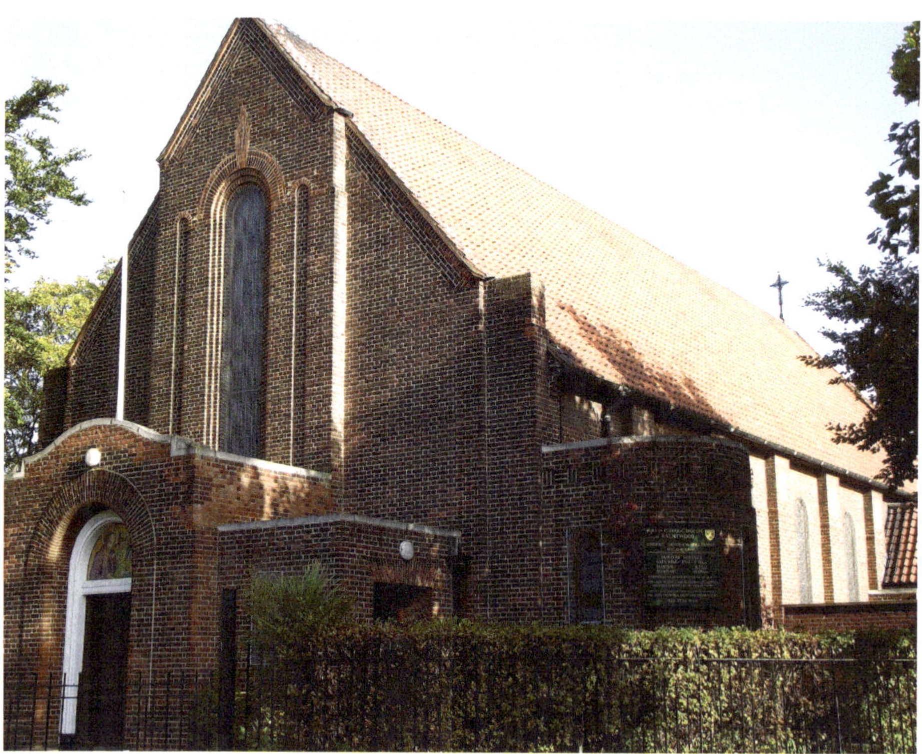

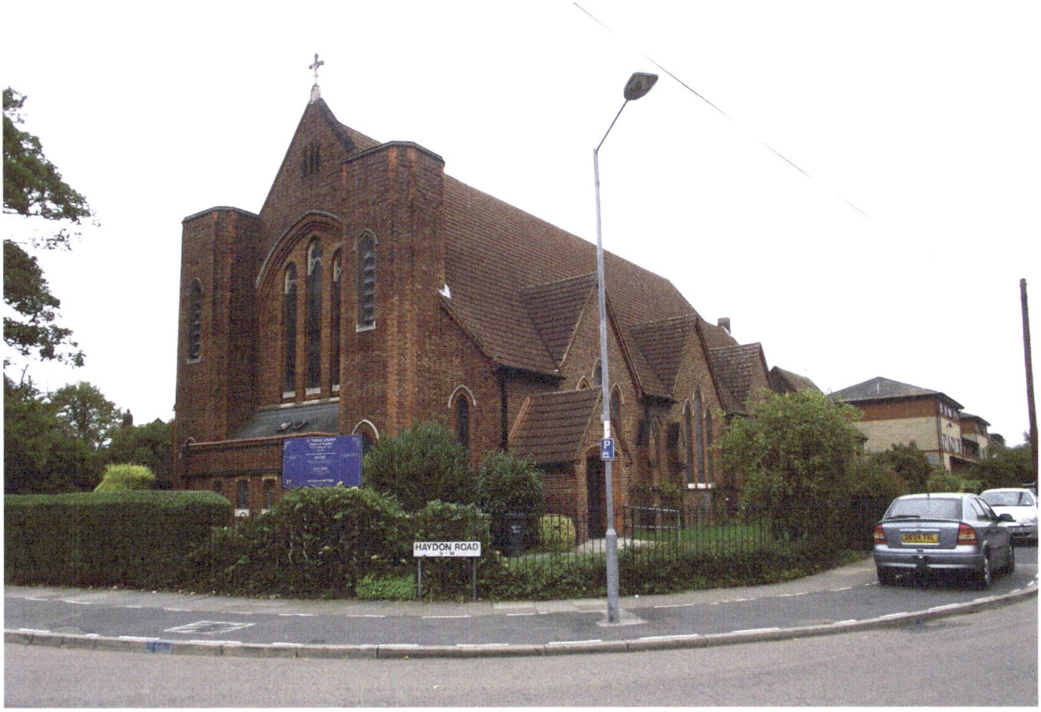

St Thomas's Church

St Thomas's church was the first church built on the Becontree estate in 1922. Its parish initially included parts of Dagenham, Ilford and Barking. This was the whole of the Becontree estate until other churches began to be built.

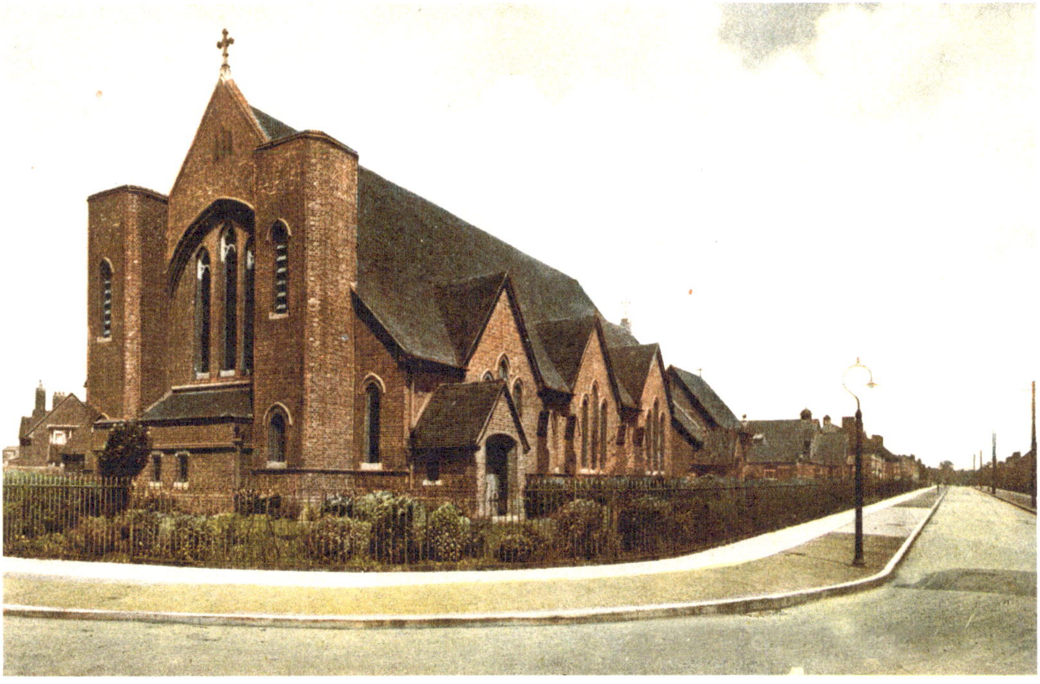

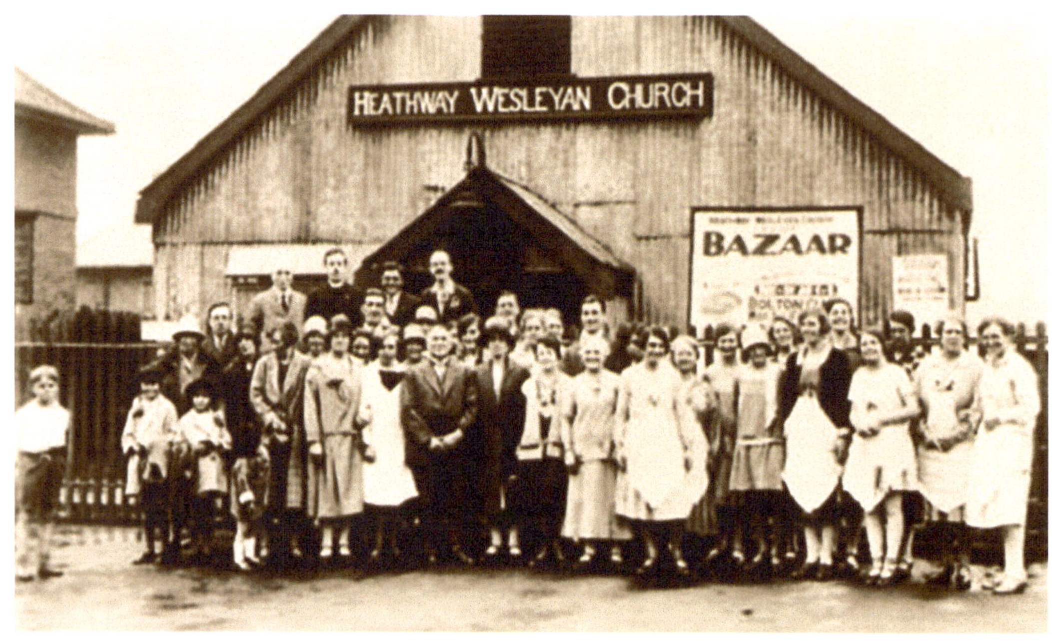

Heathway Church

A Wesleyan Methodist church was opened in a small corrugated-iron building in Heathway in 1925. This is shown in the old image. In 1930 it was replaced by Dagenham Central Hall, a much grander building with a large dome on top. This was demolished in the late sixties or early seventies. It is now the site of more modern church.

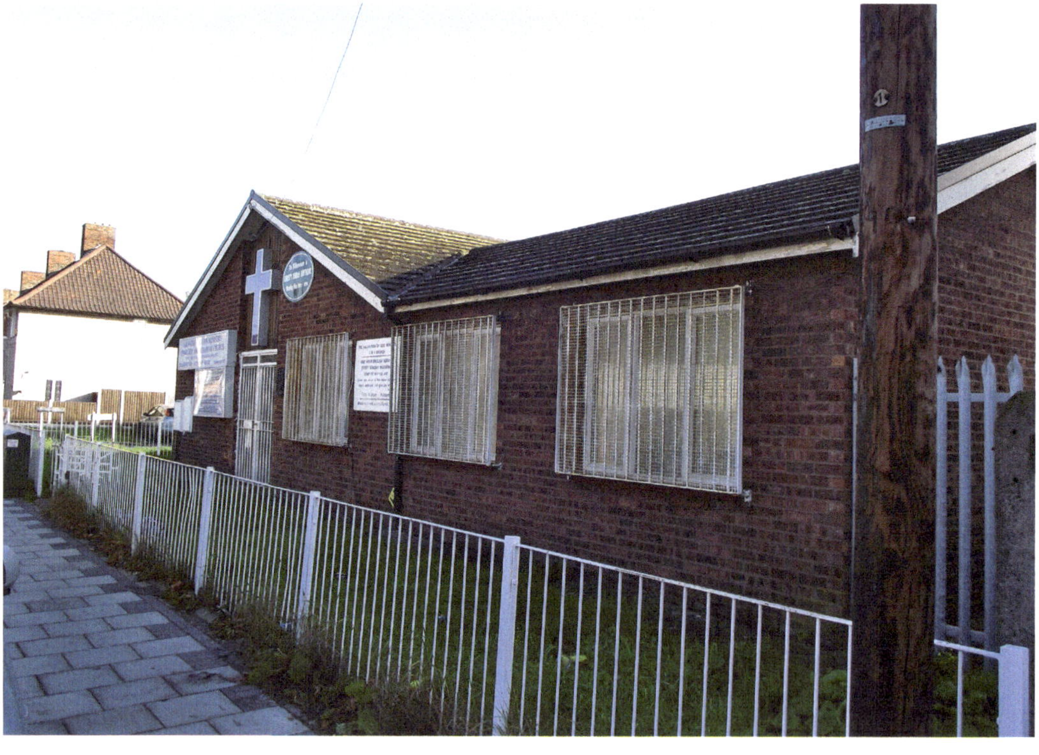

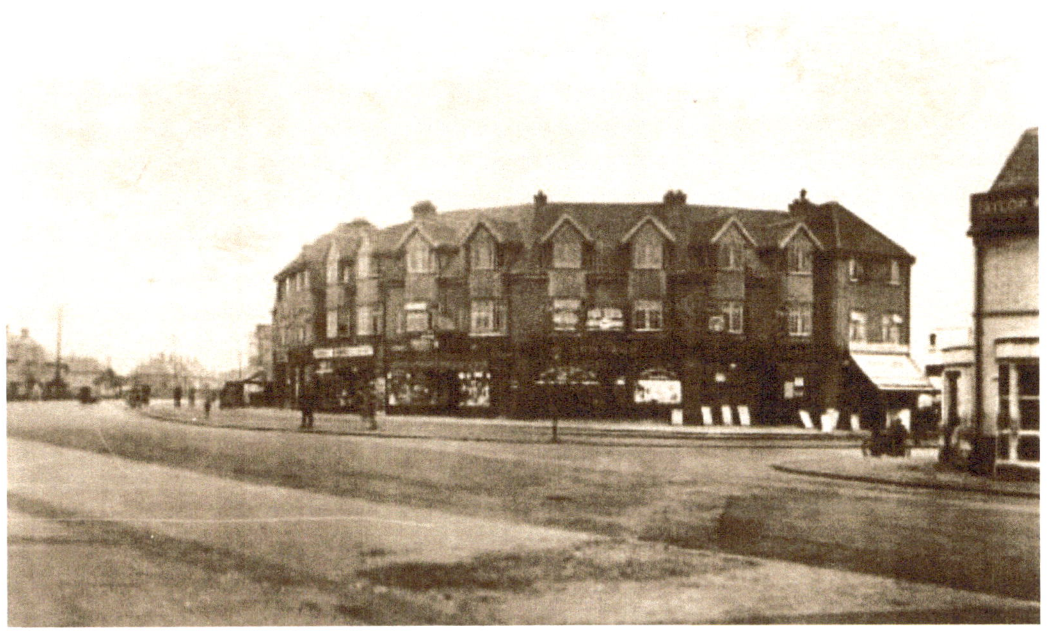

New Road

The old photograph names the road as Rainham Road. It does go towards Rainham but is now called New Road and was part of the A13 until a new A13 was built nearer the river. The old parade of shops which had declined terribly has now gone and although there was supposed to be new development in the area it is yet to arrive.

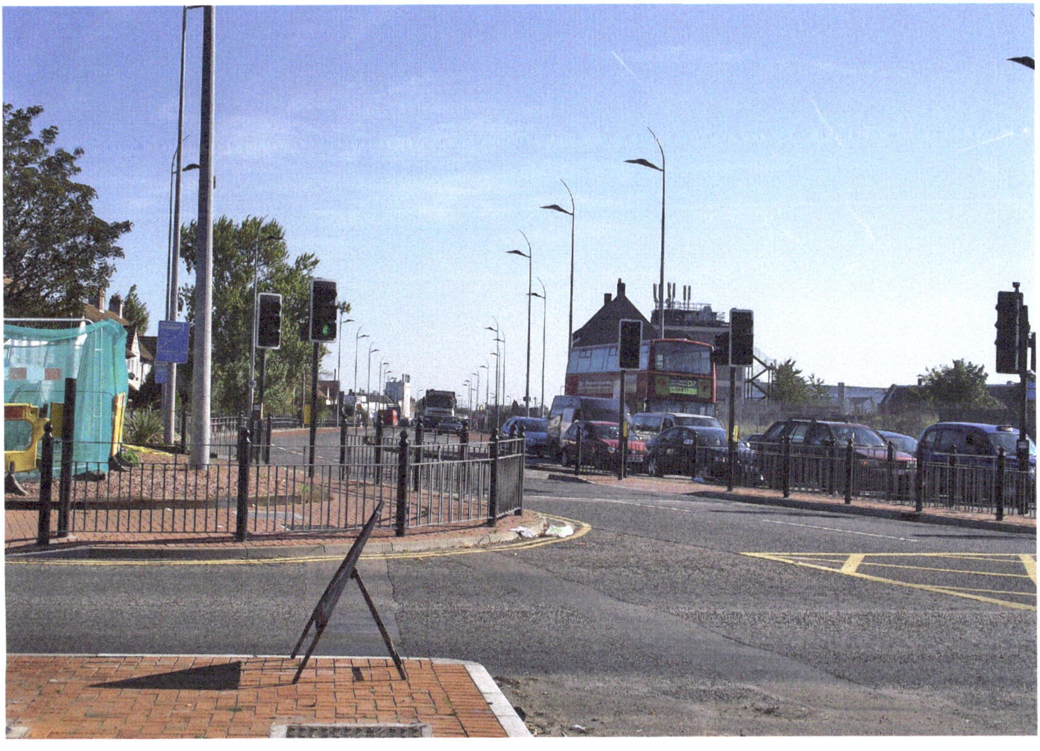

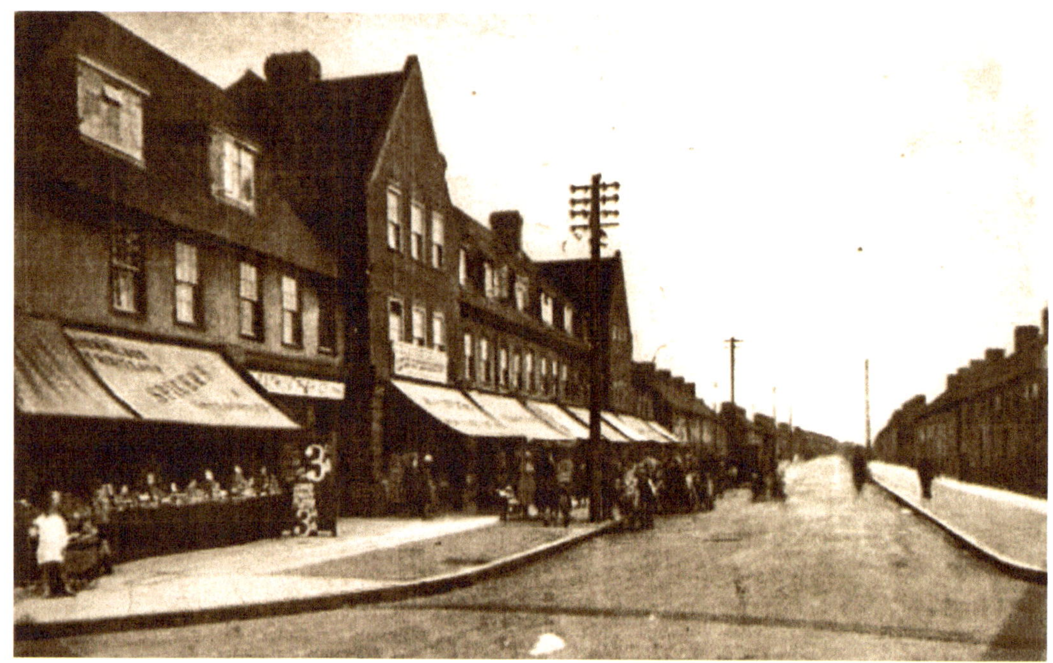

Hedgemans Road

Hedgemans Road runs from Gale Street close to Becontree station to Heathway near Heathway Station. It runs parallel with the railway line. The old photograph shows some of the shops that spread round the corner from those that line the hill over Becontree station.

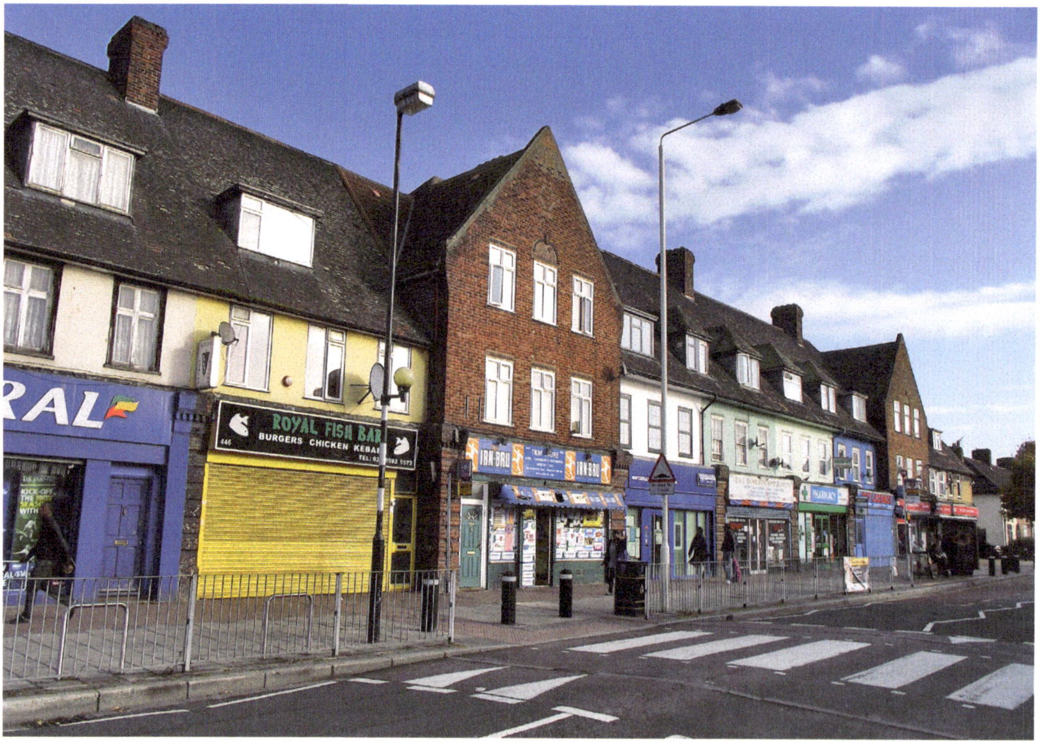

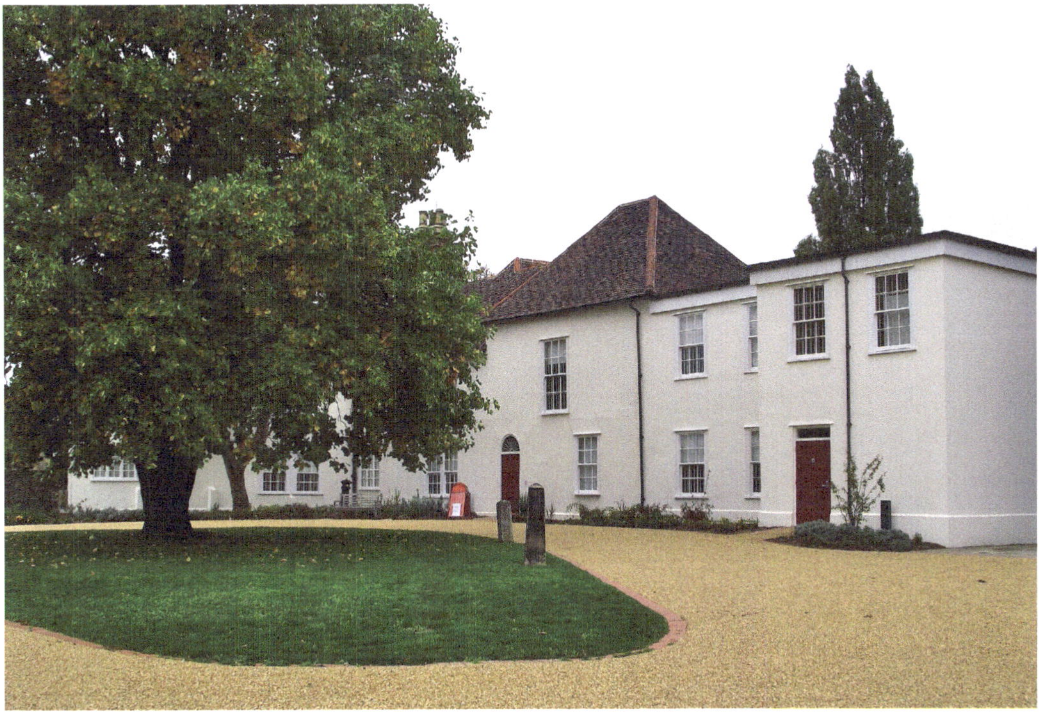

Valance House

Valance House is the only surviving manor house in Dagenham. It was built in the reign of Elizabeth I. The house has been owned by a number of different families throughout its history, and is now a local museum.

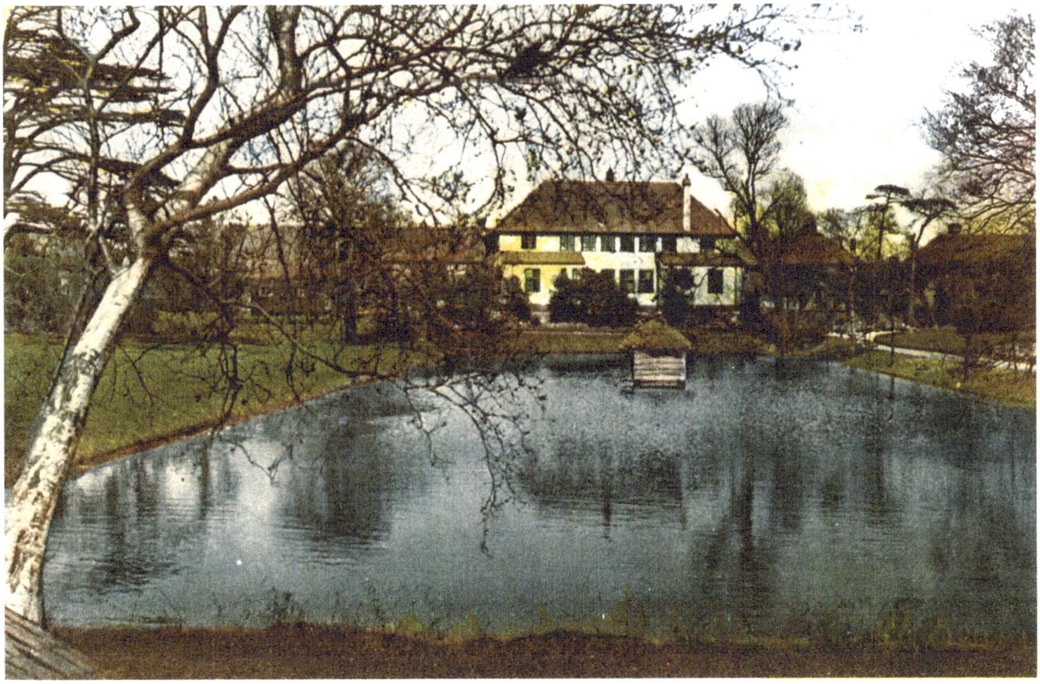

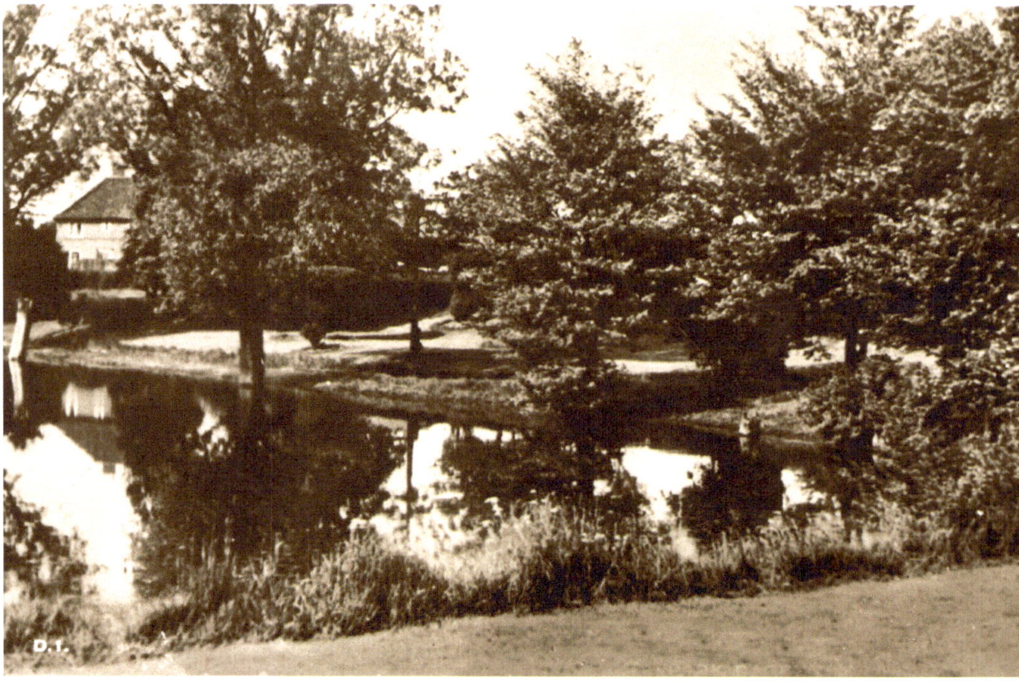

Valance Park

Valance Park connects with Valance House and includes part of the grounds of the old manor house. This includes part of the moat which is now used by local fishermen and other park users.

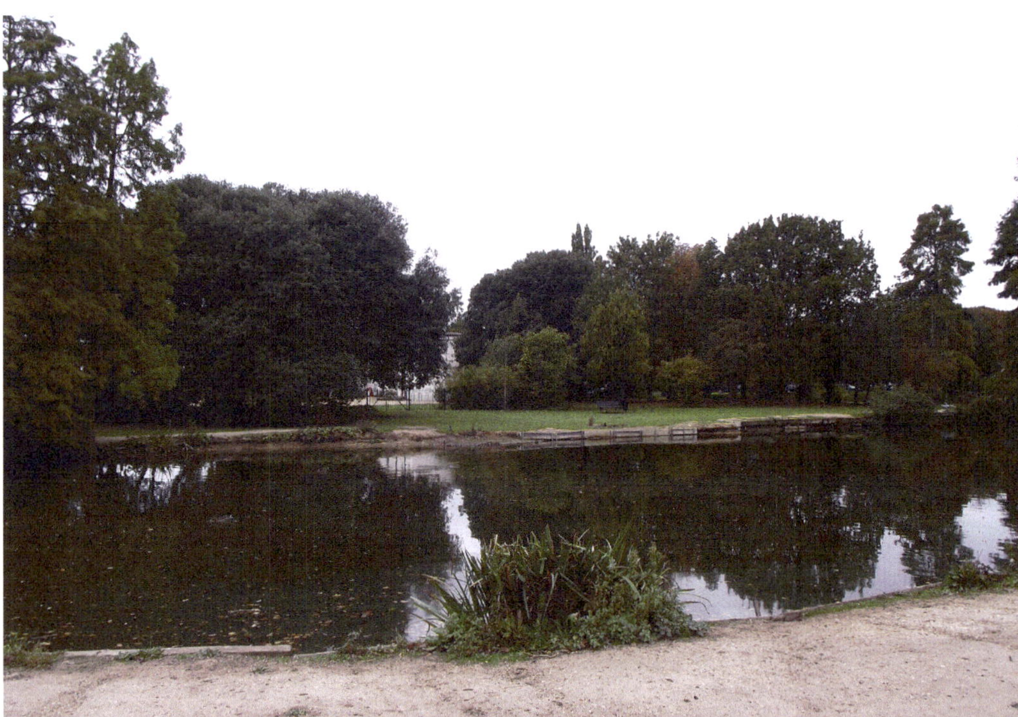

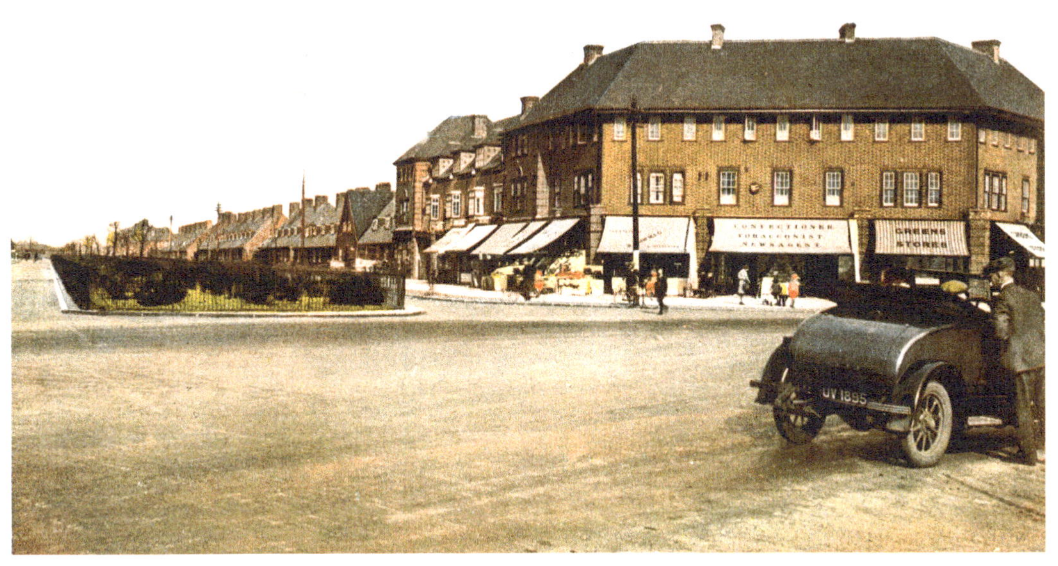

Becontree Avenue

The new Becontree estate had several small parades of shops to cater for the new inhabitants. Having so many of these small shopping areas meant that no one had to travel far for their shopping, as shown by the parade at Becontree Avenue. The grassed area in the old photograph was the site of a railway when the estate was being built.

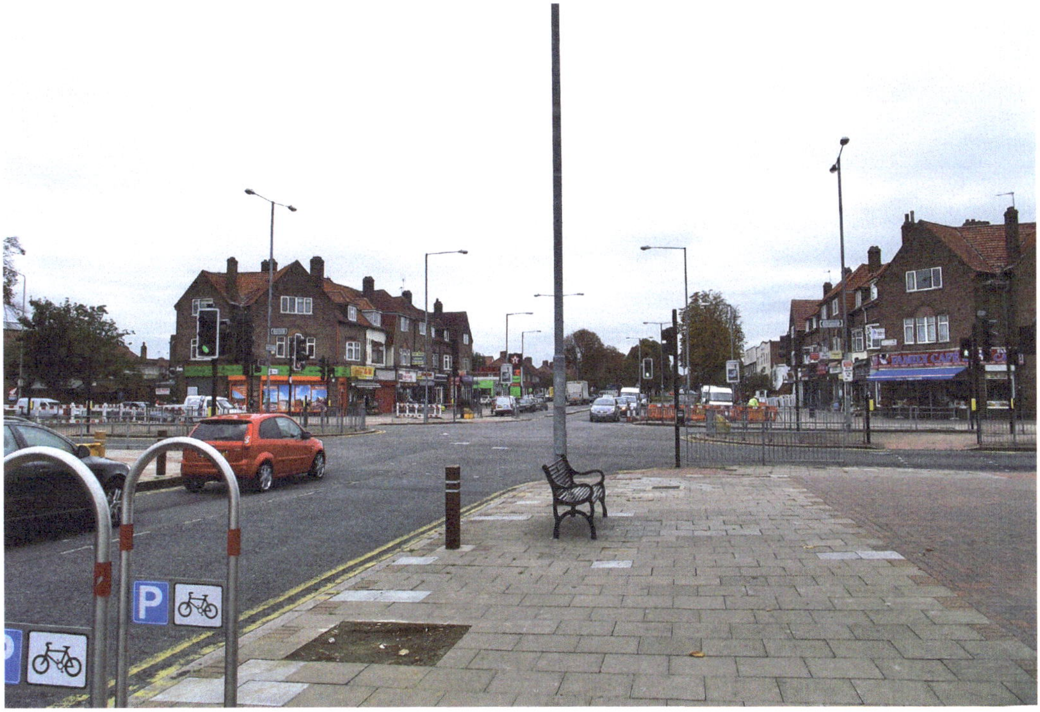

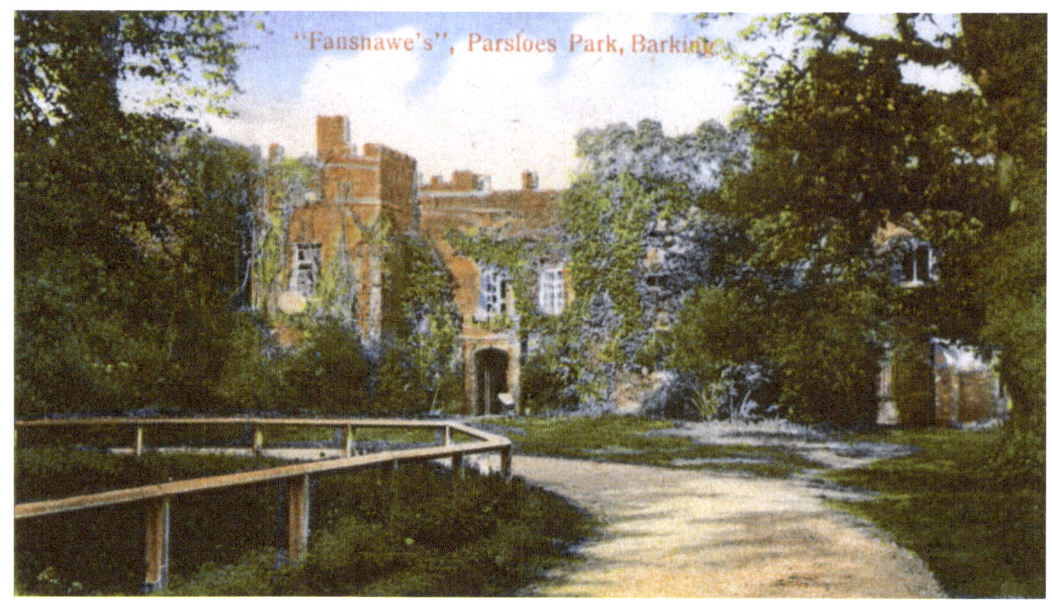

Parsloes Park

The house in Parsloes Park was owned by the Fanshawe family for over 300 years, unlike its neighbour Valance which often changed hands. By the middle of the nineteenth century it had been enlarged and given a Gothic appearance. The Parsloes Manor became derelict in the last few years of its life, and was eventually demolished in 1925.

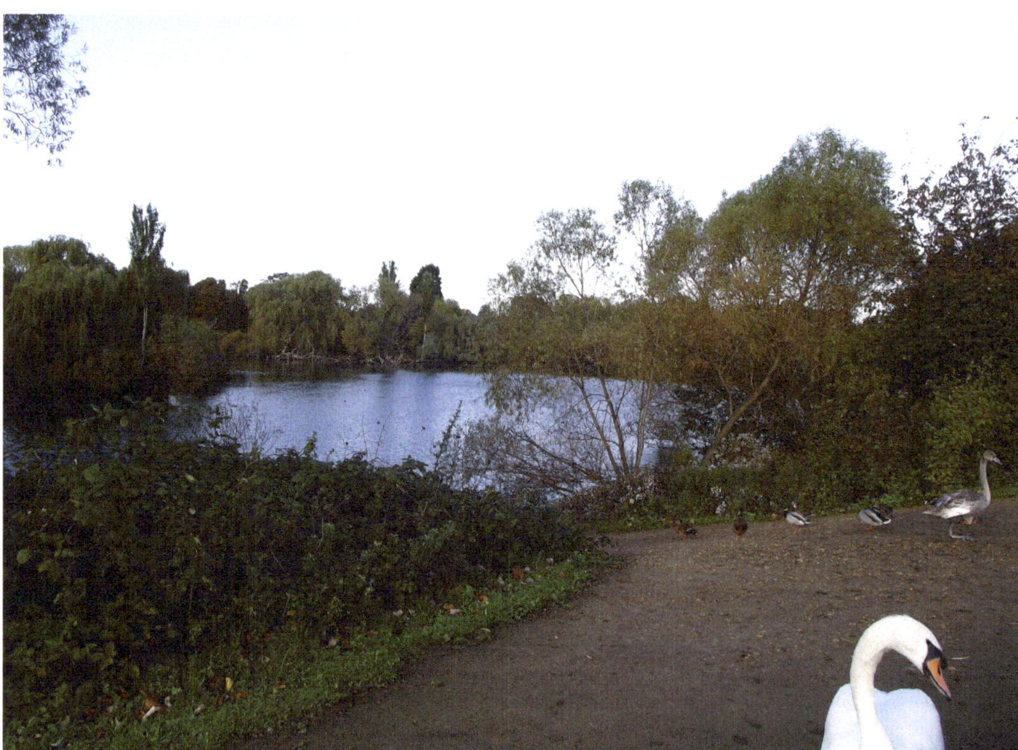

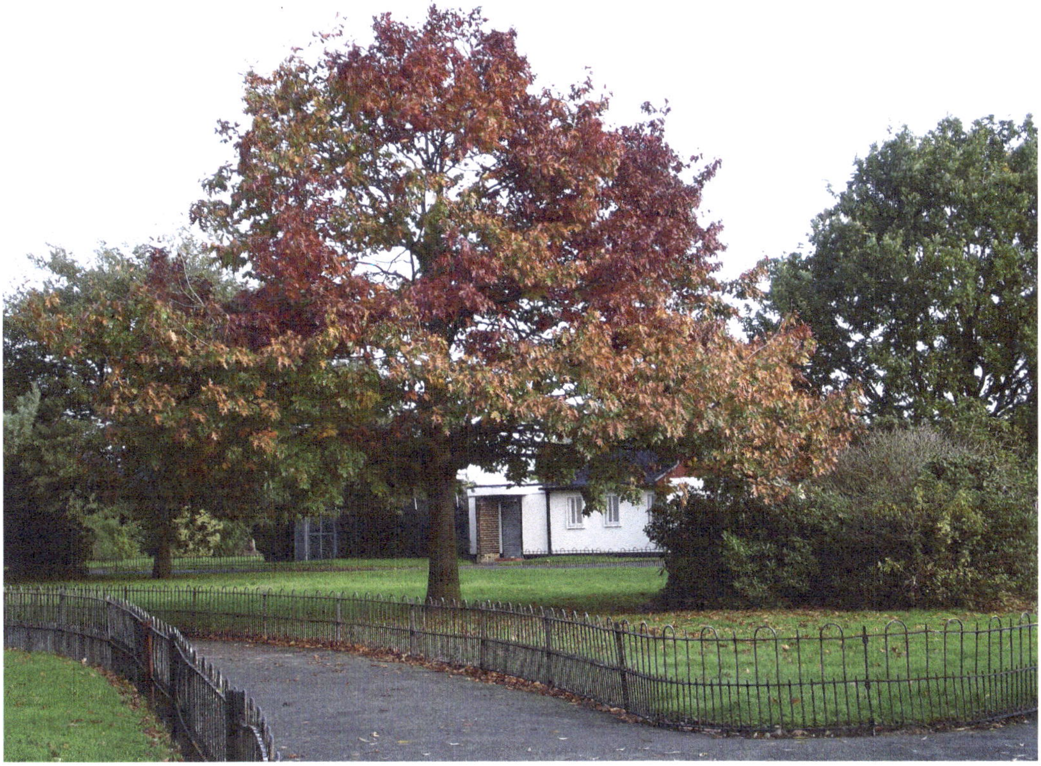

Parsloes Manor

Much of what is now Parsloes Park was once the grounds of Parsloes Manor. Up until the early twentieth century, the park was well known for racing a type of horse-drawn vehicle. It was known as trotting. There is still a large lake in the park that was once home to a number of flamingos.

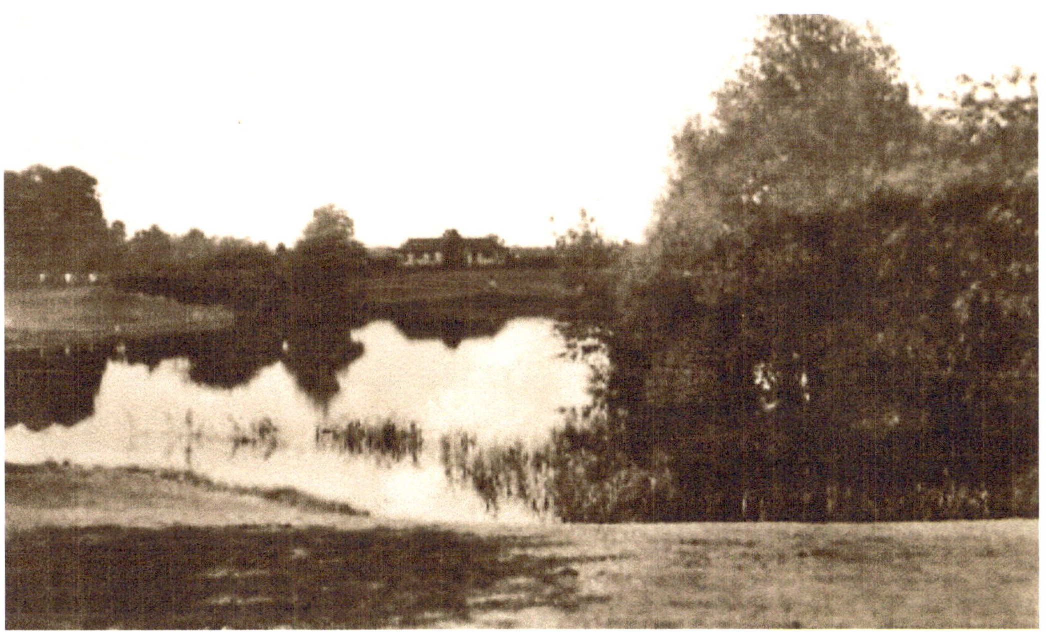

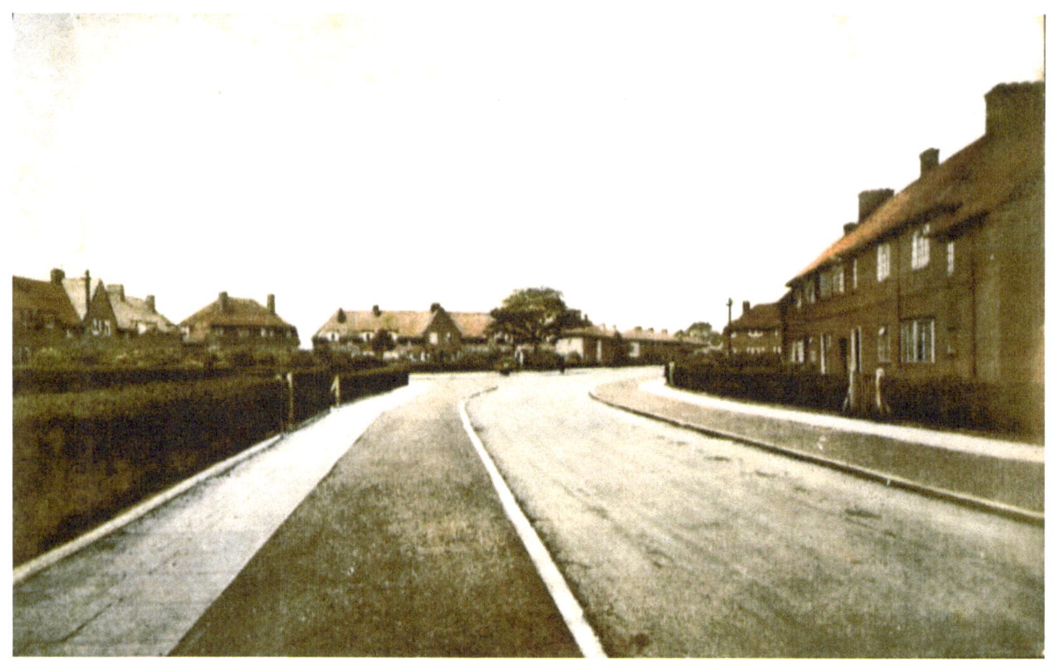

Angle Green

Angle Green is a small grassed area on Burnside Road. There is nothing unusual about it so why someone should have produced a postcard of it is a mystery. There cannot have been many customers apart from people who lived there. As the modern image shows, little has changed since the old photograph was taken.

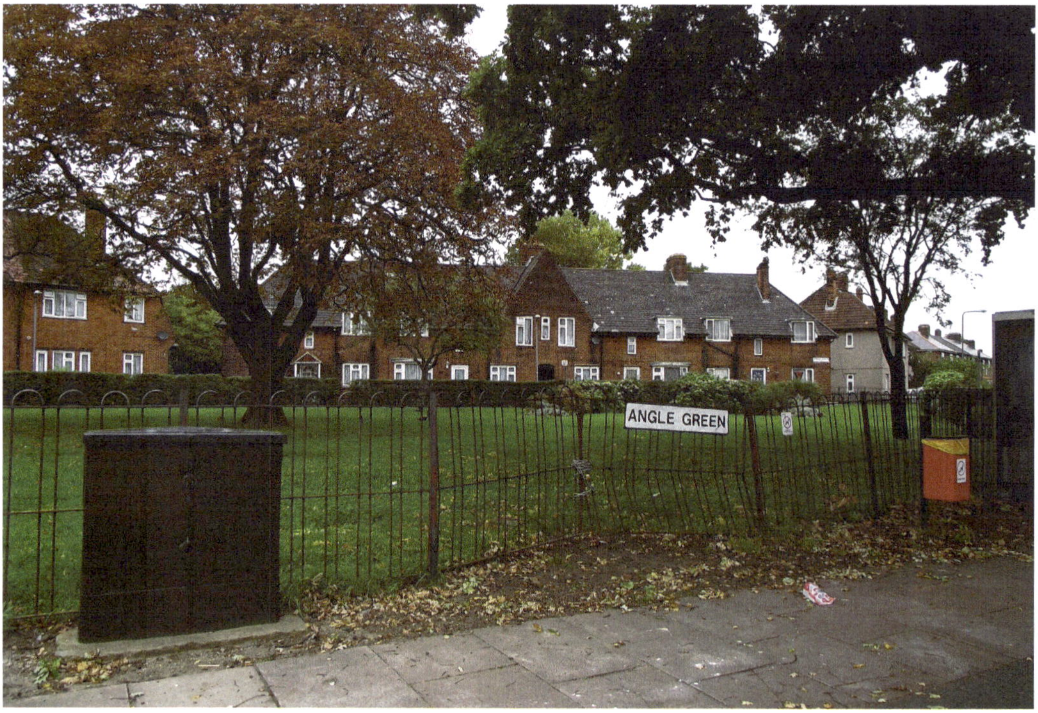

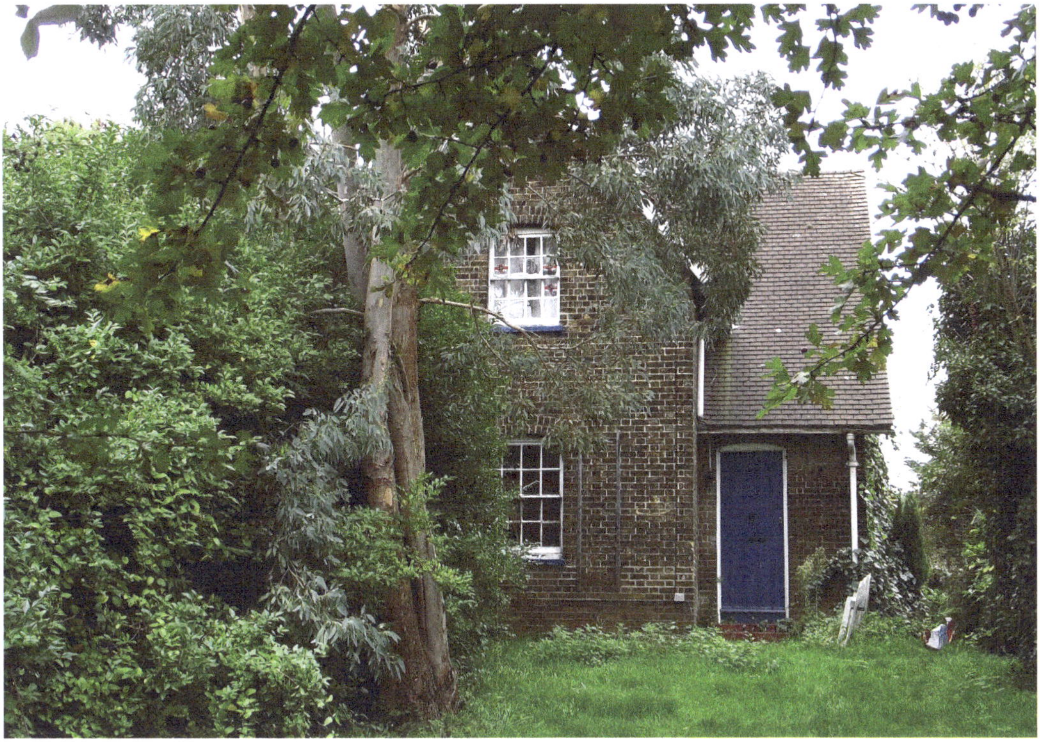

Warren Farm

Warren Farm is a very old establishment and has an eighteenth-century brick barn. The barn was originally built to store produce from the estate of Marks Manor. In 1855, the manor was sold to the crown. Although the farm still exists, it is probably known to many people through the large car-boot sales held there on Thursdays.

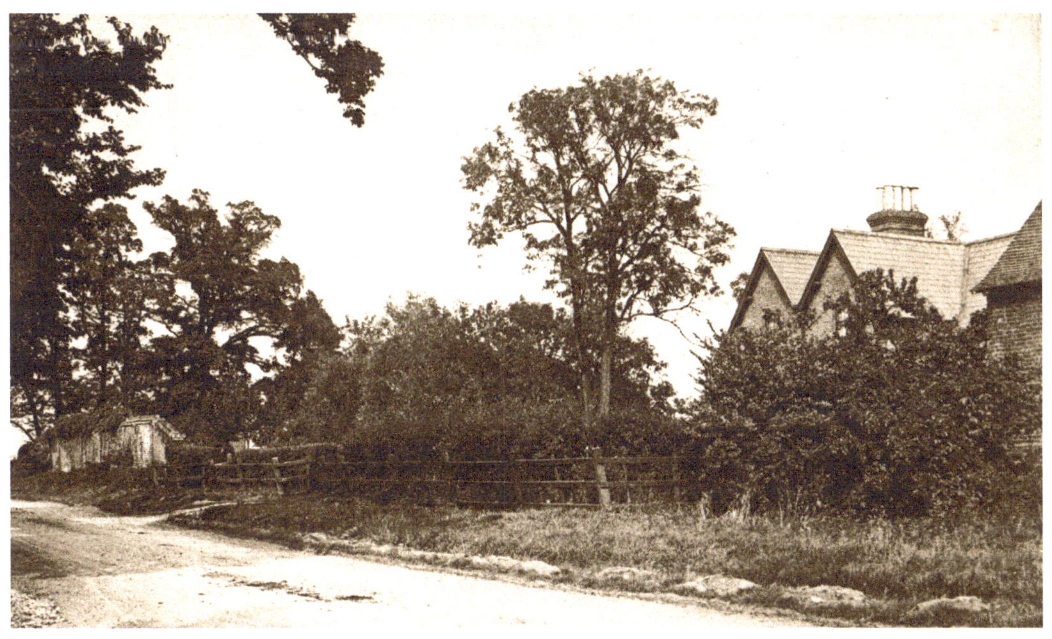

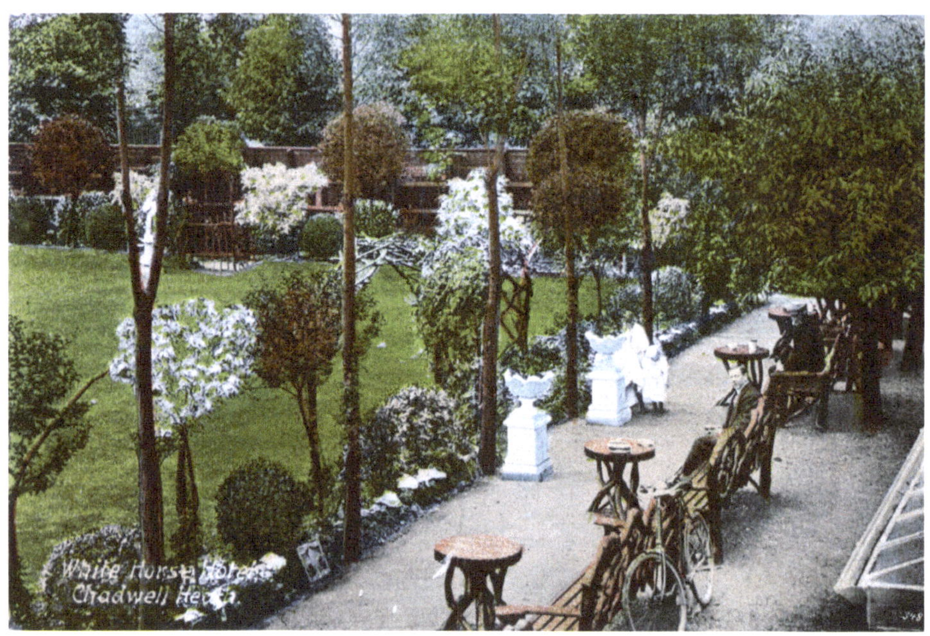

The White Horse

The White Horse is one of the oldest inns in the area, dating back to the seventeenth century. It seems to have had some problems as the landlord in 1602 was at the Quarter Sessions for disorder by excessive drunkenness. In 1621, another landlord was prosecuted for keeping a common bowling alley. It was rebuilt at the end of the nineteenth century and still has a very nice garden but, as the old image shows, it has changed a lot in recent years.

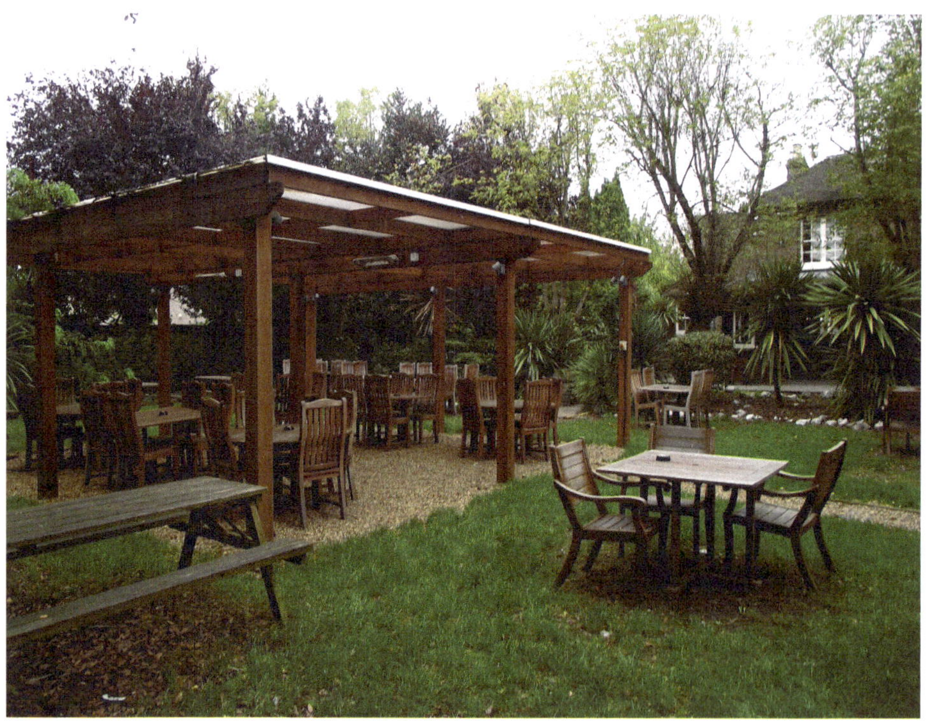

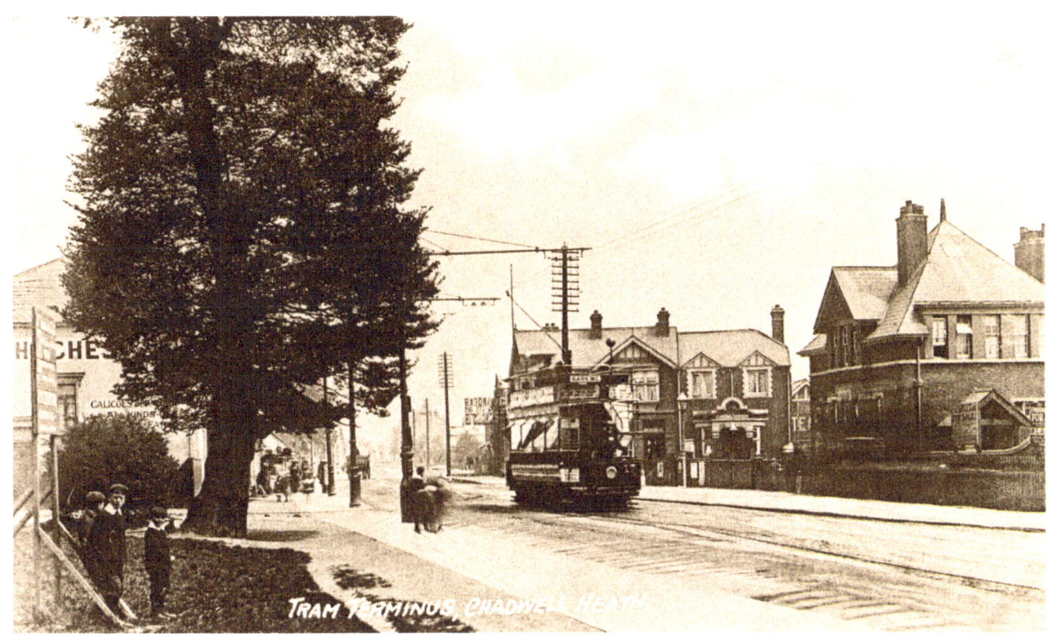

Trams Chadwell Heath

The old police station in High Road, on the right of the photograph, is now a pub named the Eva Hart after a survivor from the *Titanic* who lived in Chadwell Heath until her death in 1996. The trams began running in Chadwell Heath at the beginning of the twentieth century. The terminus stood in High Road. The trams also ran from Ilford to Barking. They were replaced with trolley buses in 1938.

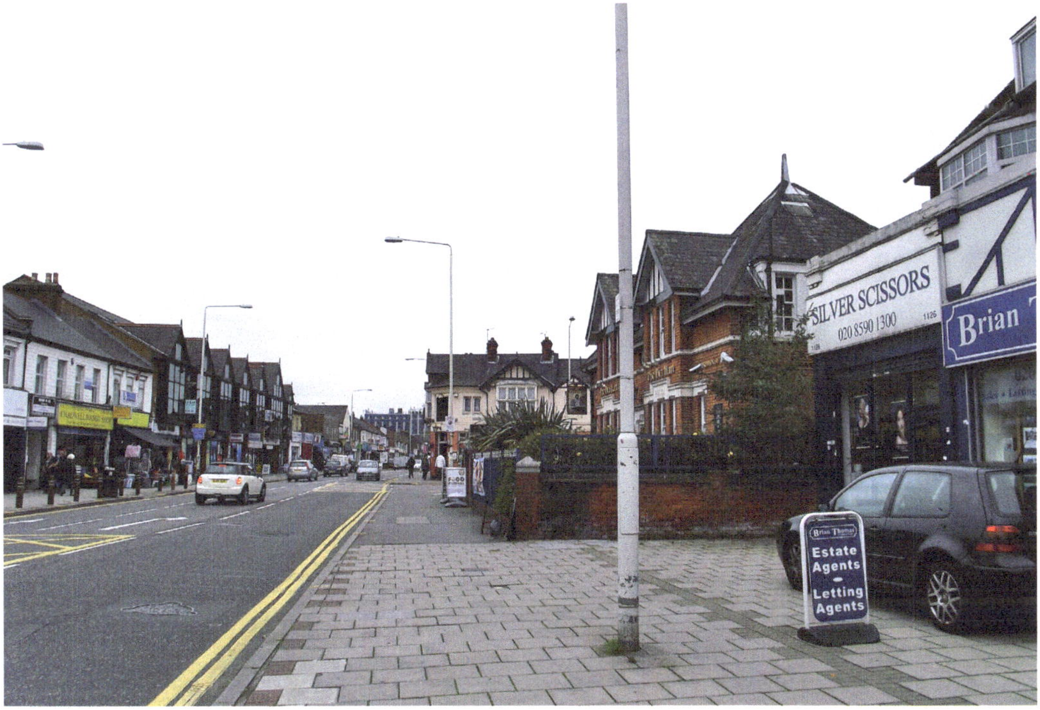

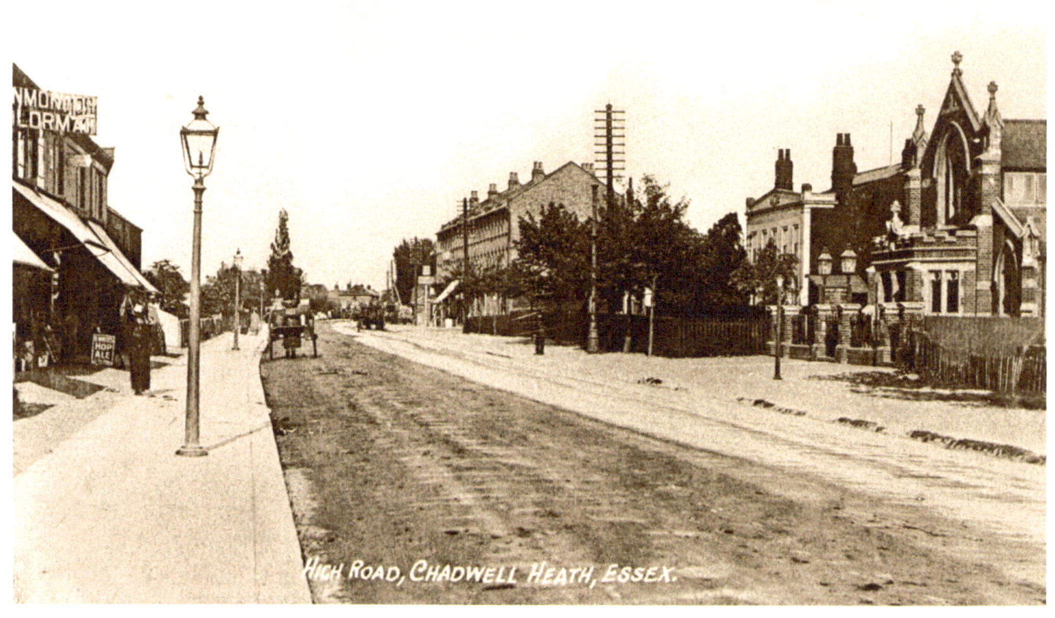

High Road Chadwell Heath

The High Road in Chadwell Heath stands on the route of the old Roman Road from London to Colchester. The old view shows an old church on the right which is still there, although some of the other buildings seem to have gone.

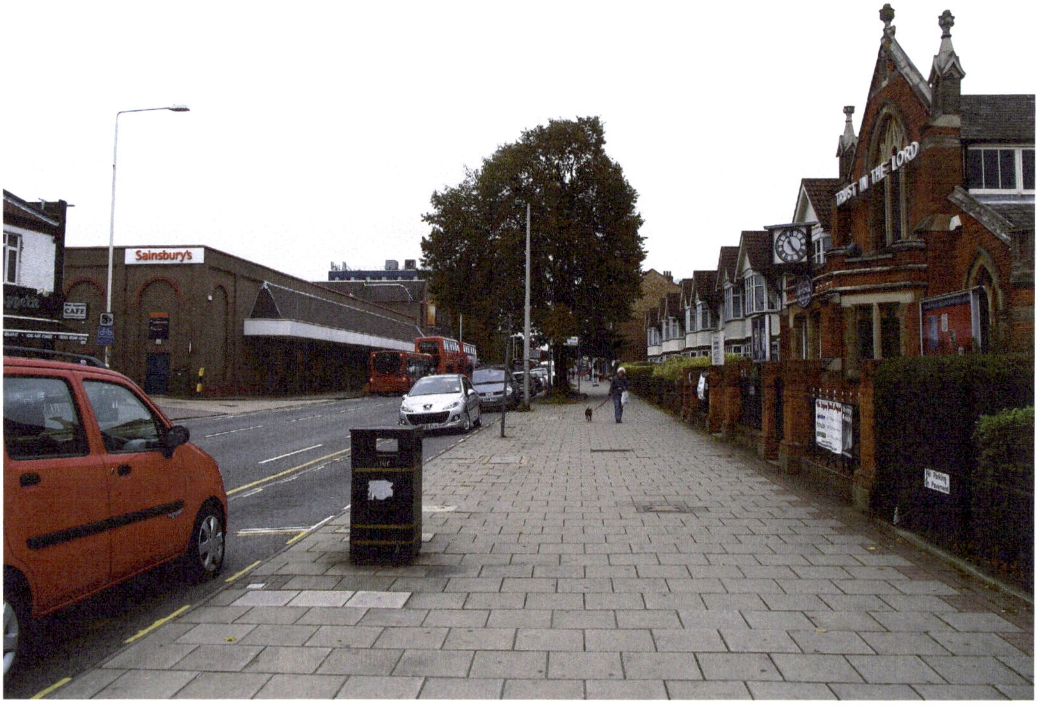

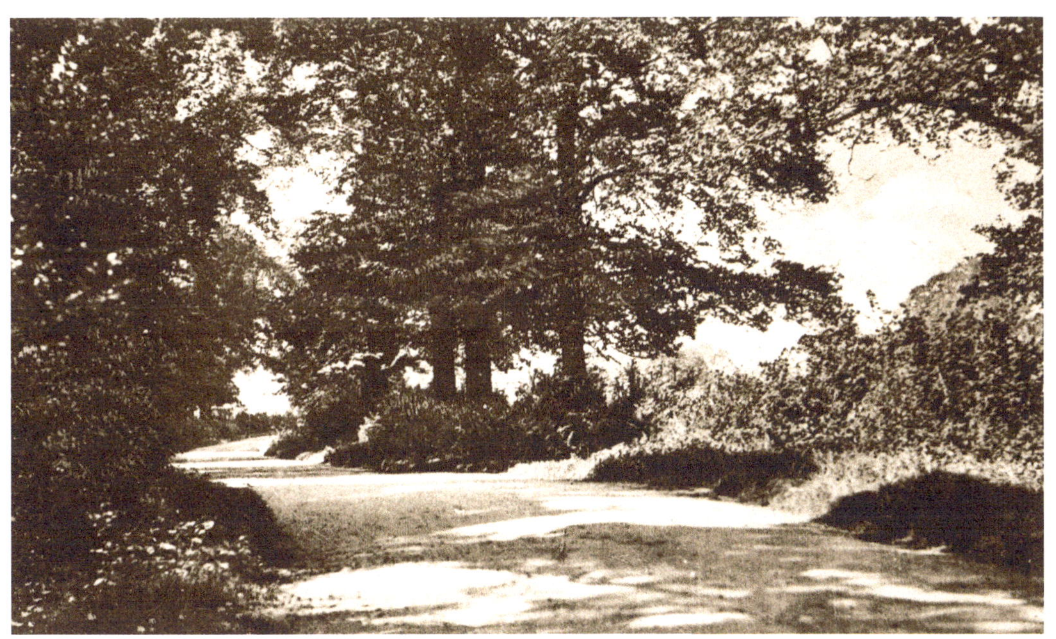

Rose Lane

The name Rose Lane was attached to a farm known from the fourteenth century. Although once a very rural lane it now runs through the centre of Marks Gate estate. In 1956, St Mark's church was built in Rose Lane as a district church of Chadwell Heath. Although the estate belongs to Dagenham it is actually in Romford.

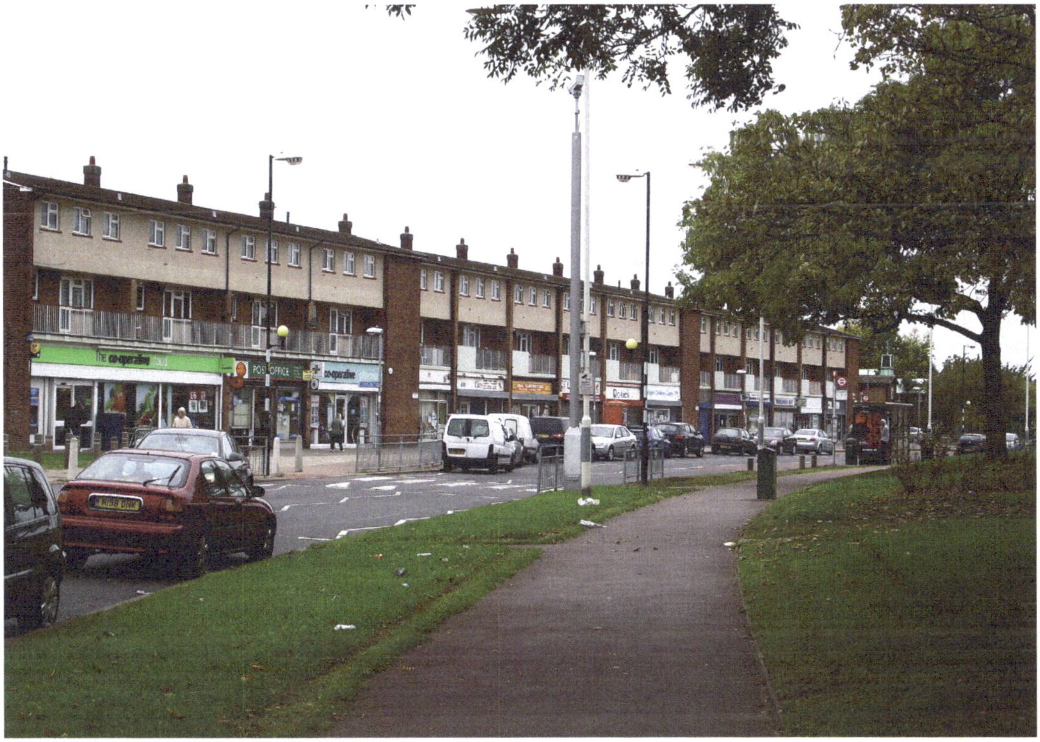

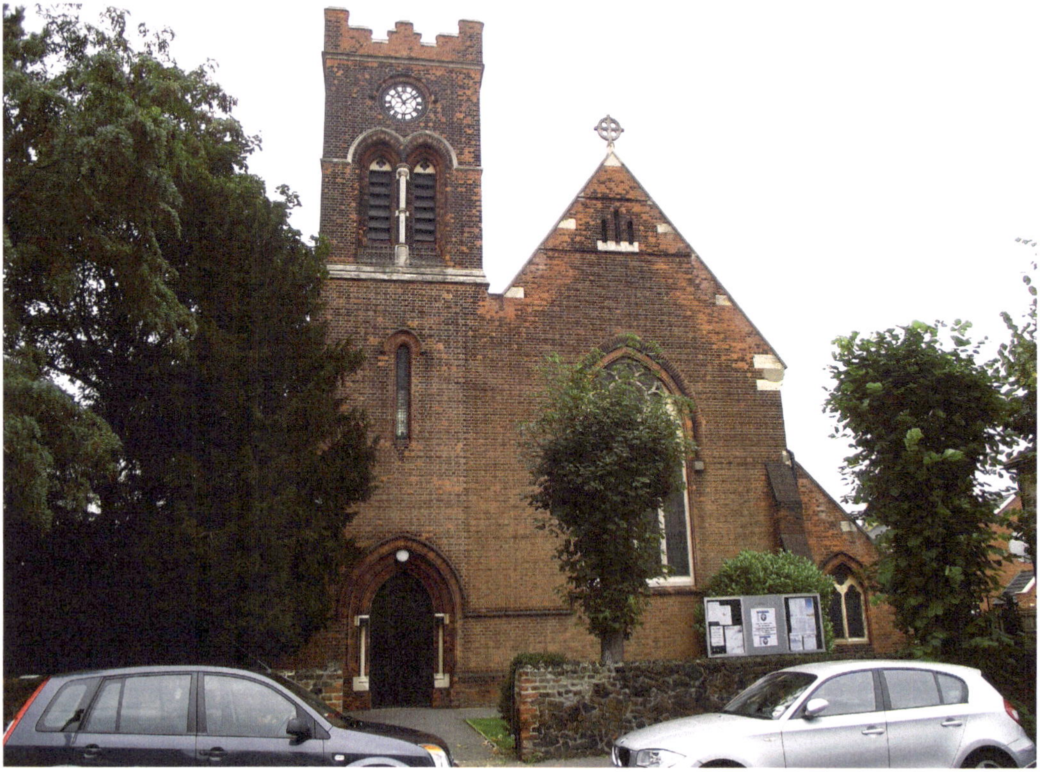

St Chad's

Apart from Dagenham church, the area once had no other churches. The vicar J. Moore began to hold services in Chadwell Heath in around 1880. St Chad's eventually opened in 1886. It was known as a chapel of ease to the parish church of Dagenham. In 1895 Chadwell Heath became a parish.

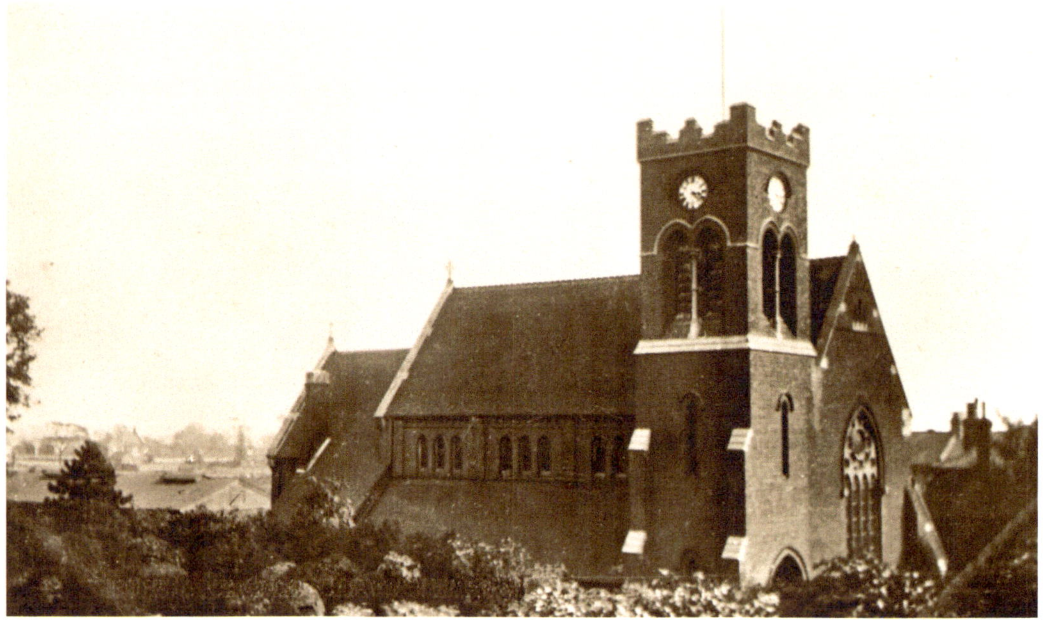

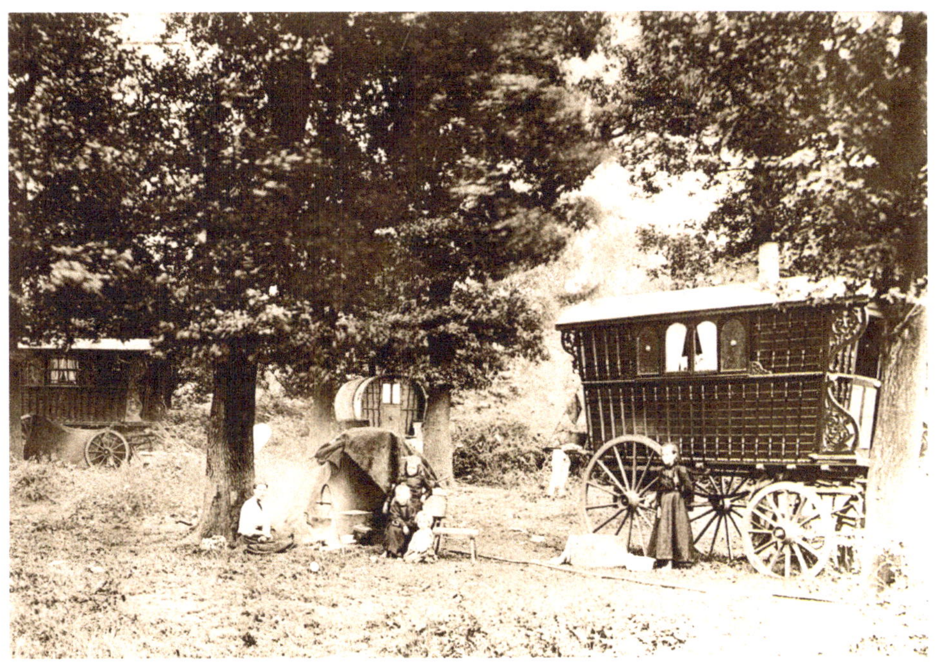

Gypsy Caravans

In the past, Hainault Forest was known as the Forest of Essex and originally covered much of what is now Dagenham. Gypsy encampments such as the one in the old photograph would have been common. Traveller sites today tend to be more permanent as this one at the Chase in Dagenham shows.

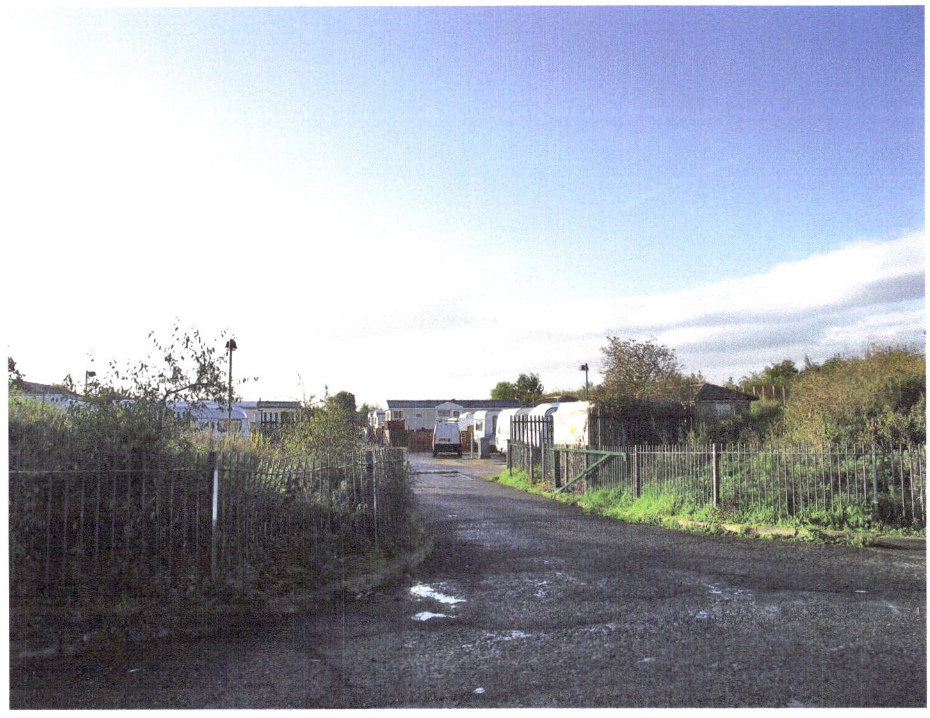

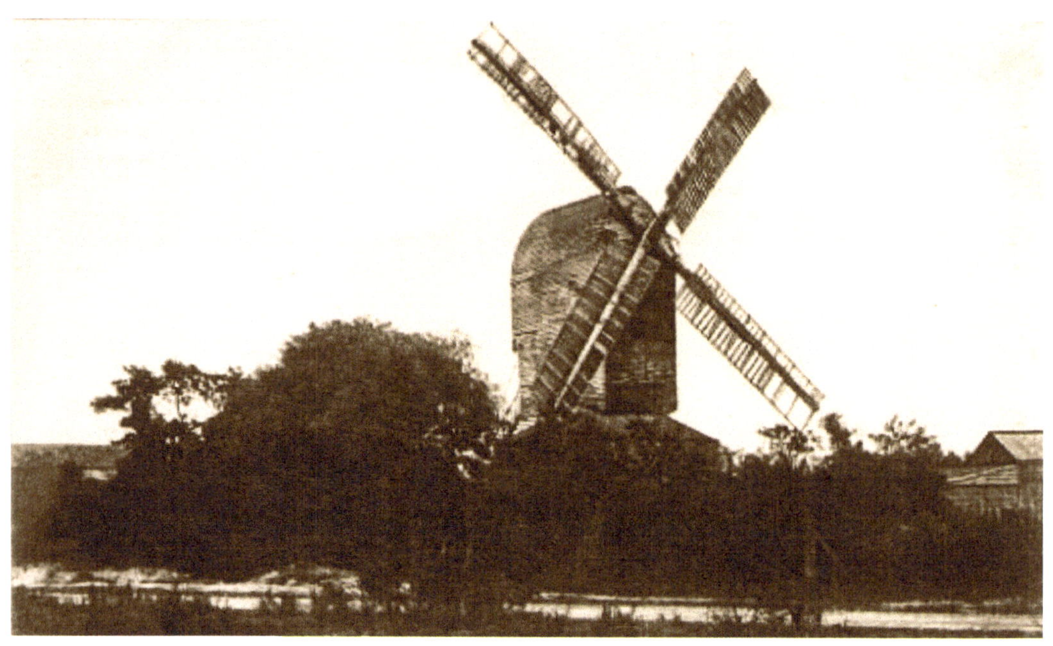

Moss Mill

Moss Mill stood in Mill Lane Chadwell Heath. The mill was demolished during the First World War. The old mill house survived much longer and was a home to several families around the Second World War, including my own family. There is no trace of the old house now.

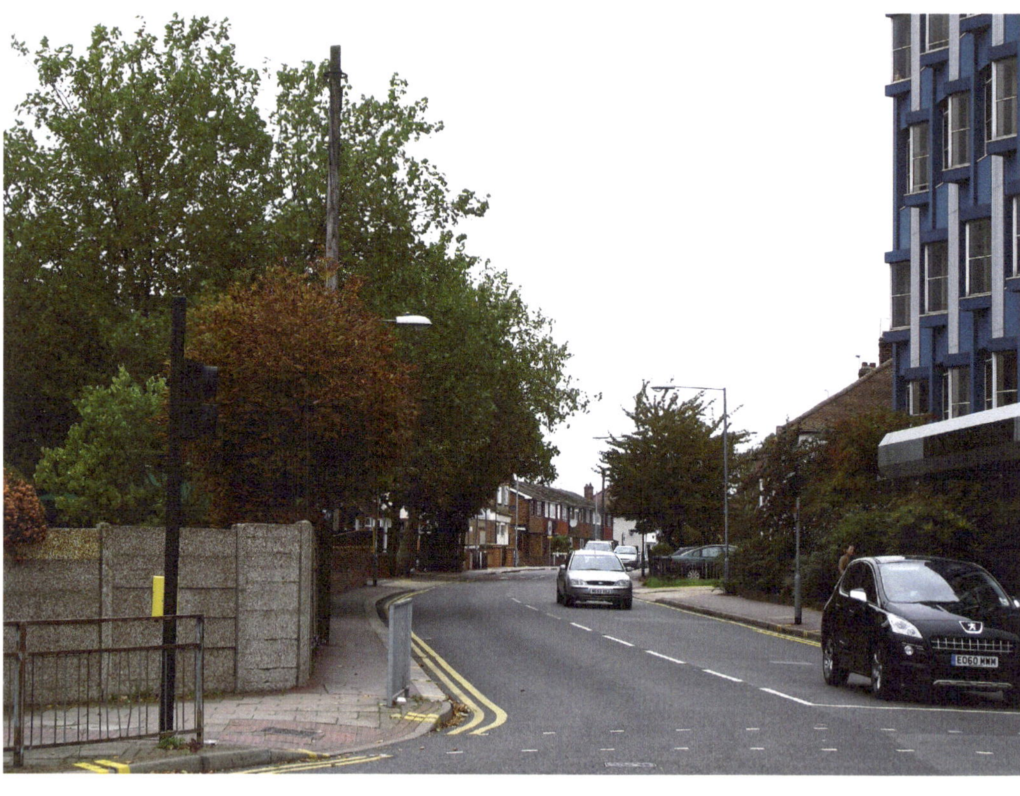

Printed and bound by CPI Group (UK) Ltd, Croydon, CR0 4YY
16/07/2026
02169566-0002